OUR WAR

OUR WAR

Days and Events
in the Fight for the Union

Mike Pride

Mike Pride

MONITOR PUBLISHING CO.
Concord, New Hampshire

Designed and composed in Fournier MT at Hobblebush Books, Brookline, New Hampshire (www.hobblebush.com)

Printed in the United States of America

Publisher's Cataloging-In-Publication Data
(Prepared by The Donohue Group, Inc.)

Pride, Mike, 1946–
    Our war : days and events in the fight for the Union / Mike Pride.

    p. : ill., maps ; cm.

    Issued also as an ebook.
    Includes index.
    ISBN: 978-0-9818215-2-8

    1. New Hampshire—History—Civil War, 1861–1865—Personal narratives. 2. United States—History—Civil War, 1861–1865—Personal narratives, American. 3. Soldiers—New Hampshire—Diaries. 4. Soldiers—New Hampshire—Correspondence. 5. Civilians in war—New Hampshire—History—19th century. I. Title.

E655 .P75 2012
973.781   2012948946

Published by:

MONITOR PUBLISHING CO.
P.O. Box 1177
Concord, New Hampshire 03302-1177

www.concordmonitor.com

To Monique,
who gives me heart,
and in memory of her father,
Frans Praet (1923–2012),
a good man

CONTENTS

PART III ✴ TO THE BLOODY END

MAPS

BY CHARLOTTE THIBAULT

AT THIS WAR MEETING ON KEENE'S CENTRAL SQUARE ON MAY 22, 1861, TILESTON A. BARKER, A WESTMORELAND BOOT-MAKER, AND HERBERT B. TITUS, AN EDUCATOR FROM CHESTERFIELD, WERE AMONG THE SPEAKERS. BOTH SIGNED UP THAT DAY AND WENT TO WAR WITH THE SECOND NEW HAMPSHIRE VOLUNTEERS.

A JOURNEY OF DISCOVERY

AS GEORGE TOWLE RODE NORTH toward the Arkansas River one day during the summer of 1861, swarms of green-headed flies attacked his horse so savagely that he had to stop and wait for nightfall to continue his journey from Texas to New Hampshire. Two days later, across the river on the Fourth of July, horse and rider faced even greater danger. Towle was boiling coffee just after sunset when he heard pounding hooves. Before he knew it, "a band of 50 or 60 Indians, half-breeds, & white desperadoes" surrounded him. They took his horse, pistol, and rifle, roughed him up, declared him a "damned abolitionist," and proposed to hang him. Glancing about, Towle was relieved to see no tree tall or sturdy enough for the job. His captors fell to drinking and playing cards. When all was quiet, he tiptoed to his horse and led it away through high grass. At a safe distance he mounted and rode toward home to volunteer for duty in the Civil War.

GEORGE TOWLE

Of the thousands of New Hampshire men whose lives the war transformed, Towle may have been the only one who had to survive green-headed flies and southern desperadoes to enlist. In Concord, the capital, the popular night constable walked three blocks, became the state's first volunteer, and started recruiting others. Three militia companies in Manchester, New Hampshire's largest city, voted to enlist en masse. Eleven young Amherst men marched to town hall and volunteered. Up in Littleton, the first man to arrive at a makeshift recruiting office granted Evarts Farr's wish to cut in front of him and sign up first. Orrin Brock of Pittsfield went out to pick checkerberry leaves for a local distillery but changed his mind and hitched a ride to a recruiting station.

The war turned Concord into a war capital and pushed peacetime political differences into the background—at least temporarily. It tested the ideals of free speech and a free press, sometimes with sad results. It required wives to assume their husbands' home duties and set many women to work making mittens, shirts, bandages, and baked goods for men far away. From the near-illiterate to the eloquent, it converted thousands of people into avid letter-writers. Rushing to his first battle, Sergeant Oscar Robinson of the Ninth New Hampshire shed almost everything he was carrying, including his food, but hung onto his pen and paper. Samuel Duncan, a one-time Dartmouth College tutor, and Julia Jones, a teacher from East Washington, fell in love by mail.

In his inaugural address seven weeks after the rebel firing on Fort Sumter, New Hampshire's new governor defined the war's cause without mentioning slavery. Nathaniel Berry's aim was to avoid a divisive topic at a time when both parties agreed on the urgency of saving the Union. But once soldiers reached the South, they knew their loved ones back home wanted to hear about the black people they encountered, and they fed this curiosity. Brave deeds by black regiments later undercut some white soldiers' racial prejudices, but it was a slow, uneven process.

The ultimate and most profound change wrought by the war was sudden death—death in battle, death by accident, death from disease, death from foul medical practices, death by execution. About 33,000 New Hampshire men, a tenth of the population, went to war. More than 5,000 died, and more than 10,000 were wounded. The effect of each death was profound, as illustrated by the elaborate Concord funeral of Charles W. Walker, one of the first to die. The novelty soon wore thin as relatives pored over casualty lists from Bull Run, the Peninsula, Antietam, and Fredericksburg. Some New Hampshire infantry units—the Second, the Fifth, the Seventh, the Ninth, the Twelfth—earned reputations as "fighting regiments," a compliment to the men who served in them but also a fearful phrase to their families. Death came to define even the Sixteenth New Hampshire, which served just nine months and barely faced hostile fire.

Before 1863, townsmen joined and fought together, creating a bond among them and a connection with people at home. But as death and illness thinned the ranks, it became more and more difficult to find new volunteers. To fill draft quotas, towns and cities resorted to paying large bounties to immigrants and out-of-town strangers. This strained budgets and alienated townspeople from soldiers at the front. It led to the unseemly practice of affluent draftees buying substitutes while the draft swept poorer men off to war against their will. Many substitutes deserted, hurting Union morale.

This book tells the story of how the Civil War affected Union soldiers and civilians. It follows the arc of the war from the heady days of 1861 to the despondency of 1863 to the weary but satisfying triumph of 1865. It is a non-traditional history told through the events of fifty days of a four-year war as seen from a New Hampshire perspective. Some episodes involve masses of men and famous battles, but most are about ordinary people struggling to survive. This approach allowed me to do what I love: free eloquent voices from archives and find lost and little-known stories. It meant I could ask the participants themselves the questions most readers have about the war: Why did so many men go so eagerly? What was it like to fight? What did white soldiers think of black people? How did they view the shift in the war's objective from preserving the Union to freeing the slaves? How did they "keep up good courage," to borrow a phrase of the time, in the face of mass killing and deadly epidemics? Where did women fit into the narrative? Taken together, these stories should give readers a broad sense of the Union war experience.

Researching this book has been a journey of discovery. I love reading other people's mail. Who doesn't? But there is something especially powerful in the desire of soldiers to share their strange and terrible experiences with relatives back home. Even as soldiers and civilians grew apart during the war, the men never lost hope that their words could make homefolks understand what they were going through. Reading letters, diaries, memoirs, and newspapers of the period confirmed the idea that generality is the enemy of truth. The soldiers were not necessarily original thinkers, but their opinions of politics, race, and the cause varied widely. The war also created a profound sense among them that they were characters in American history. Hints of this appear in several chapters, including one on the craze for war relics. In the two chapters that touch most directly on the subject, a man wounded at Antietam and a reporter who covered the battle return to Sharpsburg before a year has passed to reflect on what happened there.

George Towle, the man who braved insects and roughnecks to come home to fight for his state, expressed the deepest sentiment that most northerners shared about the war. The starting point of Towle's 2,100-mile journey was Bandera, Texas, a Hill Country village fifty miles north of San Antonio. He had enjoyed several years as a surveyor in Bandera, where he was respected and liked. Because he had attended military school in the South, Texas officials offered him a commission to fight for the Confederacy. Towle loved life in this beautiful and bountiful country "among a people rude and rough but hospitable and honest," and yet he declined the offer. "I am a Union man," he wrote. "I could not fight against the promptings of my heart. I could not fight against that flag."

OUR WAR

A COMPANY OF THE 15TH NEW HAMPSHIRE VOLUNTEERS,
A NINE-MONTH REGIMENT, LINES UP AT TRAINING
CAMP ON CONCORD HEIGHTS IN AUGUST 1862.

WAR!

"When our land is filled with widows
and orphans, and our homes draped with
mourning, as they will be in two short years,
and we then find our brothers of the same
race still unconquered, all will be for peace.
Then why not make it now before all these
tremendous sacrifices have been made?"

—*Democratic Standard*, Concord, May 4, 1861

April 15, 1861

THE FIRST VOLUNTEER

EDWARD E. STURTEVANT LIVED A LONER'S LIFE, prowling the dark streets as Concord's night watchman and sleeping by day at the police station. Yet from the governor to the ink-stained printer's helper, everyone in New Hampshire's capital seemed to know him. He was the cockeyed, cigar-chomping constable whose curiosity drove him to attend all manner of events and to chase down any celebrity who came to town. Single and sturdy, he pitched in wherever a strong arm and a willing spirit could help. He fought fires, policed conventions, captained a local militia called the Calathumpian Fusiliers, and joined the Sons of Temperance. In the spring of 1861 Sturtevant told friends that if war came, he wanted to be the first volunteer. They made sure he got his wish.

Sturtevant had not always been a policeman. In the summer of 1843, when he was sixteen years old, his parents sent him to Concord to apprentice as a printer at the *New Hampshire Statesman*. More than his native Keene, the state capital hummed with social and political life. While learning his trade and making his name as an able compositor, Sturtevant took it all in. He came of age in Concord, the good son building a Spartan life for

EDWARD E. STURTEVANT

5

himself, sending his parents money whenever he could, and writing them vivid letters about his adventures. He volunteered as a guard for James K. Polk's visit to town and met the president in the State House. When Sam Houston spoke there, Sturtevant found him handsome but joked about their handshake. "I took hold of his hand with a *terrible* grip, supposing that it would be hard as the d—l! but I smashed it all up in my hand, thinking that it was rather a soft one for the Hero of San Jacinto to have." Sturtevant went to balls and occasionally mentioned women in his letters but never by name. "I keep clear as you are probably aware of all the things in human shape that wear petticoats, and I think I always shall," he informed his family at the age of twenty.

A letter home in the winter of 1844 showed the range of Sturtevant's roving as a young man about town. On a Sunday night he went to a carpenter shop crammed with Millerites, followers of a man who prophesied the imminent second coming of Christ, and could not stifle his laughter over their odd behavior. He attended an exhibition at a literary institute, the services of a reform preacher, and a talk in which the abolitionist rabble-rouser Stephen S. Foster damned Henry Clay as "the vilest reptile that ever walked across the American continent." On a raid to enforce the town's new prohibition ordinance, Sturtevant rode a fire engine to hose out a cellar full of sots. He visited the state prison to hear a violist accompany Methodist singers and helped put out big fires both there and at a factory in the village of Fisherville. "The factory girls as well as the men helped work the engines when the men were tired," he wrote, crediting the women with saving a part of the building. He went to town meeting and marveled at how the abolitionists turned the proceedings into a two-day debacle—"nothing but row!"

Of the scores of incidents he described over the years, two foretold the grit he would show as a soldier. In 1847, when he was twenty-one, he had a toothache in "one of my little stubs." Neither of the dentists he visited could pull it. The pain was "life & death," and Sturtevant decided to yank it himself. He borrowed tools "and went to work myself and got it out by cutting, prying, and pulling—and it was a hard job any way you can fix it—and I almost fainted away—but I got it out—and have stopped its aching!" Later, during a two-year stay in Richmond, Virginia, as a printer, he hung his Liverpool-made silver watch at his work bench, and someone stole it. He never got it back, but his failure was not for want of trying. He followed the man he thought had stolen the watch to Washington and had him arrested, but the police found no watch. Sturtevant next confronted three toughs at his printing job in Richmond. They drew knives and pistols and demanded a retraction, which he refused to give. Co-workers rushed to his side, and the three men backed down.

Perhaps this amateur sleuthing turned Sturtevant toward police work. Although in demand as a printer after returning to New Hampshire, he increasingly found himself in the middle of things. On a printing job in Manchester during the summer of 1854, he witnessed riots in the streets. The Angel Gabriel, the self-anointed street preacher John S. Orr, incited a crowd of American Party rowdies to assail Irish immigrants. "He calls the Irish Catholics *mickies* and the way he pours it into them is not slow," Sturtevant wrote. "He blows a brass trumpet as a signal to commence his harangue." On the Fourth of July, club-wielding Americans wrecked the shanties of Irish families and smashed windows at St. Anne's Catholic Church. Despite reservations about the American Party, Sturtevant pronounced himself satisfied that "the Irish Catholics can't quite yet raise their black flag, with the Pope standing one foot on Washington's neck."

Back in Concord the next spring, he poked fun at the American Party even as it gained popularity. Because of the secrecy of the anti-immigrant, anti-Catholic society that spawned the party, the Americans were also called Know-Nothings. Sturtevant pretended he wasn't sure if the Know-Nothings had convened in the capital or not, saying he had seen "a great number of good looking men here in the city, who came and went away as quietly as if they were afraid somebody would see them." Their champion, Governor-elect Henry Metcalf, almost didn't make it to his inauguration. "He lodged at the Eagle Hotel, and came very near suffocating from the fact that he didn't understand shutting off the gas in his room," Sturtevant wrote. The odor was one "not very often smelt." An open window saved Metcalf from asphyxiation.

About this time Sturtevant began seizing liquor, breaking up illegal lotteries, and collaring drunkards as a full-time police officer. He chased down counterfeiters, horse thieves, and burglars and answered a complaint about a vile-smelling slaughterhouse. Often he escorted prisoners to other towns and cities by day and then worked an overnight shift. In many letters he enclosed twenty, thirty, or thirty-five dollars for his aging parents in Keene. After one New Year's shift he wrote them from the police station that he had welcomed in the year near the Free Will Baptist meetinghouse, walking his beat during the holiday for the fifth straight year. By the spring of 1861, at the age of thirty-four, he had established himself as a trusty lawman and been elected captain of the Granite Guards, a militia company. As war talk heightened, he resolved to be the first man to defend the flag.

April was a mean month in New Hampshire. Cold, wet days mocked the longing for spring, and mud replaced snow and ice. National events moved in step with the weather. Already a last-ditch peace conference had failed and seven southern states had seceded. Now secessionist troops seemed determined to shell or starve the military garrison out of Fort Sumter in Charleston Harbor.

Amos Hadley, editor and proprietor of the *Independent Democrat*, walked into his office on a Saturday afternoon. The newspaper, the capital's Republican mouthpiece, was one of several on Main Street, which ran along a plateau just west of the Merrimack River. Concord was a city of 11,000 residents, but because it was a political center and a railroad hub, it seemed larger. Hadley had put out the *Democrat* two days before, and Saturday was normally a quiet day. Not this one. News from Charleston arrived shortly after he did: The rebels had fired on Fort Sumter the previous day. Townspeople soon filled the *Democrat* office and fell into debate. Most considered the shelling a brash act that wiser heads would soon repudiate in favor of peace. A smaller group saw it as the start of a long, bitter war.

The next day the excitement shifted to the telegraph office at the Columbian Hotel on Main Street near the State House. Even though it was Sunday, Joseph W. Robinson, the proprietor, opened the office. Well-dressed people who had just left the city's downtown churches gathered there eager for news. At about noontime, Robinson obliged them: Fort Sumter had surrendered. Many in the crowd gasped, and the mood grew somber. Citizens of their own country had attacked an American fort and forced it to strike its flag. Older residents said they had never before felt such alarm.

Sturtevant walked his beat that night and turned in early on April 15. He boarded at the Phenix Hotel, where Abraham Lincoln had stopped on his speaking tour of the state the previous year, but slept at the police station. After the telegraph at the Columbian clacked out Lincoln's call for 75,000 three-month volunteers to suppress the rebellion, friends woke Sturtevant with the news. He rushed to the adjutant general's office and volunteered, then pitched a tent in the State House yard and began signing up more men.

The crusade to save the Union had begun. In Concord, as elsewhere, residents gathered to declare loyalty to the country, recruit young men, and decide how to help the families the soldiers would leave behind. As martial music filled the air, those who had uniforms put them on. Preachers lent holiness to the cause. Ladies' clubs collected money for the soldiers. One group bought Ai B. Thompson, soon to be a lieutenant, a silver revolver inscribed with a motto Thompson must have hoped was not prophetic: "It is sweet to die for one's country." When Thompson wrote home to Plymouth to inform his parents that he had joined, they were split in their response. "Were I some younger I would go myself," his father, J. H. Thompson, wrote. His mother C.B. was skeptical: "I was sorry to learn that you had enlisted but since you have I hope that you will prove faithfull. . . . I fear you will have hardships to indure that you little think of."

In response to Lincoln's call, Governor Ichabod Goodwin asked for a thousand volunteers. Sturtevant moved his recruiting office to the Phenix, where printers, railroad men, carriage makers, farmers, and others flocked to join up. Within two weeks he had enlisted 223 men. "Concord is full of the war spirit," Hadley wrote in the *Democrat*. "The news from the South has completely roused the patriotism of our people." At a war meeting at city hall, Thomas P. Treadwell, a leading Democrat, framed the nation's challenge and its solution. "How can the Union be preserved and perpetuated?" he said. "This is the all-absorbing question of the day. The only answer to this question is—it must and shall be preserved, peaceably, if we can, forcibly, if we must." Franklin Pierce, the former president, lived in Concord but missed the meeting. The next night, from the balcony of the Eagle Hotel, he assured a crowd he would have been there had he known about it. Pierce had long been a friend of the South, but on this night he expressed at least a tepid solidarity with his fellow citizens.

As unifying as the news from Sumter seemed, not all Democrats could go even as far as Pierce had. The sharpest dissent came from the likeliest quarter. The pro-southern *Democratic Standard* declared: "We are for a peace policy." The North should defend itself only if southern armies invaded, the paper said. To invade the South would cost untold lives, it predicted, as the people there defended their homeland to the last breath.

In promising to stand by these opinions, the *Standard* knew it was risking reprisal. Its editor warned Republicans to respect his right to free expression no matter how unpopular his ideas might be. "Do you propose to mob our dwellings, destroy our property, burn our homes, because we dare to exercise the undoubted birthright of American citizens, and hold you to account for your political conduct, while we take no part against our country?" the paper asked. If war advocates did try to silence him, he wrote, they could expect "a civil war at your own doors." No harm came to the paper or its proprietors in response to his baiting—at least not yet.

PASTOR HENRY E. PARKER

At the South Congregational Church the Sunday after Lincoln's call, Sturtevant marched many of his recruits to their pews. Pastor Henry E. Parker, soon to go to war as a regimental chaplain, addressed their presence. The church had often been a scene of personal and even public grief, he said, but the many tears he saw in his congregation this day sprang from "emotions the like to which were never felt here."

On a night twelve years earlier, when Sturtevant was still working as a printer, he had come to this church on a different mission. When a fire broke out downtown, he heard the first alarm and decided he must give the second. "I hallowed about five minutes but could not raise many—and then went and broke down the door to the South Church and got hold of the bell rope, and rung the bell, which seemed to wake people up. I stayed and rung the bell for an hour and a half, and therefore did not see the fire when it was the hottest, though the whole street was as light as day."

Now, in a moment just as urgent, the state's first volunteer was back at South Church, determined to give his all to put out the fire that threatened his country.

June 6, 1861

'OUR TRUE POSITION'

THE WAR BEGAN AFTER NATHANIEL BERRY was elected governor in March but before his inauguration in June. Nothing in the state's past had prepared it to muster and equip multiple infantry regiments, but hundreds of men volunteered, and two regiments comprising 1,826 men and officers began training. Amid the military bustle of the state capital, Berry's task as the new governor was to spell out the cause for which New Hampshire's sons might soon be dying.

The occasion was Election Day, a misnomer since it was in fact the annual inaugural festival. Bitter partisanship dominated public debate most of the time, but not on Election Day. In its seventy-eighth year, it had once been a street carnival with tent shows, Negro fiddlers, and booths that sold gingerbread cakes, lemonade, and stronger drink. The day still called for a parade and a street party. Because of the war, an inaugural church service, a tradition suspended in 1831, was revived for Berry's day. The Reverend Parker preached for an hour and ten minutes, asserting that no matter how dark the present might seem, the good book held comforting precedents. "The idea of a civil war is terrible, but civil wars do not of necessity destroy a nation," he said. "Indeed, more good than evil has often resulted from them."

The inaugural events lasted two days, as political leaders made time for military pomp. Trains delivered veterans' groups and local militias to be seen and feted in the capital. Bands played martial airs. At the head of the parade pranced the Governor's Horse Guard, numbering 103 sabers and led by Colonel

NATHANIEL S. BERRY

George Stark of Nashua, the Democrat whom Berry had defeated in March. The parade detoured five miles to collect the governor-elect at the train station in the village of Fisherville. By then a drenching rain was falling. Horse Guardsmen pulled their cloaks tight. Riding in an open barouche drawn by six dapple gray horses, Berry and his party ducked beneath umbrellas. He punned about the storm to a lunch crowd at the Phenix Hotel. "It is such a rain as we can bear patiently," he said. "Thank God it was not the reign of Jeff Davis." Berry was to deliver his main oration before a joint session of the Legislature. Although he was expected to speak about fiscal prudence and other traditional concerns, all New Hampshire, not just the legislators, awaited his remarks about the war.

Berry had never held major elective office, but experience had prepared him for the moment. He was a self-made man, sixty-four years old, with a beetle brow, thick eyebrows, and thinning hair. When he was six years old and living in his native Maine, his father, a shipyard mechanic, fell into the Kennebec River and drowned. With little formal schooling, Berry learned the tanner's trade and acquired his own tannery at the age of twenty-four. Eventually he settled in Hebron, a tiny town on Newfound Lake in central New Hampshire. He served as a Jacksonian Democrat in the Legislature but later joined a movement that broke with the party over the extension of slavery. He ran unsuccessfully for governor on the Free Soil ticket for five straight years during the 1840s. When the Republicans nominated him in January 1861, the Democratic *New Hampshire Patriot* dismissed him as "one of the fossils of the old abolition party" and predicted his election would hasten a war. Berry had indeed spent a decade out of politics, but he was a respected probate judge. On town meeting day in March, fifty-two percent of voters chose him.

Berry opened his inaugural speech by accusing the southern states of intentionally misreading the country's founding principles. If states could simply "sunder their bonds of loyalty and duty to the general government," he said, the United States would have no foundation. Secession was now a fact, as southerners had seized Fort Sumter, mints, arsenals, and other federal property "in high-handed acts of treason." The only choice for New Hampshire was to join the other loyal states in putting down this rebellion. Berry urged legislators to appropriate a million dollars for the war while also understanding that saving "the great experiment of free government" could cost much more. "It may be that our country must be shaken from centre to circumference by the mighty struggle; that *liberty* must be again baptized in blood," he said.

Berry uttered not a word about slavery. He would soon be calling on sons of Democrats and sons of Republicans to die in the war. He knew the newspapers would soon be back at it, Democrats calling their adversaries Black Republicans and abolitionists, Republicans branding Democrats hunkers and traitors. On Election Day at least, the people of New Hampshire needed a common cause, and Berry gave them one.

June 21, 1861

COMMON GROUND

AS THE FIRST NEW HAMPSHIRE VOLUNTEERS crossed Seneca Creek in Maryland, they beheld a novel sight. Back home, they had read and talked about slavery, but here in the fields along the road they saw actual slaves plowing corn. Some soldiers could not resist calling out, beckoning the slaves, and asking if they did not wish to be free. What the slaves made of this is not recorded, but the incident angered their owner, a farmer named Almutt. John L. Dufief, a friend of Almutt's, decided the leaders of the offending regiment should answer for their men's behavior. After all, the soldiers had threatened the legitimate property of a Union man in a Union state. If they were truly fighting to preserve the Union and leave states free to choose their own institutions, they should not tempt slaves with thoughts of freedom.

The man Dufief contacted was Stephen G. Abbott, the forty-one-year-old Baptist minister serving as the First New Hampshire's chaplain. Abbott had volunteered at the request of his neighbor, Mason Tappan, the abolitionist congressman who was also the regiment's colonel. Abbott was inventing the job as he went along. He gave sermons, prepared a hymnal, and visited the sick. After Tappan offered his men the use of his congressional franking privilege for their letters home, Abbott learned to forge Tappan's signature. Some days he signed it 400 times.

When Dufief's letter arrived, the soldiers were as new to their duties as their chaplain was. Three-month volunteers, they had left Concord to a festive sendoff as New Hampshire's contingent of the first 75,000 men called into service by the president. Once they reached Maryland, their pickets chatted with rebel soldiers across the river. When the enemy fired on the First from a safe distance, the men competed to scoop up musket and rifle balls rolling into their camp. They were eager for souvenirs and curious whether the balls were made of pewter, lead, iron, or copper. The men didn't know it, but they lacked the skills and equipment needed for effective service. They didn't even have pants. Tappan was

MASON TAPPAN

glad to hear that a hundred pairs would be waiting for them in Washington, but the men needed more pants than that and they needed them now. "Our camp & fatigue duties have been hard and continuous, & many of the men are literally *naked*," Tappan informed the state's top military officer. "They are obliged to march in their *drawers* & I have nothing to mend with but to patch them with our towels."

Pants or no pants, some of the soldiers had upset farmer Alcutt. For years northern Free Soilers and Republicans had assured Unionists with southern leanings that they had no intention of interfering with slavery where it already existed. But here, before a major battle had been fought, in a state where Union feeling was lukewarm, northern soldiers were encouraging slaves to throw off their chains. "This is *all wrong*, and ought to be stopped," Dufief informed Chaplain Abbott. If the soldiers would just leave slavery alone, they might save the country and have a pleasant time of it. "May God in his mercy avert this horrible war, and all learn to respect the laws and the Constitution, and continue as a nation unto the end of time, a happy, prosperous and united *people*," Dufief wrote.

On June 21, from the regiment's camp in Poolesville, Abbott made his reply. He did not contest the facts or dispute Dufief's complaint. "Should any of our men be detected in tampering with the slaves for the purpose of aiding them to escape," he wrote, "they would meet with severe and merited punishment." He did not know what the rules would be in seceded states, but the First New Hampshire had not come to Maryland to free the slaves. The soldiers saw slaves on every march and gave shelter to none. Slaves who entered the regiment's camp on their masters' business were sent back when the business was done. Although some of the men might question the morality of slavery, the regiment was duty-bound to recognize slaves as property and their masters as rightful owners of property. "Not a slave will be permitted to go one mile or rod with us, from his master, with our knowledge," Abbott wrote.

He dismissed the incident itself as the act of a few men in a regiment of nearly a thousand. Behind it, he wrote, was nothing more than natural Yankee curiosity. The men had called to the slaves because they were "constitutionally and hereditarily addicted to asking questions." Northerners of all persuasions wanted to know what the slaves thought. Abbott himself wanted to know, but out of respect for "the extreme sensitiveness of the people at just this time," he would not ask. Abbott clung to the hope that the country could talk its way through its differences. Discussions between northern soldiers and southern civilians "will do more than all the bayonets in the country to harmonize feeling and effect a desirable and permanent peace," he wrote. He had no doubt both sides wanted such a peace, and "every day's march and every day's residence here" bolstered his confidence that it might yet come to pass.

June 26, 1861

ONE LIFE

PERHAPS NAÏVETÉ ABOUT WAR'S TRUE COST explains the funeral Concord prepared for Charles Webster Walker. He was not the first soldier from New Hampshire to die. That distinction belonged to Luther Ladd of Alexandria, a Sixth Massachusetts man who had been shot in the streets of

Baltimore on April 19. But Walker was the first man from Concord to die, and his death came while the city was being transformed, with soldiers training on its plains and politicians struggling to meet war's demands. A soldier's death brought home the gravity of the moment. "It seemed more like a dream than a reality," Clara Farnum wrote her cousin. "It was so sudden and, under the circumstances, seemed worse than as though he had been killed in battle."

Walker's ancestors had come to Concord in the early eighteenth century, but he did not inherit an easy life. When he was in his teens, his father sent him from Fryeburg, Maine, where he had grown up, to board with his Uncle Abiel Walker, a Concord shoemaker. Charles apprenticed in a bookbinder's shop, but not for long. His brother Galen, the Massachusetts deputy warden, offered him a job at the Charlestown prison, where, through happenstance, he rose swiftly through the ranks. On December 15, 1856, an inmate serving time for cutting his wife's throat with a razor handed Galen a note that said, "Mr. Walker, you have not used me well." As Walker read the note, the inmate stabbed him in the chest and neck, killing him. Charles was made deputy warden. Two weeks later, a copycat stabbed the new warden in the neck. Promoted again, Charles decided to move on instead. By one account he did not wish to be hired out of sympathy or for the sake of convenience. It seems just as likely that recent events suggested a career other than prison administration.

In 1861, Walker was back in Concord, where another brother, Lyman, now lived at the family homestead. Charles was engaged to a teacher, but neither their plans nor his work kept him from volunteering with the first wave of three-year soldiers. Thirty-eight years old, he joined as first lieutenant in the Goodwin Rifles, a company of the Second New Hampshire. The regiment trained on the state's seacoast under Colonel Gilman Marston, a congressman like Mason Tappan of the First New Hampshire. After Walker visited home in early June, Clara Farnum, a friend of his fiancée's, wrote her cousin that he was full of stories about camp life and "lively and cheerful as ever."

The regiment soon left for Washington, D.C. The journey was novel and festive at first. A large crowd saw the men off at the Portsmouth train station, and chapters of the Sons of New Hampshire fed them in Boston and New York. They traveled from New York to New Jersey by steamboat—the first salt-water voyage for most of them. At Elizabethport, they were loaded onto open platform and gravel cars, not passenger cars. Though dismayed by this, they counted it a minor hardship of military life. It might have been forgotten except for what happened just after the train left the station.

One moment Lieutenant Walker was standing on a platform car, the next he was gone. A man who saw him disappear speculated that he had fallen asleep on his feet. The man shouted out, but by the time the train stopped, several cars had run over Walker's right leg. The company commander, Captain Simon G. Griffin, jumped from the train with two other men and the regimental surgeon, George Hubbard. They found Walker conscious and howling in pain. He asked to be shot. The rescue party carried him onto the train, and at the next station Hubbard amputated the leg near the hip. Walker died a short time later. A telegram waiting at the station in Reading, Pennsylvania, delivered the news to his comrades. "The general sentiment among the men was I wish it was me instead of him," Thomas B. Leaver, a corporal in Walker's company, wrote home.

The city's cornet band and fifty honorary members of the Goodwin Rifles met Walker's body at the train station. As the band played the death march, soldiers with rifles reversed and colors furled escorted the body to Lyman Walker's house. Flags along the way flew at half-staff, and Main Street's buildings were draped in mourning. The next morning, June 26, the body lay in state for three hours in the State House rotunda. "Probably never before did the people of Concord, as a mass, experience similar sensations on the occasion of a public funeral," one editor wrote. The Boston train carrying Walker's Masonic brothers arrived in late morning. They formed in the State House yard, all in uniform, swords drawn, and filed inside past Walker's body.

The pallbearers carried the casket to the funeral wagon waiting on Main Street. Lewis Downing & Sons, the celebrated Concord coach-makers, had prepared it. Workers draped the coach in white and surmounted it with four black plumes and the American ensign. They covered the two white horses chosen to draw the coach with black netting and more black plumes. The procession stretched a quarter mile. The cornet band at its front played a dirge, and the Goodwin Rifles marched behind the band. Then came the funeral car, the Home Guards of Fisherville, Mayor Moses Humphrey and other city officials, Governor Berry, his council, the House speaker, the Senate president, and nearly every state legislator. The Governor's Horse Guard rode with swords at the shoulder, followed by two more bands. It was a Wednesday, but businesses closed. All along the way people thronged to see the spectacle and honor Walker. As the last of the parade passed them, most joined the procession and marched to the Old North Church.

The church had a history relevant to present events, as did Pastor Nathaniel Bouton, who would lead the service. Walker's ancestor, Timothy, had been Old North's first ordained minister in 1730. Fifty-eight years later delegates had approved the U.S. Constitution in the church meeting house, making New Hampshire the ninth and decisive state to ratify. In 1833, on the same site, Bouton helped found the New Hampshire Anti-Slavery Society. Now, whatever politicians might say to the contrary, few doubted that slavery had brought on the constitutional crisis that led to war. The huge crowd gathered to honor a soldier who, even if by accident, had sacrificed his life for the cause. The casket was opened in the church so that people could see Walker's face one last time. Dignitaries and legislators took most of the seats in the church, but people also gathered outside to hear the hymns and anthems.

Before long the dream of easy victory would fade into long lists naming the men who had died of disease in the tropical murk of Louisiana or fallen in battle in places whose names were as yet unknown: Bull Run, Fair Oaks, Antietam, and on and on. But on this day, death in wartime was a novelty demanding pomp and ceremony. And yet any death is personal. Shortly after the Masons laid Brother Walker to rest in the Old North Burying Ground, Clara Farnum visited his grave. She saw that Walker's fiancée had left not one bouquet but three. Farnum pitied the woman and hoped she would come to see in time that enduring the death of a lover was preferable to being forsaken and forgotten.

July 4, 1861

THE LOYAL OPPOSITION

ON A GLORIOUS DAY THE PREVIOUS SUMMER, with American flags adorning the maples and elms all along Concord's Main Street, Henry P. Rolfe had emerged from a coach arm-in-arm with Stephen A. Douglas, the Democratic candidate for president. For an hour the Little Giant held forth before a crowd of five thousand people in the State House yard. The speech was lively, and under the glow of Chinese lanterns, Douglas's listeners lingered into the night to celebrate. As chairman of the event, Rolfe, a Concord lawyer and a Douglas man, could not have asked for more.

Now, nearly a year later, Douglas was gone, having died of typhoid fever on June 3 at the age of forty-eight, and the country was fighting the war he had tried to prevent. As the Legislature debated the state's role in that war, Rolfe found solace in Douglas's last political stand. On the Fourth of July, he wrote Governor Berry a letter and labeled it "private." A group of Democratic legislators had opposed a war appropriation, but Rolfe assured Berry they were not speaking for the party. "Mr. Douglas' dying legacy to the American People was for them 'to rise in their might and crush rebellion from the land,'" Rolfe wrote. "That should be the desire of all good men and patriots, and God help you as the chief executive officer of the State so to conduct our affairs as to combine for the overthrow of rebellion the greatest amount of patriotism, courage and efficiency."

Not every war bill was contentious. Meeting on the national holiday, legislators agreed on what had caused the war and what had not. The attack on the government's constitutional authority made the secessionists traitors. The war "should be regarded by all loyal men not as a sectional war, not an antislavery war, not a war of conquest and subjugation, but simply and solely a war for the maintenance of the Government, the suppression of the rebellion, and the preservation of the *magna charta* of our liberty and national unity." Both chambers passed a resolution containing these words unanimously.

It was another debate that angered Rolfe. Lawmakers approved a million dollars for the war and empowered the governor to spend it, but ninety-one Democrats dissented and signed a protest. They said Berry might abuse the power of the purse to support a war on state sovereignty. Representative Harry Bingham of Littleton argued that "upon the tyrant's plea of necessity, great liberties have been crushed under the iron wheel of military despotism." Rolfe didn't buy it. "I believe the whole object and aim of the originators of that protest was to embarrass and discourage good and loyal men of my own political cast," he wrote Berry. "God forbid that at this time I should do anything to encourage the heart or nerve the arm of this most stupendously wicked rebellion." The protest, he wrote, was "political clap trap, gotten up by a few crafty and designing men" who, lacking a majority to govern, had decided to obstruct. He didn't name Franklin Pierce as the instigator, but others did. Rolfe wrote only: "I know the men and their schemes."

He wanted Berry to know that many Democrats were "ready to make any sacrifice, to risk any danger personal to themselves in order that we may preserve to ourselves and our posterity 'a name and a country.'" As long as Berry chose carefully, Rolfe wrote, he could employ loyal Democrats with confidence.

July 21, 1861

TO BATTLE

THE SECOND NEW HAMPSHIRE VOLUNTEERS were green. They lacked the training and discipline that make an infantry regiment a mighty tool of war. They carried too much gear and too little water. Their colonel was a congressman. They had storybook notions of war, expecting the enemy to meet them in the open for a fair fight. They had signed up for three years but expected to snuff out the rebellion in months. At one o'clock on the morning of July 21, they awoke near Centreville, Virginia, ready to fight. To a man they believed the battle had been too long coming.

When marching orders arrived at their camp a mile and a half north of the Capitol, they shouted for joy. "Our boys are all dying to go; they are afraid it will be all settled before they [have] a chance to pick off some of

FRANK FISKE

those miserable traitors," Corporal Thomas B. Leaver wrote his mother in Concord. "This rebellion is playing itself out pretty fast or I am mistaken." Lieutenant Colonel Frank S. Fiske expressed one qualm. The order "contained several instructions as to details, ending with one that the surgeons should take their 'amputating instruments,'" he recalled. "I don't think I ever read any other sentence which made me feel so uncomfortable as that did." He had visions of Captain Cuttle, the portly, hook-handed sea captain in a Dickens novel. "I wondered if I could learn to use the hook as deftly as the Captain did," Fiske wrote.

The soldiers marched on July 16 wearing French army hats and gray uniforms trimmed with red cord—"the queerest-looking uniforms in the world," wrote Private Martin Haynes of Manchester. The brass buttons on their swallow-tail coats bore the state seal—a sailing ship and farmers before the rising sun. Except the Goodwin Rifles, a Concord militia company armed with Sharp's rifles, the men shouldered .69-caliber muskets for buck and ball. They carried ammunition, haversacks, knapsacks, and canteens. Some had whiskey. Those designated as pioneers bore axes and shovels. Though overequipped, they had no tents. They were to sleep on the ground. With prudence that many other supply officers lacked, their quartermaster, Captain John S. Godfrey of Hampton Falls, limited the load in their wagons to one ton per four horses.

JOHN S. GODFREY

The Second soon joined Colonel Ambrose Burnside's brigade, which included three other infantry regiments, the Second Rhode Island Light Battery under Captain William H. Reynolds, two Dahlgren guns from ships, and a few companies of regulars. The band played "Dixie" and workers along the banks of the Potomac cheered as the brigade crossed Long Bridge into Virginia. "At a quick step and with right good will we pushed on into Old Virginia," wrote a Second New Hampshire soldier who called himself "Corporal Trim." By Arlington Heights just across the river, alas, men began to fall out, "yielding to a fatigue which no exuberance of patriotism could withstand." Some ran out of water. "One poor fellow almost dead with thirst gave $2.50 for a canteen of muddy water, and some gave a quarter of a dollar for just a swallow," a soldier wrote. "I never knew before what it was to *want* for water."

At Bailey's Cross Roads they bedded down in the furrows of a cornfield with knapsacks or saddles for pillows. "I can march with the sturdiest backwoodsman," Lieutenant Ai B. Thompson wrote his

LT. COL. FISKE, QUARTERMASTER GODFREY, AND CHAPLAIN HENRY E. PARKER

father. "Slept on the ground last night and slept first rate." Felled trees obstructed the road to Fairfax Court House. The route reminded Godfrey, driving a baggage wagon, of a turnpike back home "in its worst state when abandoned. The hills are full as steep & the conditions of the road horrible." Yet the division, the first of three in Brigadier General Irvin McDowell's army, moved as one now, its fifteen thousand men impressing Chaplain Henry Parker, the former Concord pastor. "I have had nothing seem quite so much like war yet as to be with the advance of our division, see the throwing out of scouts to examine the country to prevent our being led into ambush, & then to visit the entrenchments & camps of the enemy, who had precipitantly fled," he wrote his wife Mary.

Entering Fairfax Court House at noon without firing a shot, the men reveled in bloodless victory. They stacked arms on the village green and cheered as Captain Tileston Barker, a fifty-four-year-old boot-maker from Westmoreland, yanked the rebel flag from the courthouse cupola. "The Stars and Stripes are flying from Fairfax Court House of which you have

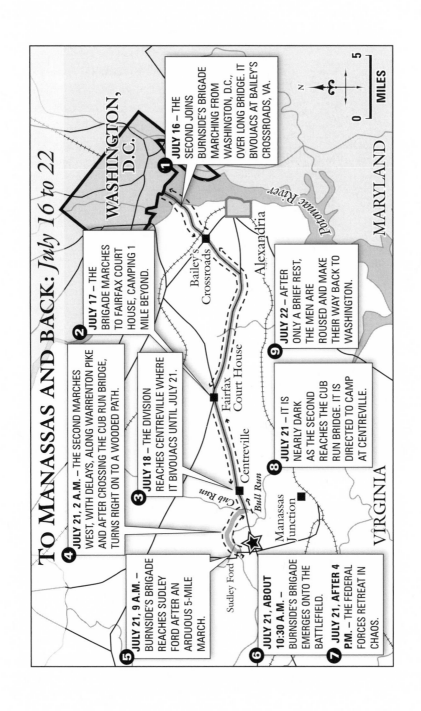

TO MANASSAS AND BACK: *July 16 to 22*

JULY 16 – THE SECOND JOINS BURNSIDE'S BRIGADE MARCHING FROM WASHINGTON, D.C., OVER LONG BRIDGE. IT BIVOUACS AT BAILEY'S CROSSROADS, VA. **①**

JULY 17 – THE BRIGADE MARCHES TO FAIRFAX COURT HOUSE, CAMPING 1 MILE BEYOND. **②**

JULY 18 – THE DIVISION REACHES CENTREVILLE WHERE IT BIVOUACS UNTIL JULY 21. **③**

JULY 21, 2 A.M. – THE SECOND MARCHES WEST, WITH DELAYS, ALONG WARRENTON PIKE AND AFTER CROSSING THE CUB RUN BRIDGE, TURNS RIGHT ON TO A WOODED PATH. **④**

JULY 21, 9 A.M. – BURNSIDE'S BRIGADE REACHES SUDLEY FORD AFTER AN ARDUOUS 5-MILE MARCH. **⑤**

JULY 21, ABOUT 10:30 A.M. – BURNSIDE'S BRIGADE EMERGES ONTO THE BATTLEFIELD. **⑥**

JULY 21, AFTER 4 P.M. – THE FEDERAL FORCES RETREAT IN CHAOS. **⑦**

JULY 21 – IT IS NEARLY DARK AS THE SECOND REACHES THE CUB RUN BRIDGE. IT IS DIRECTED TO CAMP AT CENTREVILLE. **⑧**

JULY 22 – AFTER ONLY A BRIEF REST, THE MEN ARE ROUSED AND MAKE THEIR WAY BACK TO WASHINGTON. **⑨**

WASHINGTON, D.C.

MARYLAND

VIRGINIA

Potomac River

Alexandria

Bailey's Crossroads

Fairfax Court House

Centreville

Manassas Junction

Sudley Ford

Cub Run

Bull Run

N

0   5

MILES

TILESTON A. BARKER

heard so much," Thompson wrote his father. "The rebel pickets came out far enough to see us and went back like lightning on a wire. . . . They are not chivalrous enough to stand their ground and defend their own homes." A soldier named "Norman" scoffed: "I do not know much about southern fighting qualities, but they can do some tall traveling down this way." The rebels "even left meat cooking in their camps," Private John H. Burrill of Fitzwilliam wrote. Men filched rebel blankets, tents, clothing, matches, knives, revolvers, and, at a pay table, rolls of dimes and quarters.

"Nearly everyone had some sort of trophy," wrote Corporal Trim. They took sugar, tobacco, and other staples from a country grocery. At the post office, they rifled a mailbag "filled with those inordinate boastings and conceits with which the rebels plumed themselves." Many ate supper on crockery. Chaplain Parker was served tea "in a very respectable house." His host, though a secessionist, claimed to like the invaders. "I imagine it will be very far from an impossible thing to have these seceded States return, when they have once seen our men and forces," Parker wrote. Thompson thought the day's events had exposed the rebels' strategy. They "will retreat before the advancing hosts of Lincoln's men hoping to render us unfit for action by sickness and disease from this hot weather," he wrote. "But we can stand the heat as well as they and follow them clear to the Gulf of Mexico."

Manassas, a critical railroad junction just beyond a stream called Bull Run, connected the Shenandoah Valley with eastern Virginia. Capturing it was General McDowell's chief objective in leading his army west from Washington. Winfield Scott, the general-in-chief, addressed the men near Centreville, suggesting that Manassas might fall as easily as Fairfax Court House had. Scott assured them he "shall not permit a single life to be rashly thrown away," wrote Corporal Trim. "It is thought that no other stand will be made after Bull Run and Manassas until we get to Richmond. The troops are terribly excited; it is fearful to see men with the tiger fully aroused in them." A civilian visitor rode in and found soldiers of the Second New

Hampshire bathing in a stream and horses tethered in a field. Colonel Marston told him he had heard only one complaint about his men: "They are too intelligent. They are constantly writing home."

The men awoke at one o'clock Sunday morning and washed down boiled beef with their coffee. The hour was upon them. They marched toward Bull Run "with their blankets on their shoulders, their haversacks full of hard bread, their canteens of water, with heavy muskets and cartridge boxes full of ammunition, but with hearts as light as were their falling footsteps," Thompson wrote. Each man bore forty rounds and a box of caps on his belt. Their

LIEUTENANT GENERAL
WINFIELD SCOTT

step was "almost as noiseless as the shining of the full-faced moon, which lighted them on over the turnpike thro' forest and thro' field," Thompson wrote. "It seemed to me as I watched the movement of those four thousand men as we were marching onward in the solemn stillness of the early Sabbath morn, that a phantom army was issuing forth from the mists of the night, armed with brightly burnished weapons of silver and gold." Beyond Centreville they waited three hours as the sun rose, and the heat with it. They crossed Cub Run, a tributary of Bull Run, and entered the woods on a little-used road. As a skirmisher beside the formation, Corporal Leaver dropped to his knees to "crawl and creep under the thickets" and soon fell out exhausted. It was hot and dusty, but

AI B. THOMPSON

the men marched along a path where oak leaves muffled their footfall. Like many others, Private Haynes filled his canteen with "good clear river water" from Bull Run, but when he took a sip, "I spat out the tepid mouthful in disgust, and emptied the canteen. . . . Before that day was over I would have given dollars for one square drink of that same water." Two cannon shots interrupted the morning birdsong. "Jumping forward I again joined my company" Corporal Leaver wrote.

The shots came from just below the crest of Matthews Hill, a slope of mostly cleared and rolling farmland. The left end of the rebels' line had turned to face the Yankees arriving there. Approaching the hill through the woods, Burnside's brigade was ordered to lead the attack just after ten o'clock. The Second Rhode Island infantry moved out first as some of the Second New Hampshire's pioneers advanced to clear a position for Captain Reynolds's battery. The others were told to leave their tools and pick them up on the way back. A shell exploded by accident, a piece of it striking Henry Holt of Lyndeborough in the neck. He was the first Second New Hampshire soldier to die in battle. The regiment marched out of the woods at double-quick, discarding blankets and much else, and halted to the right of the battery near the crest of the hill.

Lieutenant Thompson noted with disgust that the rebels seemed to be waiting for them to arrive just where they were placed. "We soon saw that they had every advantage of us," he wrote. "They were under the cover of woods; we could not see them, only a few of their pickets. Their batteries were all around us, except in our rear, and commanded almost every position we could possibly take to do them any injury. . . . They could see us but we could not see them." The Second "could not have been in a more unfavorable position for the enemy to cut us in pieces." The moment it deployed, a soldier wrote, "a heavy fire was opened on us from their batteries, also a shower of balls from their smaller pieces whistled through our ranks." One company commander, Captain Ichabod Pearl of Somersworth, fled in panic, his war over with the first shots.

The men exaggerated the rebel force opposite them and reacted to enemy fire as new troops do. They "opened fire, though scarce an enemy was in sight," Lieutenant Herbert B. Titus wrote. After someone spotted rebel soldiers under a fence, "they drew up and blazed away without orders from Col. or Capt.," Thompson wrote. "Our commanding officers didn't seem to know what to do. Marston is plucky and rash but he was not born to command. Lt. Col. Fiske attempted to rally the men but in spite of his

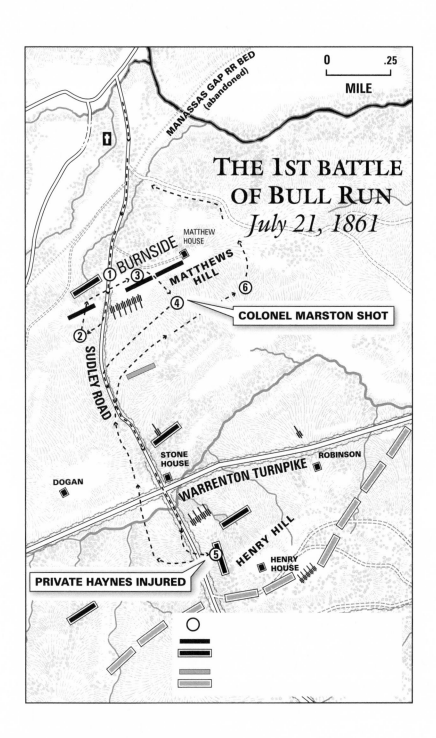

THE 1ST BATTLE
OF BULL RUN
July 21, 1861

MANASSAS GAP RR BED
(abandoned)

0   .25
MILE

MATTHEW
HOUSE

BURNSIDE

① →③

MATTHEWS
HILL

④

⑥

COLONEL MARSTON SHOT

②

SUDLEY ROAD

STONE
HOUSE

ROBINSON

WARRENTON TURNPIKE

DOGAN

HENRY HILL

⑤

HENRY
HOUSE

PRIVATE HAYNES INJURED

July 21, 1861 ▪ *To battle*

tardy efforts they retreated beyond the reach of the rebels' fire, and it was a most disorderly and disgraceful retreat." Private Haynes believed the men were just following orders. "After we had thus stood as inanimate targets for some little time, and many a poor fellow had been carried gasping and groaning to the surgeons, we were ordered to fall back and protect ourselves behind the brow of the hill," he wrote. All things considered, Captain Ephraim Weston saw only courage in his men, many of whom he had recruited in and around Peterborough. "It takes brave men to stand up for targets to be shot without having a chance to shoot back," he wrote. Private William W. Sawtelle of Amherst returned the compliment, describing Weston as "standing like a hero" under fire. "He kept his jokes going as though we were playing base ball." With Marston off to consult Burnside, Fiske strode the line, sweat pouring down his face. A cannonball blew the legs off two horses—a vivid spectacle in the regiment's primer in the carnage of war. "I had already seen men wounded and killed, but no such pitiful sight to me as that of those poor horses," Fiske wrote.

Officers had coaxed the men back to an exposed position by the time Marston returned, but just as he shouted "Attention!" a ball struck him two inches below the right shoulder and knocked him on his face. The

JOSIAH STEVENS

ball broke the bone, veered, and lodged in his chest. Ten feet away, Major Josiah Stevens "thought him shot dead," but an officer grabbed Marston's right arm to pull him to his feet. "The air was burdened with choice selections from the old colonel's matchless vocabulary," Haynes wrote. Chaplain Parker came to the rescue, helping Marston into the saddle and guiding him to a field hospital.

Now in command, Fiske reformed the regiment behind the Seventy-first New York on the hill. "I could hear the bullets strike someone, and the poor fellow would give one 'Oh' and that would be the last of him," wrote one man. Captain

Griffin ordered his men to lie down because they couldn't fire without endangering the New Yorkers. He then had to defend them when Fiske accused them of disgracing themselves. Fiske glanced up as a shell hit the ground between the feet of a standing soldier. "He seemed to me to rise a musket length in the air without any will or effort on his own, and I expected to see him fall dead," Fiske wrote. The man landed on his feet with a curse.

A horseman approached just as Fiske prepared to move the regiment again. "To my great surprise, Col. Marston was again seated on his horse and resumed command," a soldier wrote. "About this time it seemed as though the victory was ours. And had all of our officers the Courage of Col. Marston it would have been so." His arm in a sling, Marston "said

GILMAN MARSTON

he was with us again and would be with us so long as he could," wrote Thompson. It was what happened next that fixed Thompson's opinion of Marston. As the rebels pulled back toward Henry Hill and the Second New Hampshire pursued them, Marston "squatted on his haunches in a ditch packed full of men who had jumped in there to escape the rebel fire, which was thick and hot upon us." That was the last Thompson saw of Marston on the field. "To speak the plain truth," he wrote, "he was useless as a commander when unwounded and we knew it, notwithstanding his plucky speech made while his face was distorted with intensest pain."

When the regiment stopped, only the smoke from rebel firing was visible. Private Samuel Newell, a nineteen-year-old drummer from Manchester, called the enemy shells as harmless as "so many potatoes," but some found their mark. Private Haynes heard the roar of a cannon "ending in a 'thud,' which told it had got a victim down the line. Looking back, I saw a prostrate form sprawled in the dust of the road, with Johnny Ogden bending over it. 'Who is it, Johnny?' I called back." It was Private Henry Morse, a tent-mate from Acworth who had toured Washington with Haynes three weeks earlier.

Another cannonball hit four men, blowing both legs off one of them, nineteen-year-old Private William H. Quimby of Portsmouth. Nearby a ball shattered the knee of Private Lewis N. Relation of Hopkinton, who tumbled into the arms of Henry H. Everett. Everett helped carry him to safety, but he died before the day was out. Fiske declined a swallow from a soldier's canteen only to watch the man raise it to his own lips just as a cannonball took his head off. "Such a sight at home would have

LIEUTENANT COLONEL FISKE (CENTER) PREPARES TO MOUNT.

made me sick and faint with horror," Fiske wrote. Just a short time in battle led to a more clinical observation: "My principal feeling was astonishment that a cannon ball could make such a clean, knife-like cut."

In mid-afternoon the firing stopped, and a cheer started on the Union right. Believing his army victorious, General McDowell rode along the line delivering the news. The Second gave him "three rousing cheers." The rebels were indeed in trouble, but their stand on Matthews Hill had bought them valuable time. Now, rather than press his advantage, McDowell hesitated, providing even more time for rebel reinforcements to arrive from the Shenandoah Valley.

Cannon fire soon blasted the illusion of Union victory. The hardest fighting of the day began, and Burnside's men "were allowed to be spectators," Thompson wrote. After moving along the Sudley Road, they climbed halfway up Henry Hill, where they were "ordered to lie down on our faces, which most of the officers and the men obeyed," Thompson wrote. "They lay there in that disgraceful, because unnecessary, position without firing a musket or seeing an enemy." Up the hill in the distance the rebel line had re-formed its strengthened ranks. One by one, Union regiments moved up "in solid columns towards the enemies' batteries and discharged volley after volley into the rebel ranks but every one retreated in disorder and confusion leaving many dead and dying on the field," wrote Thompson. Hopes rose at the advance of the New York Zouaves, the firemen recruited in New York City by Colonel Elmer Ellsworth, who had been shot in May while removing a rebel flag from an Alexandria hotel. The Zouaves looked striking in their red uniforms but could not withstand the rebel firepower.

Two Second New Hampshire companies moved up the hill. "We stopped in the road a few minutes and I lay down under a fence," wrote Private Josiah S. Swain of Manchester. Haynes described the view: "We had a house on our front, some secessionist cannon up near it, and enough of the enemy to give us a real lively time." As he rested his musket on the fence to shoot at a rebel waving a flag, a cannonball sent the top rail skittering across the road. Splinters stung his neck, and he tumbled down the bank. "I heard one of the boys cry out 'Mart is killed!'" he wrote, "and for about half a minute I didn't know but what I was." Swain fell asleep. When he awoke, the regiment was gone and so was his musket. Men were streaming back toward Matthews Hill. "I got into a wagon and went up the hill," he wrote. "Then the retreat commenced. I got a drink of whiskey or I never could have got off the field, for it was men and horses, wagons and cannon rushing all ways, the dead and wounded at every step."

The hardships of the retreat varied from soldier to soldier, but the men of the Second agreed on the main points. All blamed other regiments for starting it, and all described panic and chaos. Fiske and others said the regiment left the battlefield in good order, but that did not account for the wounded, exhausted, and lost men scattered across the field. "I tell you, Charley, it was an awful day for all of us; men with all kinds of wounds begging for water and to be taken off, but we could do these poor fellows no good, for it was all a man could do to look out for himself," Swain wrote his brother. Corporal Leaver's first thought was that fresh troops had arrived to relieve his brigade. "I never thought of retreating until I was fairly under way being carried on with the crowd, and when I look back upon it now it is with feelings of pain to think that we should have lost all the ground that we had gained," he wrote. Captain Weston searched for a senior officer to order a halt. "I rushed among the flying column and shouted and prayed in tears and agony asking for some officer to command us," he wrote. All ignored him. "Such a rout," Weston wrote. "Why if one thousand men had come upon us with a will, they could have cut us all to pieces." Haynes described the retreat this way: "Never was an army more completely broken up and demoralized than was ours; never were the real dangers of any situation more intensely magnified than were those which threatened us; and never did men conjure up more visions of danger which existed only in their own minds than did we."

The retreat was hardest on the wounded, including those left behind. John L. Rice, a twenty-one-year-old private from Cornish, was shot through the lung late in the battle. With the help of Chaplain Parker, two comrades carried him toward the field hospital at Sudley Church, but pursuing rebels scared them. They decided Rice was a goner anyway, left him unconscious under a fence, and joined the fleeing army. Lieutenant Charles Holmes of Hopkinton had succeeded Charles Walker as orderly after Walker's fatal fall from the train in New Jersey. Hit in the right shoulder, Holmes lay on the field until Private Calvin Burbank of Webster helped him up. They walked through fields and pastures away from the road to avoid being trampled or captured. "He was bloody even to his feet as he travelled through the first half of the night," a comrade wrote. The next morning, in a downpour, Holmes walked twenty miles from Fairfax Court House to Washington. His trek ended at the home of Treasury Secretary Salmon P. Chase, who sent for the best surgeons he knew. They could not remove the ball from Holmes's shoulder, and the Chase family took him into its care.

The retreat route became an obstacle course as men discarded muskets, blankets, and knapsacks to lighten their load. Teamsters unhitched teams and galloped off two to a horse. Some sold horses to the highest bidders among desperate infantrymen. A rebel shell hit a wagon and team cross-ing the bridge over Cub Run. As Thompson approached the bridge, he passed so many abandoned wagons and deserted cannons that the bridge was "impassable for anything other than a man or two on horseback. Here was our ambulance and I wondered what had become of our wounded for when it passed me some distance back it was full." Surgeon George Hubbard knew the answer. After shellfire upended the ambulances, "We were forced to leave them and run for our lives," he wrote. Ambulances that managed to cross the bridge made "the night hideous with their groans and cries," wrote Private John W. Odlin, a musician from Concord. John

Godfrey, the quartermaster, noted that in every wide ditch "a wagon was sure to be overturned bottom upward into it and then the harness was cut and the horses mounted by from one to four enterprising individuals and started on full speed." Godfrey's wagons made it back to Washington with their original contents and more. "My teamsters picked up many things on the road & if we had only been empty we could have got thousands of dollars worth," he wrote. In some places the ground "was covered a foot deep with spades, shovels, picks, iron pails, boxes of bread, horse shoes, rope and every conceivable thing an army could want."

The men had been marching and fighting since one in the morning, and they were thirsty. "Every step we would see some poor fellow who would beg us not to leave him there to die, holding up his hands in supplication, with blood streaming from his wounds and mouth parched with thirst," wrote Sergeant Frank Robinson of Manchester. He and other soldiers lifted a comrade but couldn't carry him far. "We dropped the man—that look I shall ever forget," Robinson wrote. Early in Private Swain's flight, he passed up a chance to steal a horse for fear the owner might be nearby. "I called myself a fool afterwards for not getting a horse, for I never came so near dying as that time," he wrote. "I had got but three miles, I could neither swallow nor spit; I drank water much blacker than your boots. We had to drink where all above and below were washing their wounds in it, and men going through mud, blood and all. . . . Every mud hole we came to was at once in a center of men dying of thirst." Private Haynes, who had emptied his canteen of the tepid water of Bull Run before the battle, now gladly "scooped up a few sips from a mud puddle through which men and horses and wheels were ploughing their way."

As men from the Second approached Centreville in clusters, the rebels stepped up their pursuit. "Their cavalry would keep coming down on our rear and pick off those who could not keep up with the rest," wrote one soldier. "Their cannon followed us and every few minutes a ball would come whistling among us. . . . They could drive us just where they pleased for we did not come back with our Regiments. The companies were all mixed up." A man in front of Private Haynes "who was congratulating himself upon his escape from the dangers of the day, had his head severed from his body." The situation could have been worse. "If they had pursued us with half their force they might have cut us in pieces or taken every one of us prisoners, so panic stricken was the whole Federal army," Thompson wrote.

July 21, 1861 ▪ *To battle*

Despite the panic Thompson did his duty as an officer. He gave two exhausted men his water and helped them along until they collapsed in the bushes. He caught up with Sergeant Charles Cooper, a fellow Concord man who had been shot in the thigh and lost his ride when the regiment's ambulance was abandoned. Thompson helped Cooper to a muddy brook, where they drank their fill. Moving on, Thompson found the roadside "strewn with soldiers who had lain down from sheer exhaustion and fallen instantly asleep." The men he collected included Corporal Leaver, who could no longer lift his rifle. "I strapped a rifle on my back and took a musket on my shoulder and carried them to camp," Thompson wrote.

The men straggled into their old bivouac beyond Centreville, slumped to earth "like overworked oxen," and fell fast asleep. Thompson's group had been in camp for fifteen minutes when the order came to fall in for the march to Washington twenty-seven miles away. Leaver could not stay awake, and soldiers loaded him onto a wagon. Haynes awoke thirsty again, but someone had emptied his canteen. "If I could have got hold of that sneak thief, the casualty list would have been one bigger," he wrote. Colonel Marston reached the camp on horseback, but he was in agony. Chaplain Parker helped fix up a baggage wagon for him, other wounded officers, and Surgeon Hubbard. Fiske's last sight of the bivouac was of Hubbard and another surgeon amputating the leg of Sergeant Isaac Derby of Westmoreland by campfire and candlelight.

Most of the men either sleepwalked to Washington on rubber legs or fought slumber on horseback. "It was with great difficulty I could keep from falling off my saddle again & again by dropping to sleep in it," wrote Parker. The chaplain found the retreat worse than anything he had witnessed in battle. "I had read of defeats & retreats," he wrote, "but little did I expect to be ever in the midst of one; and I pray that I may never be again. . . . The horrors of the battlefield, the falling soldiers, the wounded men & horses, the mangled slain are terrible but not so sad as such a retreat: the sight of a whole army disorganized and demoralized." Even the robust Thompson sat down to rest. When the wagon carrying Marston happened along, "I hailed them, was fortunate enough to get a seat with the driver and rode the rest of the way to Washington." The driver nodded off, and Thompson took the reins. Private William Sawtelle, who marched the entire way, pronounced himself "very lame, the bottoms of my feet being something like raw beef."

In Washington, the night had been long and anxious for Benjamin Brown

French, a New Hampshire man who had been marshal of President Lincoln's inaugural procession four months earlier. French's house guests had gone to see the battle and returned in panic at midnight. One of them, Colonel John S. Keyes of Concord, Massachusetts, shouted upstairs for his mother to pack for the 4:15 a.m. train. Why such haste, French asked. "We are whipped all to pieces," Keyes answered. His guests gone, French "walked down in the City and soon found, to my sorrow, that our 'grand army' had made a grand run." Soldiers stumbled into the city "some without guns—some with two. Some barefooted, some bareheaded, & all with a doleful story of defeat." French spied the wagon carrying Thompson, Marston, and the others. Seeing "2d Reg. N.H.V." painted on its side, he crossed the street. Hubbard, sitting in the driver's seat, told him Marston had made it into the house on his own, bowing to the ladies in the doorway as he passed. Later that day, a surgeon removed the bullet from Marston's chest.

The men struggled to rationalize their defeat. "We were not beaten this time in the fighting, but by an unfortunate combination of adverse circumstances," Haynes wrote his girlfriend, Cornelia Lane. Many suggested "masked batteries" had given the rebels an unfair advantage. "The enemy was too cowardly to come out in the open field, but stayed in the woods all the time," a Manchester soldier wrote. Although the armies were of equal strength, most men believed they had been greatly outnumbered. They might have won the day anyway, Haynes wrote, "but for that unaccountable panic communicated to two or three broken regiments by teamsters who had driven their teams into places where they were not wanted, and who took the order to change positions as a signal for retreat." As Godfrey issued blankets and linen pants by the hundreds to replace the ones the men had discarded, he questioned the necessity of the retreat. "From all accounts the rebels were as badly frightened as we were and ran as bad," he wrote. "A third army could have whipped them both." To him, the real culprits were newspapers that had "been constantly calling out for a fight."

Senior officers, including Marston, were popular targets for blame. "Every order was a blunder and every movement a failure," wrote Thompson. "Had the men been left to themselves with their muskets and ammunition they could and would have done the enemy serious injury, but as it was I don't believe they killed a single rebel except what the rifles may have picked off." In his battle report, Fiske accused unnamed officers from other units of ordering his regiment into poor positions. Captain Griffin wrote that after the first hour of battle "our regiment acted apparently independently, having very little connection with its brigade or with any other troops." Griffin and the Second's other captains signed a call for Marston's resignation. Griffin later called this "an outrageous act of insubordination" caused by "greenness," but at the time he doubted that Marston knew anything of military tactics. Chaplain Parker wondered if McDowell hadn't sealed the army's doom by fighting on the Sabbath. "We selected the day of battle," he wrote. Still, in his mind the army, not the cause, had suffered defeat. "I still believe this cause is God's and that it is safe with him," he wrote. "He will in some way bring good out of it."

SIMON G. GRIFFIN

The morning the march to battle began, Lieutenant Herbert B. Titus, an educator by profession, was ordered to stay in Washington to supervise sixty "mostly sick, but a few lazy, drunk, and devilish" soldiers who could not or would not go. Relieved on Saturday morning, he paid a man fifteen dollars to drive him to his regiment behind "as sorry a nag as ever desecrated the sacred soil of Virginia with his lazy tread." The nag's owner was "anxious to see the expected fight and 'fun.'" They arrived just in time for Titus to go to battle. Afterward he rushed to tell readers of the *Sentinel* back home in Keene the real story before rumor and exaggeration clouded the facts. "The holiday of war is over, and we have met its stern realities," he began. These realities hinged on two questions: What had his regiment done and who was responsible for its actions? "I saw brave men as ever faced the cannon's mouth placed in position where they were mowed down by shot and shell, totally unable to do anything in return," he wrote. "I saw brave men stand their ground and cowardly officers skulking and sneaking for a covert." The soldiers' valor heartened him. "What cannot such men accomplish when properly led?" He called the defeat "the very best thing that could happen to us at this stage of the war."

Like any parent, Corporal Leaver's mother wondered what her son had felt during battle. Dread, he wrote, though "not of fear of the present, not of death, but of the unknown future and of what was hidden behind the grave." Even standing beside two men who were hit "did not make me feel any degree alarmed for myself." Nor did he want to flee. "All was wrapped up in one single idea and that was to shoot my rifle," he wrote. "There was a good deal of satisfaction in the thought of what I was fighting for and I felt that I was doing right in doing the rebels as much harm as possible."

It took time to count the regiment's losses. "Many sad and sorrowful faces there were at our roll call after the battle, to hear their names unanswered," wrote Private Charles Mace, a Dover native. "Every newcomer was hailed at a distance with a faint hope they might be our missing ones." Casualty reports were erratic. In August, the newspapers listed twenty-five men from the regiment imprisoned in Richmond. Many were wounded and one had died. Three weeks later a second list arrived from a captive comrade, William H. Walker of Somersworth. "We are very kindly treated here," he wrote. His list contained forty-two names.

John L. Rice's name was on both lists. This surprised the men who had left him for dead with a bullet hole through his lung and the people in Cornish who had held his funeral. Two days after the battle, Rice awoke, still lying under the fence where he had been abandoned. Flies swarmed around his wound and maggots squirmed there "in constantly increasing numbers," but he could not move. The Bensons, a local couple who had been caring for the wounded at Sudley Church, found Rice and persuaded a rebel surgeon to examine him. The surgeon called the case hopeless, but the Bensons brought Rice food and water from home each day. Amos Benson cut off Rice's uniform shirt and scraped away the maggots. After ten days, Rice was loaded on a boxcar for Libby Prison.

Like Rice, the Second New Hampshire survived to fight another day. Over time, as Bull Run receded into memory, the men smoothed off the rough edges of their performance on July 21, 1861, and took justifiable pride in having fought in the war's first great battle. In the short run, as Lieutenant Titus had written, it was a day of lessons learned the hard way. Not least of these was how difficult it was to explain a battle to people who hadn't been in it. As Private Swain wrote his brother Charley, "A man cannot tell much about anything, after a battle, for it is all a whirl, but it did not seem so in battle. I thought I could tell everything, but cannot." Anxious about loved ones and friends, curious about the great clash at Manassas, people back home read the soldiers' letters eagerly. But only the soldiers themselves truly understood the ordeal they had endured and the grim reality of the fighting to come.

August 2, 1861

AN EYE FOR AN EYE

JUST BEFORE THE EXECUTIONER PLACED a handkerchief over his face, Private William F. Murray stared out with apparent indifference upon an army of witnesses. There were thousands of them, ordered to Fort Ellsworth in Alexandria to see him hang. From the scaffold erected along the timber wall of the newly built fort on Shuters Hill, Murray may have gazed beyond the soldiers and down King Street toward the Potomac River. This was Alexandria's main thoroughfare, its two-story and three-story brick buildings near the river housing taverns, inns, and brothels. The war had ignited a boom, drawing thousands of Union soldiers to town with sorrows to drown and sexual urges to satisfy.

During the week after the Bull Run battle, Murray had joined the crowd. Possibly the presence of several New York Irish regiments in Alexandria attracted him. He was Irish, born in Dublin in 1831. A family man, he had joined the Second New Hampshire Volunteers from the tiny town of Lincoln. He was an outsider, an Irish Catholic in a company of mostly younger Yankees with names like Ames, Barker, and Merrill. At the court martial that condemned him, he appeared to be dim, lonely, and despairing. He left no known account of his experience at Bull Run, but most likely he turned off the road to Washington during the retreat and walked into Alexandria looking for a good time. He was there on Friday, five days later, armed with his musket, bayonet, and cartridge box.

As Chaplain Peter Tissot discovered, Murray had plenty of company in the taverns and whorehouses. Tissot moved about Alexandria that week ministering to his New York regiment, the Irish Rifles. In a heavy rain the day after the battle he found the men huddled in the mud at Fort Ellsworth without food or shelter. After they moved to a slave pen in town, solace arrived in the person of the paymaster. "We had 'Pay Day' and of course drinking," Tissot wrote. "Such a picture of hell I had never seen."

That very day, Mary Butler was released into this hell from the workhouse, where she had been confined either as a pauper or "for correction." Ellen McCarthy, a prostitute, took Butler in. In the evening Murray was one of McCarthy's customers. Afterward, he went drinking elsewhere, filled his canteen with whiskey, and returned to McCarthy's place. As they drank the next morning, she offered to put him in a room with Butler. The record is unclear about what happened next, but apparently Butler took Murray's money and provided nothing in return.

A neighbor out to fill a bucket with water saw Butler a short time later walking down King Street. When a man shouted for her to stop, Butler looked over her shoulder and said she would be right back. "Stop!" the man shouted again. She kept walking. The man ran toward her, raised his musket, and pulled the trigger. Her dress afire from the gunshot, Butler fell to the ground smoldering and bleeding. "Help me! Help me!" she cried. "Ellen, I'm dying!" McCarthy called John Dooley, a soldier staying in her house, and he and a bystander chased Murray down and subdued him. On the way to the provost marshal's office Murray said he had shot Butler because she robbed him. Dooley handed the marshal Murray's musket, its barrel still hot.

Back on King Street, the burning dress was pulled from Butler's body, but there was no saving her. McCarthy and Margaret Adams, the woman who had seen the shooting while fetching water, prepared the body for burial. The coroner confirmed that a gunshot wound in the back had killed Butler. "It entered near the spine, nearly opposite the heart, and passed out in the region of the heart," he reported. The wound was "as large as my hand," Adams said. "Her heart came out of the hole." As the women and Dooley lifted the body into a coffin, a musket ball rolled out of the wound. It was still round rather than misshapen, a mystery that would go unsolved after Dooley gave it to the officers at Murray's court martial.

On orders from General McDowell the court martial convened two days after Butler's death to try Murray for murder. "This Case requiring immediate example, the commission will sit without regard to hours," wrote James B. Fry, McDowell's chief of staff. Nevertheless, the commission first tried Thomas Jackson, a soldier accused of stealing a dollar's worth of tobacco on the wharf in Alexandria. Jackson was acquitted.

Murray's two-day court martial was as remarkable for what wasn't said as for what was. The commission showed no interest in putting the sordid circumstances of the crime on the record. When the judge advocate caught McCarthy in a lie, establishing that she had spent time with Murray before the slaying, no one asked what they had discussed. When McCarthy said she had shut Murray and Butler in a room together, no one asked why or what happened. McCarthy and Dooley evaded questions about what he was doing at her house, and no one followed up.

For a man with his life at stake Murray offered a feeble defense. He pleaded not guilty but called no one to testify for him. His questions of witnesses elicited only hints of what had happened. He did not claim alcohol had affected his judgment or dispute McCarthy and Dooley's dubious testimony that he had been sober when he shot Butler. He never offered an alternative account of events, denied the murder, or suggested that any witness had lied or misled. His closing statement focused on the availability of liquor, and he stopped speaking in mid-thought. On the second day of the trial, four days after the killing, Murray abruptly said, "I have nothing more to say," and sat down.

Whatever the ten officers of his court martial knew about the killing beyond what appears in the record did not move them to mercy. Murray had shot an unarmed civilian. They convicted him and sentenced him to death. Because it was a capital case, McDowell had them polled. The result was clear: "In the case of Murray nine (9) members voted for the sentence, one (1) against." McDowell ordered Murray hanged the next afternoon before "all the troops of his command who can be spared from their duties."

There is no way of knowing whether Murray thought his death would serve a purpose, but others did. Taking a cue from McDowell, the *New York Times* correspondent wrote that the hanging "will exercise a wholesome restraint upon the lawlessness of the soldiers." In a civil war in which the North's hope was reunion, its army had to protect citizens in the seceded states. The war had made life cheap, as many of those present at the hanging had just seen at Bull Run, but it did not signal open season on southern civilians. "The execution was meant to strike terror into the men," Father Tissot wrote.

On August 2, it fell to Lieutenant Chester K. Leach to march his company of the Second Vermont the three miles to Fort Ellsworth for the execution. "We had a regular sweat of it, going to the fort and back," Leach wrote his wife Ann. The regiment arrived an hour early, at three o'clock, and joined a throng that Leach estimated at six thousand to ten thousand men.

Murray was not alone as he prepared to face his fate. His chaplain, Henry Parker, was absent, but Tissot and Father Peter Kroes, a Jesuit from Georgetown College, spoke with the condemned man. Feeling "a little uneasy" about his service on the court martial, Colonel J. McLeod Murphy brought holy water for Murray. Tissot wanted to speak to the crowd but felt himself "too shabbily dressed to face such a large audience." Whether it was the religious attention or some inner strength that steeled Murray, he played his final scene with dignity. The *Times* reporter remarked on his "steady gait" in approaching the noose. Lieutenant Leach agreed: "He marched on the platform perfectly calm, attended only by the executioner. When the rope was put over his head, he took off his cap and replaced it, & put his hands behind him to be tied." Witnesses differed on whether he said anything. "Murray called on his friends to sustain his family in their hour of trial," the *Times* reported. Leach saw neither Murray nor the executioner speak. When the trapdoor dropped, the body disappeared. "I think he did not struggle much by the looks of the rope," Leach wrote. The *Times* praised the good order of the hanging. Despite the crowd, its reporter wrote, "everything passed off without unnecessary excitement."

Soldiers gave varying accounts of what they thought Murray had done. Some mistakenly believed the victim was black. "No more negro women were killed by the soldiers after that," wrote a sergeant in the Fortieth New York. Perhaps because the colonel of Leach's regiment had presided over Murray's court martial, he came closest to the mark. "A woman of ill fame got his money and he shot her," the lieutenant wrote his wife. The scuttle-butt in his company was that "he paid her before and she ran."

Murray's regiment did not see him die, but the men knew about his case, of course. Corporal Thomas B. Leaver lamented the damage Murray had done to the Second's reputation and the freedom the men would lose. Before the murder he had gone sightseeing in the capital several times without a pass. "There will not be many more such tragedies as the troops are now kept very strict and are kept in their encampments," Leaver wrote his sister. "It comes rather hard on those that behave themselves."

The execution caused other men to reflect, but not necessarily on the message McDowell had intended. Captain Newton Martin Curtis of the Sixteenth New York, who had given his chance to witness the hanging to an eager comrade, considered the value of the death penalty. "I soon came to believe," he wrote, "that it was not only not beneficial, but a positive injury." Leach reacted more viscerally: "I have seen a sight today such as I never saw before nor expect to see & can't say that I ever want another of the like sort." Another soldier considered the execution one more lesson in the reality of war. "It seemed we were to see death in all its forms," he wrote.

August 8, 1861

FIGHTING WORDS

THE MOB ON CONCORD'S MAIN STREET was hundreds strong and growing. Men ripped down the *Democratic Standard's* business sign and set it ablaze, kindling for the fire to come. Hearing gunfire inside Low's Block, they smashed out the third-floor windows. Some rushed upstairs intent on a "clean sweep," a "complete gutting" of the offices. Type, cases, proofs, newspaper bundles, ledgers, tables, desks—anything they could lift— cascaded out the windows and crashed onto the hard dirt of Main Street. Everything combustible stoked the fire. And with that, a rival newspaper happily reported, the *Standard*, "a disgrace to the city and State," was "summarily 'abated.'"

The *Standard* was a casualty of war, its demise a smudge on the ideal of freedom of the press. Its editorial policy set by Edmund Burke of Newport, the paper had espoused an extreme Democratic, pro-southern position for five years. The Republican Party had ascended in New Hampshire during these years, but as long as the country was at peace, people who abhorred the *Standard's* views tolerated their publication. The coming of war and the defeat at Bull Run sharpened the paper's opinions and tested the public's patience. When soldiers were bleeding and dying in battle, what could be dismissed during peacetime as a dissenting opinion took on the scent of treason.

Even in an era of partisan newspapers run by strident editors, the *Standard* was extreme. Its content made it seem as though the *Richmond Dispatch* or *Charleston Mercury* had opened an office in a northern capital. Indeed, the *Standard* reprinted stories from southern papers. Burke and the Palmer family, which ran the paper, railed at Republicans as abolitionist lunatics. The paper's voice on race and slavery was perverse and unrelenting. The black man's normal state was abject barbarism, it said, but "aided by the white man, and only through the medium of slavery, he becomes partially civilized and Christianized. . . . He is the mere infant of the human family, ever needing nurture, restraint, and correction." Created for labor in the tropical heat, the black man "can snuff its pestilence, and eat its spontaneous fruits, and grow fat. But being a mere sensualist, after supplying his physical wants, he has no more aspirations for the higher and better life than the wild beasts which dispute with him dominion of the forest and the desert."

Republicans might predict easy victory in the war, but such confidence passed over the offices of the *Standard*. Northern troops could never win because southerners would never surrender, the paper said. "When our land is filled with widows and orphans, and our homes draped with mourning, as they will be in two short years, and we then find our brothers of the same race still unconquered, all will be for peace. Then why not make it now before all these tremendous sacrifices have been made?" If Republicans had their way, the *Standard* warned, freed slaves would stream north "to become competitors and equals of the Northern laborer—to become loafers and paupers—to become thieves and murderers—to mingle with and depreciate and demoralize the white race."

The *Standard*'s owners sensed the peril their opinions placed them in. "Even the lives and property of Democrats have been threatened merely because they exercise the sacred right of freedom of thought and speech in denouncing the wicked authors of this awful war that is upon us," the paper editorialized after the fall of Sumter. The *Standard* reprinted a *Boston Journal* article accusing it of "treasonable meanness" and saying the slave power financed the paper as "a sort of gutter for conveying all kinds of lying misrepresentations of the South." The *Journal* even suggested that the public inflict upon the newspaper "the treatment due to traitors." In print, John B. Palmer, the *Standard*'s publisher, stood up to such threats. The paper would "adhere to the flag of the Union, and stand by the constitution and laws of the country," he wrote. "It will maintain to the last extremity, with our blood if need be, the freedom of speech and the press." Palmer was confident that all Democrats would avenge "the blood of the first democrat of the Granite State" assailed by a Black Republican mob.

Underestimating Palmer's grit, George H. Hutchins, the owner of Low's Block, decided a bloodless coup might silence the *Standard*. He ordered Palmer to vacate the printing office and counting room by June 30. Palmer had been renting the space for six years at fifty dollars per year and was paid up through June. In an open response to the eviction threat, he wrote that Hutchins had often warned him of the danger Republican mobs posed to his newspaper. Palmer treated these messages "with the contempt they deserved" and heaped scorn on the messenger. Hutchins, a flour dealer, was "a rabid Black Republican" who stood to profit from the war his party had started. "The motives of many of the patriots figuring in this war are quite as mercenary," Palmer wrote. On his lawyer's advice that the lease was annual, not quarterly, he vowed to stay in Low's Block until the end of 1861 and to defend his property "while I have a breath left in my body."

On August 5, the First New Hampshire Volunteers came home, their three-month enlistment done. Those who stayed in the city waiting for pay or preparing to join a three-year regiment heard about the *Democratic Standard* and its references to the war as "vile" and to Jefferson Davis as "a patriot." A few of them went to Low's Block on August 8 for copies of the latest issue. Its lead editorial called Bull Run "a total rout, and a disgraceful, ignominious flight." It praised the rebels' "consummate skill" and cast the retreating Union army as "a set of stragglers, shoeless, hatless, without arms, and utterly demoralized." These words stung all the more for the truth they contained. Denied copies of the paper, the soldiers left in anger.

Civilians and a few soldiers soon gathered in the street below. John Palmer heard a clatter on the stairs. He left his seventy-four-year-old father, Brackett Palmer, in the counting room and shut himself and his brothers in the printing department. Charles Clark, a boy of fifteen who had served as a clerk for Captain Edward E. Sturtevant in the First New Hampshire, led the invading force of three soldiers and several civilians. They tried to break in the door but retreated when the Palmers challenged them. Three Palmers rushed to the window, one wielding a pistol, one a musket, the third an axe. John Palmer later said he shouted to the mob that "they had in contemplation the destruction of my property, and if they carried out their plan, it would lead to their own destruction and civil war in the Granite State." Palmer's foes said he dared the crowd to come and get him.

John Kimball, the city marshal, and John M. Hill, a Democratic businessman with a newspaper background, entered the offices to negotiate a truce but only made things worse. Kimball asked the Palmers to surrender their weapons, and John Palmer handed him his pistol and prepared to leave. Then Kimball, considering the size and mood of the crowd below, changed his mind. He told Palmer, or at least Palmer said he did, to keep the pistol. If the Palmers did not help defend their property, he said, no one would. "I became more desperate than I should have been had I not seen him," Palmer later wrote.

At this moment a single gunshot sealed the fate of the *Democratic Standard*. Possibly through carelessness, Palmer pulled the trigger of his pistol and fired a ball through two floors and into a shop at street level. Although it caused no injury to the seamstresses working there, it brought a raiding party up the stairs again. Marshal Kimball blocked one door and Hill the other, but young Clark kicked a panel out of a door and stuck his head through. Palmer fired again, the ball tearing through Clark's hat. When the door crashed in, the Palmers fired twice more, shooting off a finger of Private Marshall Hurd and wounding Private Frank Hersey in the left arm. The gunshots sent the crowd in the hallway scurrying back downstairs. They also incited the mob on Main Street, which had swelled to hundreds. Some men lobbed stones and bricks through the windows of the *Democratic Standard*.

The Palmers had had enough gunplay. As the mob made yet another rush, father and sons escaped into nearby insurance offices and hid. In the *Standard* offices, rioters smashed the tools used to make up the type, dismantled the press, and broke windows. Anything they could lift sailed to the street below, where the mob cheered and fed the fire. The Palmers sold alcohol-based patent medicines from their offices. As the intruders raided this stash and sampled of it, their fervor rose until all that remained was part of the hand-press, papers, broken glass, and empty bottles strewn about. The destruction lasted two hours—with no police intervention, as both Palmer and the Democratic *Patriot* noted. The Republican paper asserted that once the crowd heard that men had been shot, "No police department could restrain or withstand the excitement." The intruders found the

Palmers and led them through the mob outside. Old Brackett Palmer was spared a beating, but his sons "were assailed by blows from fists, rocks, sticks, &c.," a reporter wrote. The Palmers stopped at Kimball's office, where the crowd clamored for revenge, and boarded a coach to the state prison, the one place they would be safe for the night. The crowd ignited a tar barrel on Main Street in celebration, and with that the riot ended.

The *Patriot*, the state's leading Democratic paper, considered the much smaller *Standard* a nuisance but came to its defense. Its destruction was a strike against "a principle of most vital importance to ourselves, to the press, and in fact to the whole community—*the right of freedom of thought, opinion and speech*," editor William Butterfield wrote. He called the attack planned, not spontaneous, and identified its planners as leading citizens, not soldiers. The mob was "countenanced and encouraged by the open approval of responsible men standing by as gratified spectators," he wrote. A few policemen could have dispersed it, but the police "calmly folded their hands, ignored their official oaths, and permitted the grossest outrage upon private rights and public order to be committed, in broad daylight, without an effort to prevent it." The *Patriot* linked the riot to the war, writing: "We are called upon to bear arms against open enemies of the country abroad. But can we be expected to listen to that call while we have far more danger- ous enemies—lawless mobs—here in our midst?"

To Amos Hadley of the Republican *Independent Democrat*, the issue was not freedom of the press but loyalty to the country in time of war. The *Standard's* columns had long "teemed with the meanest kind of trea- son," he wrote, "but as our community is an order-loving, law-abiding one, nobody thought of 'abating' it by force." What doomed the paper was "blackguardism upon the brave and patriotic soldiers" of the Union army. Hadley condemned "the mob spirit" but wrote that it was Democrats who had long condoned violence to silence opponents. He cited the caning of Charles Sumner, the abuse of Republican lecturers, and the destruction of abolitionist newspapers. The *Standard* had brought itself to ruin through "the utterance of treasonable sentiments, shameless siding with the enemies of our country, aiding and abetting the rebellion against our Government, and mean abuse of the soldiers of the Union," Hadley wrote. *The Daily American* in Manchester editorialized that it would not support mob justice even for good ends but added: "A 'mob'—a tumultuous, disorderly and riotous assemblage—is one thing; a mass meeting of the people, rendered indignant by treason or sympathy with treason, and prohibiting its continuance among them, is another and altogether different thing,"

How far could a newspaper go in criticizing its government in wartime? Where did freedom of the press end and treason begin? Was mob violence ever justifiable? In peacetime, perhaps, these questions might have been debated rather than merely raised after the order-loving people of Concord destroyed the *Democratic Standard*. But war has a morality of its own, and a way of sweeping aside high ideals.

August 22, 1861

'I AM READY FOR THE WARS'

BEFORE LEAVING THE WEST, Edward E. Cross informed his best friend he was coming home. "I am ready for the wars," he wrote Henry O. Kent. The question was what these words meant. When Governor Berry offered Cross a colonelcy on August 22, 1861, authorizing him to recruit and train an infantry regiment, he took a good deal on faith. Cross had joined a militia in his native Lancaster in his youth but had gone west in his late teens. Now he was twenty-nine and except for occasional visits had been absent from New Hampshire for years. Tales of his military exploits in Arizona and Mexico had drifted back to the state, but many of these he had written himself in his colorful style. His one asset in Concord was Kent,

EDWARD E. CROSS

whom he had known since boyhood and corresponded with ever since. If anyone knew what he meant when he said he was ready for the wars, it was Kent, and Kent had Berry's ear.

Cross had arrived in Arizona in January 1859 to start the territory's first newspaper, to help foster American rule, and to make his fortune in the silver mines. The Apaches were obstacles to white settlement, stealing livestock from the herds that sustained miners and soldiers and sometimes kidnapping or killing white people. Federal policy toward the tribes was taking shape. Thompson M. Turner, a tubercular newspaperman who came from Cincinnati with Cross and his party, put it this way: "Place the Indians on reservations north of the Rio Gila, establish military posts along their limits, and shoot every Indian found off the reservations. No other plan short of total extermination in an indiscriminate massacre of men, women and children, will rid the country of their continued depredations." Turner had no faith in treaties and knew the territory's army detachment was much too small to restrain the Indians.

Cross earned a reputation for usefulness and brainpower in Arizona, especially about military matters. He became a familiar figure at Fort Buchanan, the region's army post, and a confidant of its commander, Captain Richard Ewell. As a volunteer dragoon, he chased Apaches with Ewell's soldiers. In editing *The Weekly Arizonian*, he proved to be a quick study, lucid and fearless. These qualities led Don Miguel Antonio Otero, New Mexico's delegate to Congress, to hire him to assess military affairs in the territory.

After visiting forts across the vast region, Cross gave Otero a report that can only be described as a tour de force. He recommended closing five forts where settlers were many and Indians few. "The troops should be moved into the Indian country," he wrote, specifying a manpower level for each garrison. Because pursuing Indian bands after they stole livestock was futile, Cross favored tougher measures: "better to strike home upon the Indians at once and retaliate instead of pursue. . . . Sudden and effective blows may be struck home upon the Indians whenever they commit depredations, their ranches destroyed, their women and children seized." He reminded Otero that this required plenty of good horses at Buchanan and other forts. Cross tied his military ideas to the economic interests of settlers. To ensure "vast revenue" for the mines and their investors, he wrote, the government must neutralize the Apache threat and maintain a safe route to the Gulf of California. "Without these privileges, money, labor, & human life will be expended in vain." American forces should harass the Apaches "until they beg for peace, and are willing to settle on a reservation where the Pinal and Coyotero bands might be collected." He advised that Indian agencies be abolished and their duties assumed by soldiers. "Those who do the fighting should make the treaties," he wrote.

Like other miners, Cross hoped the United States would continue its territorial expansion at Mexico's expense. The Boundary Mine, which the St. Louis Silver Mining Company had hired him to run, was in the Santa Cruz Mountains twenty-five miles from Fort Buchanan and only four miles north of the Mexican state of Sonora. Its owners were preparing to ship a steam engine, grist and saw mills, and other equipment west from St. Louis. The plan was to install three furnaces capable of smelting eight to ten tons of silver ore per day. Protecting this investment was paramount, and taking Sonora would help secure it. "The Apaches ought to be prevented from desolating and plundering the State of Sonora, as they have done for many years," Cross wrote. "If garrisons of American troops are thrown into Sonora, then Fort Buchanan may be abandoned." He was not alone in this view. Turner, his journalist friend, wrote that the only question was "when Sonora shall become an integral part of our great Republic."

Had business interests not united them, Cross and his fellow immigrants might have been at each other's throats. They were men of strong opinions and quick triggers. Even common goals for the territory did not stop Cross from fighting a rifle duel with Sylvester Mowry, a sniffy ex-army officer whose honesty Cross questioned in print. Fortunately for them, they both missed. Mowry's main business was the Patagonia Mine, of which Ewell had been an original incorporator. Herbert T. Titus, the man who bought Ewell's share, had battled Free-Soilers in Kansas in 1856 and later joined William Walker's renegade military expedition in Nicaragua. Whatever differences these men might have, they were all white Americans, a distinct minority, who longed for a safe place to do business. "We have no law here," Cross wrote Kent. "Everyone goes around with six-shooter, rifle and Bowie knife for between Apaches, Mexicans and bad white men, one needs arms always." Cross counted sixteen violent deaths in six months. Turner's dispatches to the *Missouri Republican* seldom failed to report a murder, kidnapping, or robbery.

As the months passed, Cross assumed several roles in the law-and-order campaign while enduring the ups and downs of mining. In March 1860 he visited Turner, the newspaper correspondent, just as he and a partner took full ownership of the Boundary Mine. Cross spoke "in the most flattering terms" of the mine's prospects. "If the Indians do not molest them, the employees of the St. Louis Mining Company will have nothing to fear but the rattlesnakes," Turner wrote. "These venomous reptiles infest the locality to an extent quite annoying to timid people; but a few hogs domesticated in the vicinity will soon clear them out." What excited Cross was news that the mine held veins of gold as well as silver. A recent assay of gold ore samples had put their value at twenty dollars an ounce, he told Turner. To a census-taker in 1860, Cross estimated his wealth at $7,500. A few months later, however, the new owners fell out in a dispute over the richness of the veins and abandoned the mine. Apparently this gave Cross more time for soldiering. After the Apaches stole livestock that summer, he joined Ewell and his men on a raid that was more a show of force than a practical mission. Ewell did not expect to bring the animals back despite Apache promises to return them. "The best possible success would be followed by no other guarantee but promises, and they were profuse in them already," he wrote. The patrol returned empty-handed. Cross implored Secretary of War John B. Floyd to reinforce Fort Buchanan. "If possible be kind enough to order another company of mounted men to this post," he wrote. "The Apaches are swarming around us—killing, robbing and carrying off captives. Capt. Ewell is a brave & vigilant officer, but what can he do with one company of mounted troops?" Then, at the headquarters of Cross's old mining company on July 23, Sonoran laborers turned on their American bosses, killing an engineer, a chemist, and a machinist and stealing equipment. A German cook was arrested as an accomplice, and Cross sat as the man's judge and rode into Sonora to demand justice of officials there. He returned to Sonora in early 1861 to fight in an uprising that he hoped would weaken the Mexican government's grip on the state.

The fall of Fort Sumter ended what progress settlers had made in Arizona. The government abandoned Fort Buchanan, and security for the mines vanished with the soldiers. The war split the garrison as it had split the country. While Captain Ewell went south to fight for the Confederacy, his lieutenant, Richard S. C. Lord, went north to fight for the Union. Cross did not hesitate: the Union was in his blood. He had always considered himself a warrior, and in Arizona he had been one. When he rode to California to catch the first steamer for New York, he left a life he loved for a chance he loved more. Writing from San Francisco on July 3, he suggested to Kent and Berry that experience had prepared him to raise a cavalry squadron.

When he told Kent he was "ready for the wars," he probably meant he had honed his military skills and learned to value discipline, order, and decisive leadership. He had endured long marches through hostile country, carried arms with a purpose, and tested himself. He had seen that half-hearted measures against a stubborn enemy did no good. At Don Miguel Otero's behest, he had studied the big picture and mastered it. Perhaps most important, he had survived two and a half years in a lawless land where a poor decision, a wrong turn, a rattlesnake, or simple bad luck could mean sudden death.

The fates of some of Cross's Arizona colleagues illustrate the point. Cross gave a eulogy for Frederick Brunckow, the engineer and assayer killed by Mexican workers and mutilated by wolves. Indians slew Elliott Titus, brother of the Patagonia Mine's co-owner, and Horace Chapman Grosvenor, a woodcut artist who had come to set up a mining company. Apaches killed William Wrightson, the Cincinnati printer and engineer who had invited Cross to Arizona. Thompson Turner, their journalist friend, was leading his horse through a ravine when three men jumped him and beat him to death with stones.

HENRY O. KENT

Back in New Hampshire, Cross could not have asked for a better ally than Kent. While Cross's politics blended the anti-Catholic, anti-immigrant views of the American Party with Democratic positions, Kent was a rising Republican in a state where the party of Lincoln held power. He was editor of the *Coos Republican*, the party organ in Lancaster, and represented the town in the Legislature. He was helping the state's adjutant general form and provision regiments and choose their leaders. No one knew Cross's qualities and experiences better than Kent.

As Cross sailed home, the state was raising infantry regiments after the Union debacle at Bull Run. Congressmen commanded the first two New Hampshire regiments, and Enoch Q. Fellows, a West Pointer, led the third. Colonel Thomas Whipple of the Fourth New Hampshire had fought in the Mexican War and been captured in 1847 in Vera Cruz. Cross had spelled out his qualifications as he saw them, writing Kent that "Indian fighting has made me a tolerable partisan officer" and asking his friend to use his pull with the governor. "I tender my services to the state of my nativity in this day of peril," he wrote Berry himself, vowing to take "any position which may be assigned me." He appeared on schedule at the State House for an interview with the governor and left expecting an offer to lead the Fifth New Hampshire Volunteers. When the offer came, he asked for and received permission to choose his own officers.

Time and events would tell how ready for the wars Edward E. Cross actually was.

February 21, 1862

PICTURE MAN

HENRY P. MOORE

MUSICIANS OF THE THIRD NEW HAMPSHIRE BAND were eating supper around the campfire when Captain James F. Randlett walked up with a man in tow. He had brought a rebel prisoner for them to meet, he said. His joke lasted only a moment before Private John W. Odlin recognized the visitor. "Who was it but our friend H. P. Moore just from Concord, and natural as life," wrote Odlin, a twenty-year-old cornet player. Their hearts filled with "home feeling," the musicians hugged Moore and shook him by the shoulders.

Henry P. Moore left no known written record of his wartime experiences. If he wrote to his wife or kept a journal of his travels in South Carolina and Georgia, these writings were either lost or remained in private hands. But Moore did leave scores of pictures. To make them he lugged his boxy camera, photo plates, curtain, and tripod to camp streets and cemeteries, rooftops and fort walls, plantation houses and slave quarters. He photographed soldiers, naval crews, freed slaves, cannons, and ships in harbor.

The war had created a photography boom. As the state capital and the mustering point for thousands of volunteers, Concord had half a dozen photo salons that catered to soldiers. Their principal product was the carte-de-visite, an albumen portrait pasted on a two-and-a-half-by-four-inch card. Often with chests puffed out, waists sucked in, and weapons in hand,

A CARTE-DE-VISITE OF NATHAN M. GOVE, WHO ENTERED THE THIRD NEW HAMPSHIRE IN 1861 AS A TWELVE-YEAR-OLD BUGLER (HIS FATHER WAS IN THE BAND). ON THE CARD'S REVERSE IS THE MARK OF THE PHOTO SOLON WHERE THE PICTURE WAS TAKEN.

men posed for these pictures and gave them to loved ones or swapped them with comrades-in-arms. Salons in large towns and cities everywhere did a brisk business making pictures of wives and sweethearts for the soldiers to carry with them.

Itinerant photographers worked many army camps, but the Third New Hampshire had none—or at least no good one. "He is just the man we want," Odlin wrote of Moore, "for it has been impossible to obtain pictures of any kind worth having, or durable enough to retain their color even a month." Moore's ambition went beyond the carte-de-visite trade. "He comes with the intention of taking views of the camps and plantations, and has had over one hundred applications for large sized pictures," Odlin wrote. Moore planned to make eight-by-five-inch group pictures, landscapes, and domestic scenes and sell them for a dollar each with discounts for bulk buyers. Evidently the plan worked. He came south again in 1863 and photographed other regiments. After this second visit, the musician Benjamin Stevens wrote that Moore's orders totaled $3,000—a huge sum in a time when an army private made thirteen dollars a month.

Moore's enterprise was a logical extension of his work back home. He had started as a sketch artist and lithographer, making New Hampshire city and town views. The public, he knew, was interested in places as well as faces. Once he learned photography, the new technology, he saw its capabilities in the same way. His journey to Hilton Head allowed him to test the market for pictures of the distant outposts where New Hampshire men now camped. Probably he arrived in the Third's camp with a good idea of what he would find. His friend Odlin had reconnoitered Hilton Head and described everything from a new barracks for the "sable children of the South" to "the mysterious rattling" of domino games in camp. Because a Concord newspaper published Odlin's letters home, Moore had almost certainly read about Hilton Head before seeing it.

Odlin's regiment and others had moved onto the island the previous November after Union gunboats captured the forts there. Their object was to set up and protect a supply base for the blockade of Charleston and Savannah. The duty was sleepy. Although the soldiers sometimes patrolled, their main enemies were bugs and disease. The regimental band had it even easier. Many knew each other from the Fisherville village band, and most played "backfiring horns." The bells faced the rear over their shoulders so infantrymen behind them could march to the tune. "I am having fine times

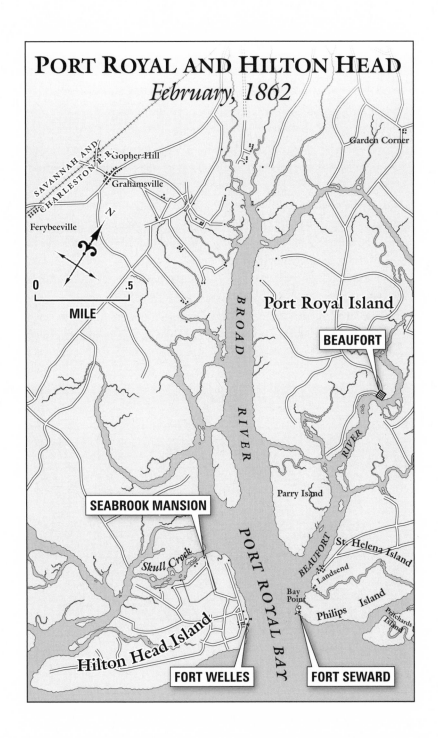

PORT ROYAL AND HILTON HEAD
February, 1862

SAVANNAH AND
CHARLESTON R. R.

Gopher Hill

Grahamsville

Ferybeeville

Garden Corner

N

0 — .5
MILE

BROAD RIVER

Port Royal Island

BEAUFORT

RIVER

Parry Island

SEABROOK MANSION

Skull Creek

BEAUFORT

St. Helena Island

Landsend

Bay Point

PORT ROYAL BAY

Philips Island

Pritchards Island

Hilton Head Island

FORT WELLES

FORT SEWARD

here, plenty to eat, and but little work to do," musician Josiah Dadmun wrote his girlfriend in Concord. "This is just the kind of life to suit me, and exactly agrees with my lazy disposition."

The day after Moore's arrival, Odlin accompanied him to Fort Welles, a coastal stronghold built by the rebels early in the war. It was George Washington's birthday, and the two men and George Lang, another Concord musician, had just sat down to a lunch of mackerel when gunships in the harbor fired a salute. After the flag was raised to cheers from the soldiers, the fort's cannons replied. "The very guns that were once used to try to effect our destruction, thundered forth their recognition of Washington's birth-day," Odlin wrote. A forty-two pounder boomed just above and behind them, its blast nearly knocking them over and the sand it threw up stinging their shoulders and necks.

By the following week Moore had set up a tent to house his operation, collected props for portraits, and opened for business. The soldiers tried to convince him the tent he chose had previously been the small-pox ward, but they couldn't fool him. Soon they knew him as an entertainer as well as a photographer. He played his banjo and sang.

SOLDIERS AND PROPS BEFORE MOORE'S
TENT. THE MEN TEASED HIM THAT THE TENT
HAD ONCE BEEN A SMALLPOX WARD.

THE THIRD NEW HAMPSHIRE BAND.

COMPANY I OF THE THIRD NEW HAMPSHIRE.

The regimental band mustered on February 28 wearing blackened boots and white gloves, a sight that pleased both the regiment's officers and Moore. The officers gave the musicians the afternoon off, and Moore asked them to pose. Afterward, a few of them sat near their mess tent for a more casual picture. The group portrait shows twenty-one soldier-musicians, the twelve-year-old drummer boy Nathan Gove of Concord, and the black boy who carried the bass drum. Odlin and the black boy flanked the formation, with Odlin seated at the far left in the photograph and William Butler standing jauntily before the bass drum on the far right.

Butler, a former slave who made it into several of Moore's frames, took this last name rather than call himself Seabrook after his former master. The Seabrook family's cotton plantation was one of several on which the soldiers now camped. The plantation house served as headquarters for Fellows, the regiment's colonel. When James Seabrook bought the 1,600 acres thirty years earlier, 156 slaves came with the purchase. Butler, who looks in the picture to be about twelve years old, had no schooling before the soldiers arrived, but band members gave him a uniform and taught him. Odlin soon observed that Butler "has already learned to spell and can read many words correctly."

Moore took many pictures of soldiers outside tents, but his eye soon wandered, and he followed it. To create perspective on the island's flat, sandy landscape, he climbed to the highest places he could. From the roof of the signal station, a plantation house several stories high, he pointed his camera in at least four directions. Atop the Seabrook mansion he shot the vast grounds out back with Fellows and other officers posing below and cotton from a shipwreck drying on the lawn. Moore's pictures gave families back home a sense more vivid than words of the terrain where the men pitched their tents.

Moore also photographed a place sacred to the men. Malaria was "the great curse of the sea coast," wrote John C. Linehan, a musician. Camp diseases were killing many men, and the dead were being buried two miles from Fort Welles. During the regiment's first weeks on Hilton Head, "the Dead March was played on every side, and files of men with reversed arms and slow step, told the observer that another one had fallen," Odlin wrote. "We buried eight, side by side, beneath a palmetto, and their comrades played last tribute to them by vollies of musketry over their open graves." Edward F. Hall, a private from Exeter, wrote his wife Susan that the sixteen who had died by mid-March were "the most robust and hardy men we had. . . . They are taken down very suddenly with violent headache and pains all through the limbs and in a short time loose their reason and become insane, and die, some in twenty-four hours, some in four or five days." Some of the men were assigned to create a new cemetery in a grove of small pines. When it was done, the regiment marched there one day with the band. "Most of the pines have been left for ornament," wrote Hall. "It is laid out in squares, one square for each company, about large enough for ten graves, with paths around them." The dead could now lie closer to

COL. ENOCH Q. FELLOWS'S HEADQUARTERS
ON EDISTO ISLAND, S.C., 1862.

MOORE CLIMBED TO A ROOF TO PHOTOGRAPH
THE WHARF AT HILTON HEAD.

camp, and several had already been reburied there. In Moore's photograph, three men from Company G occupy the front rank. Amasee Niles, whose headboard is in the middle, died at sea on November 9, 1861, the regiment's first casualty. Originally from Haverhill, Niles had enlisted at Concord at the age of nineteen. The men protested when an officer wanted him buried at sea. A soldier wrote home of the cemetery dedication that no other event "has awakened more interest among the soldiers than this, and the friends of the fallen will learn with pleasure that they here rest in peaceful sepulture among kindred and friends." Private Hall had a more sober thought: "I hope we shall not be so unfortunate as to fill it."

THE THIRD NEW HAMPSHIRE'S NEW CEMETERY, CLOSER TO CAMP.

March 31, 1862

THE NAMESAKE

SERGEANT LOUVILLE BRACKETT was "missing." Day after day, week after week, month after month, the word hung like a dark cloud over his sister Susan in the far north. Was he wounded? Captured? Dead? Had he run away? Brackett and several other men from Milan, a tiny lumbering town in New Hampshire's northernmost county, had gone together to Lancaster to enlist shortly after the first call for troops. They wound up in Company F of the Second New Hampshire, trained at Fort Constitution on the state's short coast, and headed south. At Bull Run none of Brackett's comrades saw him fall. For days after the battle, stragglers wandered into the regiment's camp and men there pored over ever-changing lists of captured, dead, and maimed comrades. Brackett never showed up. No list included his name. He was simply missing. Back home, Susan Brackett, the only daughter of a farmer with seven sons, read about the battle and waited.

Some of Louville's acquaintances tried to soothe her. The first word came from Welcome A. Crafts, his first sergeant, and it resolved nothing. Crafts knew Susan, though not well, and tried to be kind by equivocating. Louville had left the field safely, "seeming to bear a charmed life and to be impervious to shot or shell," he wrote. Comrades saw him going through the woods as the retreat began, but when things became chaotic, they lost track of him. "We hope that he is only taken prisoner and that he may be exchanged for some that we took." Even if he was wounded, Crafts assured her, the rebels had promised humane care. "We know not but feel (and hope and would advise you to feel) hopeful—yet prepared for the worst." From there Crafts descended into a weepy sermon. "There is sweet consolation in the reflection that he who dies in the service of his country is but perishing in the cause of God & humanity," he wrote. "The liberty of enslaved millions will come through the blood of heroes. Just such in all ages of the world men have offered themselves up on the altar of their country—have bled and died to *establish* while we die to *perpetuate* those glorious institutions which bless our beloved land. O Susan I know your grief will be that of a devoted and affectionate sister. . . . We will mingle our tears as you mourn a brother lost & I a companion in arms, a comrade in the bloody fight & the dangerous retreat."

Given the choice between an optimistic outlook and a bond of grief with Sergeant Crafts, Susan Brackett chose hope. Absent proof, she clung to every rumor that Louville was alive, every doubt about his death. Her brother had been one of more than 900 infantrymen in his regiment. Soldiers look out for other soldiers. Didn't it stand to reason that if he had been killed, one of them would have seen it happen?

Among Louville's band of North Country volunteers, Private Henry S. Hilliard of Colebrook was Susan's most faithful informant. He was twenty-three, a year older than Louville, and they became friends. It is possible Louville was illiterate, as Susan's wartime letters contained none from him, but Hilliard apprised her of their doings even before the Bull Run battle.

From Camp Constitution, where the regiment trained, he wrote her that Louville "appears to like military life, which I do not." From Washington, he described how they had sat in the House gallery on the Fourth of July and heard a talk by Galusha Grow, the new speaker. Aware of all the uniforms in his audience, Grow said: "No flag alien to the sources of the Mississippi will ever float permanently over its mouths till its waters are crimsoned with human gore. And not one foot of soil can ever be wrenched from the jurisdiction of the Constitution of the United States until it is baptized in fire and blood." This speech inspired Hilliard to share his thoughts about the cause. The army's purpose, he wrote Susan, was to preserve "our *free & independent government* by crushing out the most ignominious rebelion that ever was known to exist *on the face of the earth*. We are not bloodthirsty villains waging war against peacible citizens for the sake of plunder but *lovers of humanity, lovers of free institutions*."

When Hilliard next wrote, more than seven weeks had passed since Bull Run. He and his comrades had witnessed the start of Speaker Grow's predicted bloodbath. Battle had hardened them with the "horrible incidents that have transpired in their view, so that they care no more for a man's life than they do for a beast's." Hilliard's girlfriend Lulu had written him that Susan was ill. "I fear that you take the loss of poor Louville too hard," he wrote. "Although he was a brother and a very affectionate one you must be reconciled to his fate." Hilliard had accepted his friend's death "without a murmur, as he was offered up on the altar of his Country, & in a just & holy cause. He has undoubtedly found a resting place with the brave & holy." When Susan still expressed doubts, Hilliard wrote more bluntly. "There is not a shadow of doubt but he was killed upon the field, as no information has ever been received of his being wounded or taken prisoner," he wrote. When someone suggested to her that Louville was a prisoner in Richmond, Hilliard told her this was "not to be relied upon. . . . & furthermore I have seen a perfected list of the names of the prisoners & his name was not on the list. I do not wish to add on coal to the fire of affliction which is burning in your heart. Neither do I wish to keep you in suspence, which is the worst affliction there is, therefore I will state candidly that in my opinion he was killed while on the retreat."

For Susan, absent a body, an eyewitness, or an official death report, an ember of hope remained. Six months after the battle, she asked if Hilliard had learned anything about Louville from returning prisoners. "I have *failed* to obtain any knowledge of him whatever, & I have made inquiries of every person that I have seen that has been released," he responded. He held Louville dear in memory but had long ago dismissed the idea that he would return. "It is the cruel hand of war forced upon us by wicked hands of ambitious men that deprived us of our *cherished* & *loved* friend & brother," he wrote.

Hilliard was not Susan Brackett's only correspondent. A single woman twenty years old, she attracted suitors. Corporal Edward Bragdon of the Tenth Maine "felt want of some friend to sympathize with me" but worried she might not answer. Volney Bisbee, a friend from school days, took her picture to war with him. It reminded him of "many a good time which we have spent together and may I not hope that there is a good time comming." These young men were too late. Even as she struggled to accept the loss of her brother, Susan found the man for her: Gardner C. Paine, a twenty-eight-year-old Milan storekeeper. The least romantic of her correspondents, he came across as a man making a business transaction, not courting a woman, but they announced their intention to marry in late 1861.

Four months later they met for the wedding at the home of Merrill Forest, a justice of the peace in Berlin. By then Susan had apparently reconciled herself to Louville's death. For the first time since Bull Run, Hilliard wrote to her without advising her to move on. This did not mean Susan Brackett Paine had forgotten her brother, as indeed she hadn't. The Paines named their first child Louville.

April 14, 1862

RELIC RAGE

NINE MONTHS AFTER THE BATTLE OF BULL RUN, Lieutenant Herbert B. Titus recoiled when soldiers from his own Second New Hampshire Volunteers used their "sacrilegious hands" to dig up graves on the battlefield in search of relics. Yet even he understood that if they wanted a souvenir, they had no choice: above ground, there was little left to take. Bones of men and horses still littered the field, and where the Zouaves had fought, shreds of red cloth brightened the hilly landscape. Except for a few timbers, even the Henry House, scene of the fiercest fighting, was gone. After telling Titus that souvenir hunters had removed the house piece by piece, a local man proudly showed his own prize, a length of clapboard damaged by a shell.

HERBERT B. TITUS

Titus, a farmer and educator from Chesterfield, had risen to county school commissioner and was running a teacher institute in Keene when war came. After enlisting, he promised the editor of the *New Hampshire Sentinel* a weekly letter. It was a promise he couldn't keep, but he was such an observant and thoughtful witness to war that his readers no doubt looked forward to his letters when they did appear.

One day Titus curled up in a corner of his tent in Alexandria and wrote to the patter of raindrops. "I have written a longer and very different letter from what I intended when I commenced," he told his readers in the end. In the mania for relics, he had hit upon a good topic and could not let it go. "I wonder if this relic-rage is peculiar to us Americans," he wrote. "I have seen it carried to such disgusting extremes that I am out of all patience with it." The craze started at the top when, after the Second's first campaign, Lieutenant Colonel Frank Fiske presented the state with a chair "quite peculiar in its construction" from Fairfax Court House. Major Josiah Stevens sent a professor friend in Concord two live opossums, which tried in vain to wrap their prehensile tails around their new owner's oleander trees.

Nothing was sacred. Nine months after the battle Titus happened upon the remnants of a marble gravestone at Manassas Junction. The few pieces left included a chiseled palmetto, gun, and cartridge box. The dead soldier's name was gone. Nearby Titus found a metal coffin and a monument to a Georgia soldier, George T. Stovall of the Rome Light Guards. He recorded Stovall's epitaph: "His life he devoted to his God and sacrificed in his Country's defense. His last words were 'I am going to heaven.'" The monument was meant to mark where Stovall fell. "Of course it will never be placed upon the spot intended, for the battle field is six miles away," wrote Titus, "and I suppose this too will soon be broken in fragments and pocketed by those monomaniac relic-hunters."

Titus explored Alexandria, marveling at the old city's harbor on the Potomac, the canal connecting it to the West, and its status as a railroad hub. He also noted the shabbiness of some buildings and found certain local customs primitive. Walking past a food market, he saw a local delicacy that offended his sensibilities: "robins hanging by the dozen and half dozen, exposed for sale." Titus made the obligatory stop at the Marshall House. It was here that it occurred to him to write about the souvenir craze. Colonel Elmer Ellsworth had been shot at the hotel at the start of the war, becoming a martyr to the Union. Men in Titus's regiment had taken souvenirs from the hotel the previous summer, but its destruction was only beginning then. When Titus visited, a man from Philadelphia was restoring it. Even so, sightseers and relic-hunters picked the interior clean. "Wall-paper, stairs, balusters, doors, mantels, everything divisible and portable has been taken and carried away," Titus wrote. He watched an elderly man pilfer a wood shaving from a carpenter's bench, a chip from a mantel, and a strip of wall-paper that had been hung only days before.

Back in Washington, Titus assessed the damage to the tree Congressman Dan Sickles had shot in 1859 before bringing down his actual target, Philip Barton Key. Sickles was charged with murder for killing his wife's lover but pleaded temporary insanity and won acquittal. "How many ladies have pieces of the bark, wood and branches from that tree near Franklin Square that received a bullet from Sickles' murderous pistol that missed the body of its victim?" Titus wrote. "The tree is stripped of bark as high as one can reach, and still they are peeling it up among the branches."

Titus understood the obsession with relics. The war had heightened awareness that Americans were living in historic times. And while he complained about the scramble for souvenirs, the nature of the prizes some people took, and the depths to which they sank to take them, he knew first-hand how irresistible the urge could be. Near the Henry House he suffered his own "slight attack of the prevailing epidemic." His quarry was modest and practical. He cut a few small shoots from an apple tree in the garden, put them in a potato for moisture and protection, and mailed them home. A measure of guilt went north with them. "After all I have seen and said, I half hope they will never grow," he wrote. If they did, at least it would be only after they had been properly set in a New Hampshire tree "whose bark and body bullets have never pierced."

June 1, 1862

WOUNDED

WHEN GEORGE AND WARREN BUCKNAM played military games as boys, their friends nicknamed Warren "War Bucknam." But when the real war began, Warren was a married man starting a family and George was twenty-five, single, and able-bodied. He had gray eyes, stood five-foot-eight, and liked to pick his banjo. He and Warren were both printers. In August 1861, after a former printer they knew, Edward E. Sturtevant, set up his recruiting office, George enlisted in the Fifth New Hampshire Volunteers.

As he sat writing to Warren one day from the Fifth's camp, two men who had defied an order stood handcuffed on barrels outside his tent. They had been there two hours. Another time, half a dozen soldiers were forced to march about with signs on their backs reading, "Not to be trusted." George never got enough to eat. "If they don't give us better rations than we have had, I shall make a row if I have to be buried alive for it," he wrote. "The open air gives us a good appetite." After buying two dollars' worth of pies and cakes from a sutler, he wrote: "My conscience don't smite me a bit for doing so. I never wanted to spend money so much in my life before."

At Fair Oaks, Virginia, on June 1, 1862, two months into Major General George B. McClellan's campaign to take Richmond by marching his army west across the Virginia Peninsula, Colonel Edward E. Cross ordered the Fifth into the woods toward rebel lines. It was the regiment's first battle, and for George Bucknam it lasted just minutes. Early in the charge a musket ball hit him in the back below the ribs and came out the front. He fell and could not get up. Sturtevant organized a party after the battle to find the wounded and bury the dead. Walter S. Drew, a soldier in the detail, wrote that the searchers "were greeted on every side by groans of anguish, cries of distress, and wails of despair. I have read of the valley of death but never supposed I should traverse it. The dead lay in heaps." The men put a slab over each grave naming the dead man and his company. "It was a sad duty to perform," Sturtevant wrote. "I fear a great many more of us will be in the 'sacred soil.' But we enlisted for the war, and therefore must take its chances." After Bucknam was brought in, Sturtevant advised his family to expect the worst, referring to him in the past tense. "I regret to say it is severe," he wrote. "He was a brave soldier, done his duty faithfully, and was shot while pressing on in front of as deadly a fire as ever any soldiers were drawn up to face."

Friends who visited Bucknam a few days later were shocked to find him on his feet complaining that his wound might not end his soldiering days. He wrote Warren that until it happened to him he had thought being shot in the back branded a man a coward. "I have greatly undeceived myself," he wrote. "For when the bullets are flying in all directions a brave man may as [easily] be hit in the back as in any other part of the body."

George was transferred to Nelson Hospital, an eighteenth-century house built in Yorktown by Thomas Nelson, a signer of the Declaration of Independence. It had been Lord Cornwallis's headquarters during the Revolution. Perhaps because Bucknam was first thought to be a hopeless case, he and Private Hiram A. Young were the only men in Sturtevant's company sent there. Others were shipped north. A week after they arrived, doctors discovered that Young's skull was fractured, operated, and killed him in the process. Peter Mooers, a Deerfield farmer and Young's adoptive father, asked Bucknam to share "the particulars about Hiram and what he left at the hospital." Bucknam replied that Young had died peacefully. Of his own condition he wrote: "I have almost lost my senses, I feel so lonesome, and besides I don't feel extraordinarily well."

Sturtevant advised Warren not to come to Virginia, as he believed George would soon be moved again. Rosie Smith, George's fiancée, felt too squeamish to go to him. "It would be a great relife to me if I could go where he is but it is Impossable," she wrote Warren's wife from her home in Hanover. "I have not the means nor the Courage neccesarry to undertake such a journey and in a sick room particularly where there are wounds, I would be very little use, for instead of being able to take care of

GEORGE BUCKNAM AND ROSIE SMITH, HIS GIRLFRIEND.

him, I would need someone to take care of me. . . . I cannot go however I may wish it."

Doctors soon shipped Bucknam north, where his family lost track of him. Warren turned to a stranger, J. F. Desmages, a former Concord man who worked for the Hudson River Railroad Company in Manhattan and tended to wounded New Hampshire soldiers when he could. "My only regret is that I cannot get the time—being a servant of others—to do tenfold more for those who have *given them selves* 'for the liberties' of their country and the rights of *man*," he wrote Warren. He located George in a hospital on Davids' Island in Long Island Sound. A doctor he spoke with knew nothing of George's case but called the island "a delightful place" where "the patients are all in *good hands*." Desmages hired a boat to the island and surprised George by calling out his name. George did not know Desmages, but Desmages knew Concord, referring to it as "that honored town," and delivered mail from home. He found the presence of hundreds of wounded men "a sad, sad sight," but he sent Warren good news: "You may dismiss *all* anxiety in regard to your brother's health." George also wrote: "I am the same old sixpence. I am awful sick of this place and am asking to get out of it. . . . It seems hard for me to know most of the other boys have gone home, and I obliged to stay here. Expect me a little."

A month later he was still in Tent 13 on Davids' Island, and his frustration boiled over. He gave no credit to the doctors. His wounds remained tender, his back hurt, and he wondered if he could ever stand a long march. The hospital was "decidedly the meanest hole that ever any body got into," he wrote. "Sick men die here for want of proper care." He could not fathom why the army did not send the worst cases home, "where some kind hand can sooth them in their dying hours." He knew military leaders feared desertion but wondered how that could be worse than what he saw around

TENTS ON DAVIDS' ISLAND, THE HOSPITAL THAT SEEMED
MORE LIKE A PRISON TO GEORGE BUCKNAM.

him. "I am now writing in a tent where three have died, in my idea, just out
of neglect, and the fourth one—it is hard to tell whether he will live or die—
he is emaciated to a skeleton." Had the man been sent home, George wrote,
his family's care could have saved him, and even if it had not, it would have
been better to die at home than on Davids' Island. "Do men love to lay
down their lives for the cause of liberty and then be deprived of the littlest
privilege he can ask for—that of dying at home?" he wrote. George likened
the government's failure to provide food and care to "picking the pennies
off from dead men's eyes." He grew cynical as his furlough requests were
denied and more men with ghastly wounds arrived at the hospital. "It can't
help being agreeable for any person that has been wounded, and has snuffed
up all the bad smells of his own wound, to be compelled after he has began
to improve in health himself to snuff all these fresh arrivals' wounds over
again," George wrote. He craved food from home but advised Warren to
send him nothing, as "any little delicacy" would be stolen or discarded. He
apologized for his bitterness but wanted his brother "to know what this
world is made of—part of it."

After nearly six months on Davids' Island, Bucknam was sent directly to
a convalescent camp, where conditions were "enough to discourage the best
natured man there ever was." Many men had nothing to wear, and those
with shorts wore them until they were "literally moving about with lice."
He wondered how the public could abide the existence of such camps and
hospitals. "There is a great many such places in our neat little Country and
our pretty little civilized community which some folks pretend are *all right*,"

he wrote. By the time he returned to the Fifth's camp in Virginia, he had even cooled on his fiancée. He had once claimed that hearing from Rosie Smith, "my Rose," lifted his spirits, but he had not seen her for eighteen months and judged her letters less rosily now. "They are generally worth reading," he wrote Susan Bucknam, his sister-in-law. While he doubted a camp rumor that the Fifth would soon be sent home, it gave him "a faint hope," and the hope fathered a daydream. "I wish I could look into somebody's windows now, just to see how it would look inside of a house, I have not been in one for so long," he wrote. "I should not care if they did consider it saucy and I would come right into the house without stopping to knock at all."

Such was Bucknam's despair, such the price of defying death. Although he was glad to be alive, it galled him that he had lived to fight another day.

August 13, 1862

THE NEWLYWEDS

THE FATES OF THE THREE MEN AND THEIR WIVES were joined in Keene, where the Sixth New Hampshire regiment was preparing for war on the Cheshire County Fairgrounds. Charles Scott, the major, had served as deputy sheriff in Peterborough, and his wife Sophia worked as a milliner. Captain Obed Dort, a druggist who also sold paint and wallpaper, lived in Keene with his wife Julia and their two young sons. He turned his store counter into a recruiting station where, in November 1861, twenty-four-year-old John Cummings and the squad of twenty-four men he had recruited in Peterborough joined Dort's company. Cummings was a bachelor—for the moment at least.

When the regiment gathered for Thanksgiving, someone noticed an apple pie with Cummings's name cut into the crust. He was about to be mustered in as a first lieutenant, but the pie signified a more personal milestone. Its baker was Katie Scott, Cummings's eighteen-year-old sweetheart and no relation to the Sixth's major. When Katie Scott became Kate Cummings at

SOPHIA SCOTT

the Sixth's camp a week later, dropping the "i" in her nickname, the wedding was the social event of the training camp. But the newlyweds had no chance to settle into marriage before the Sixth marched through a foot of snow to the railroad depot on Christmas morning.

In mid-July, after six months in North Carolina, the regiment joined the Ninth Corps at Newport News, Virginia. Scott, Dort, and Cummings had all been promoted by then—Scott to lieutenant colonel, Dort to major, and Cummings to captain. When a fever sent Scott to the hospital, Sophia Scott went to his side. His brother came with her, reporting on July 25 that Scott, while better, was "still sick and much exhausted in strength." At about this time, Julia Dort and Kate Cummings decided to visit their husbands. Kate shared this news with John in a letter filled with tidbits from home about the dinner she'd just eaten, a new hotel going up, and a man dropping dead while mowing his hay. She worried the regiment might move before her arrival or, worse, be off fighting in Richmond. "I often think how many times I have said in your presence I wish I could know something in the future," she wrote. He needn't fret about her traveling because a male friend of the Dorts was coming along. Julia Dort was also bringing her six-year-old son Arthur while four-year-old Frank stayed home with family. "It seems strange to

CHARLES SCOTT

August 13, 1862 ▪ *The newlyweds*

think that I am to see you so soon, as I shall if I have good luck," Kate Cummings wrote.

Major Dort went to meet the women and his son at the Baltimore depot, but while he was gone, the regiment was ordered away, just as Kate Cummings had feared. As her husband steamed up Chesapeake Bay, the ship carrying her passed him going the other way. This maddening coincidence overwhelmed him. "I never felt more in my life than I did then," he wrote his sister. At his new post he rented a room at a farmhouse and wrote Kate to come to him. He asked his colonel if he could go to her, but it was fighting season and the prospect of orders to move was too great. "I am placed in perplexing circumstances," Cummings wrote his sister. "I think sometimes I will go to her anyway but then I should have to give up my place in disgrace here, and possibly she may be able to get here quite well without me. . . . If Kate could have come one day sooner I could have brought her right along with me as well as not."

KATE AND JOHN CUMMINGS

Major Dort hurried off to rejoin the Sixth, leaving Lieutenant Colonel Scott to figure out what to do about the women stranded at Newport News. Scott asked for a vessel to transport the three women, little Arthur, and any able sick men. Kate Cummings heard the steamer arrive the night of

August 11 and wrote her husband that she would soon be on her way. "I felt when I started from home something was to happen," she wrote. Although things had gone badly so far, "I hope the future part of my journey is to be different. I can not go home without making one more effort to see you. I write this so if I never arrive at my destination, you may know I started."

The ship that had come for them was the *West Point*, a 409-ton side-wheel steamer just two years old. Its captain was the veteran J. E. G. Doyle. Two hundred and fifty-eight convalescent soldiers, including many from the Sixth New Hampshire, boarded the ship, as did the three women and the boy. As the highest-ranking infantry officer, Scott took charge of the troops. The *West Point* took on seventeen more men at Fort Monroe before heading up the bay toward the Potomac and Aquia Creek, where the Union army controlled an important landing.

As the *West Point* churned along the river on August 13, all seemed well. The light of a high summer's day still glowed on the river as dusk settled in. Passengers who were paying attention just after eight o'clock heard a steam-whistle blow just ahead followed by the *West Point's* answering blast. A minute later, a loud crunch jolted the ship and sent passengers lurching across their quarters. Sergeant Curtis L. Parker of the Sixth bolted out of his cabin and saw water surging along the ship's passageways. He heard a woman's cry. He raced upstairs to Julia Dort's cabin, helped dress Arthur, and led the two of them to the hurricane deck, the highest point on the steamer. It was natural to think this was the safest place to be. Already men fleeing the chaos below were filling it.

Captain Doyle knew the *West Point* was sinking. He had made a careless mistake, turning to port instead of starboard as another ship approached. His ship crushed the protective frame on the paddle wheel of the *George Peabody*, a nearly empty transport moving at high speed. The collision stove in the *West Point's* bow, "taking away about ten feet, leaving us in a sinking condition," Doyle told a reporter later that night. The *Peabody* floated away with a hole in its side above the water line, its engine and steering disabled and its captain helpless to answer the cries of the *West Point's* passengers.

As water flooded the decks, Colonel Scott ran to Doyle to see what might be done to save them. Doyle offered no hope, telling Scott the ship might sink in ten minutes. Scott returned to the hurricane deck, joining the three women, the boy, Sergeant Parker, and James A. Newell, a Massachusetts doctor who had been working at the Newport News hospital. When Scott

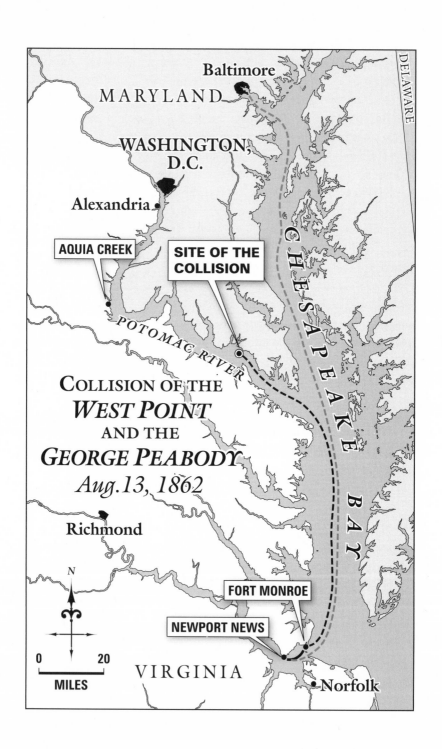

DELAWARE

Baltimore

MARYLAND

WASHINGTON, D.C.

Alexandria

AQUIA CREEK

SITE OF THE COLLISION

CHESAPEAKE BAY

POTOMAC RIVER

COLLISION OF THE
WEST POINT
AND THE
GEORGE PEABODY
Aug. 13, 1862

Richmond

N

0   20
MILES

FORT MONROE

NEWPORT NEWS

VIRGINIA

Norfolk

spotted a lifeboat floating away, he stripped, dived into the water, and tried in vain to retrieve it. As the hurricane deck flooded, the women clung to Newell as he held the boy aloft. Suddenly the deck collapsed, plunging those on it into the river. A frantic soldier pulled Parker under. The sergeant surfaced far from the ship and could no longer see the women or the boy. Nor could he find a scrap of the bow or hurricane deck to keep him afloat. As he swam away toward the Maryland shore, he realized he was too weak from illness to make it that far. When he turned back, the *West Point* had sunk in twenty-five feet of water. Only the smokestack and its iron connecting rods broke the surface. Hands and arms clung to the rods, and people thrashed about, struggling to stay afloat. Many slipped under. The exhausted Parker swam to the smokestack and wrapped his right hand around a rod. Colonel Scott held on nearby.

Passing ships stopped to rescue anyone they could. A soldier and a black servant woman had turned a pail upside down on the river, each holding one side to keep it from tipping and filling. Two Sixth privates from Haverhill, George Smith and Hiram Poole, had sat together on a wooden door. Parker held onto his connecting rod and bobbed in the river until a light cruiser came along and took him and others to the *George Peabody*, whose engine and steering mechanism had by then been repaired.

But the sinking of the *West Point* was a story of sorrow, not salvation. Seventy-six people drowned, including Sophia Scott, Julia and Arthur Dort, Kate Cummings, and eleven Sixth New Hampshire soldiers, inflicting grief all across the state. Civilians were used to long casualty lists; it was the drowning of the women and the boy that shook them. "While near relatives are almost crushed by the poignancy of their grief, all, alike, are mourners," the *Peterborough Transcript's* editor wrote. "There are no hearts that have not been touched to the quick by the news of this fatal disaster—there are not many eyes that have not moistened as the imagination has painted to them, over and over again, the group upon the hurricane deck of the sinking steamer in that dread moment, when despair was followed by heroic calmness and resignation." Only God knew why such tragedies happened, the editor observed, struggling to reach a consoling note. "As those we mourn were good and brave and true, let us be made better, braver, truer." The *New Hampshire Sentinel* in Keene, the Dorts' hometown, put it this way: "The hardships and perils of the battle field are, it would seem, enough for the human heart to bear—but the sudden deprivation of wives and children, while on visits of love and mercy, touches the deepest foundation of sorrow."

Bodies washed up on the Virginia shore. It was summer, and officials ordered them buried quickly. This caused further anguish for some survivors, including relatives of the women and the boy. A few days after the collision a boatman saw Sophia Scott's body floating in the Potomac. He pulled it into his boat and rowed to the Virginia shore, where he gave the jewelry she had been wearing to the county sheriff. Colonel Scott was in Washington to testify in the *West Point* inquiry. When he learned his wife had been found, he wanted her body returned to Peterborough to lie beside their only two children, both daughters who had died before the war. He asked Secretary of War Edwin M. Stanton's permission to retrieve it, but Stanton refused him. Scott was determined. He found President Lincoln at the Soldiers' Home, where he often stayed in a gray stone cottage to escape the heat of summer and the pressures of the White House. Scott's request annoyed Lincoln. "Am I to have no rest?" he asked, telling Scott the decision was Stanton's to make and the burden Scott's to bear. The next morning the president reconsidered and personally helped Scott gain passage downriver.

On the morning of August 27, two weeks after the collision, Scott returned to the navy yard on the steam-tug *Leslie* with Sophia's body. He had learned where thirty other drowning victims were buried, including the Dorts and Kate Cummings. Four days later, when a huge crowd turned out at Peterborough's Unitarian Church for Sophia Scott's funeral, Cummings's father was absent. He had gone south to recover her body. Major Dort retrieved Julia and Arthur as well, and friends of Doctor Newell, who had helped the women in their final minutes, carried his body home to Massachusetts. The papers reported that a drowned woman had still clung to Newell's body when it reached shore.

Of the three widowers, only John Cummings fought on with the Sixth New Hampshire. Dort resigned in September, citing the need to care for his son Frank and return to the business Julia Dort had run in his absence, and Scott took a disability discharge. After a brief leave Cummings returned to his regiment, which had just been mauled at the second Bull Run battle. "There is nothing left of them, hardly," he wrote the *Transcript*. "Eighteen men killed, wounded and missing from my company." To his mother he poured out his grief over the loss of his wife. "I cannot help but think I shall go to her soon," he wrote. "If it should be so, do not think of it otherwise than as a relief and blessing to me." A month after Kate's death he led his company into Maryland, where the charge into heavy fire across a bridge at Antietam reminded him of his childhood musings. "Mother," he wrote, "I used to read of Napoleon's battles and think it would be glorious to have a chance to take part in a battle. I have had it." His fatalism persisted. "If I should chance to be killed, or rather it should be my destiny to die here, do not feel bad about it, mother," he wrote. "Remember there is pleasure in the tho't of joining her, and that I died happy believing that we were again to meet.—All the sorrow I feel at the thought of death is that there are those who will mourn for me, but we must go sometime and as we pass on one by one those who are left must weep by turn."

September 17, 1862

RUSH TO BATTLE

THE NINTH NEW HAMPSHIRE REGIMENT stared in awe at the soldiers marching by. Stripped for battle, they wore tattered uniforms and carried no knapsacks. Some walked barefoot. When a passing veteran deigned to notice the new men, who were loaded down with gear, it was to taunt them as bounty soldiers afraid to get their uniforms dirty. The Ninth had been rushed south with little training and no ammunition. Many men couldn't load or fire their weapons. Yet here they were, set down in some of the heaviest fighting of the war so far. In the distance they could hear the guns at the old Bull Run battlefield.

The regiment had come together just weeks before, in late July. One assembly point was Lebanon, where several scholars from nearby Kimball Union Academy marched after volunteering for three years in the army. The young ladies of the academy presented them with a five-by-eight-foot silk banner reading "Amino et Fides"—"Courageously and Faithfully." The men came to town beneath this flag to enlist under Daniel C. Buswell, who would become their company commander. They received a federal bonus of a hundred dollars, twenty-five now, the rest to be paid when they mustered out. Residents of Lebanon housed and fed them for ten days, a period that Sergeant Oscar D. Robinson later called "the holiday of their soldiering."

The holiday ended August 5 when they swapped the warm beds of their hosts for "rough board stys filled with straw" at Camp Colby in Concord. Suddenly they were eating boiled beef, soggy potatoes, and tasteless bread from rusty tin plates and washing it all down with oily coffee. More than a thousand people turned out at dusk one Sunday to watch them on dress parade. What the crowd saw was an exceptional group of men, according to Marshall P. Wood, a twenty-four-year-old corporal from Rindge. "This is the best regiment that was ever got up," he wrote his wife Julia. "They have taken a great deal of pains to get the best men. Every man has been examined in every shape and manner." Wood was an odd blend of thrifty and spendthrift. He made his own ink by squirting garget-berry juice through cloth and adding just enough vinegar to make it spread, but he also spent eighteen dollars for a six-shooter—"a splendid thing"—and paid ten dollars for drum lessons in hopes of becoming a drummer.

The Ninth broke camp in Concord after twenty days. "Parting with friends is the hardest battle that a soldier has to fight," wrote Lieutenant Thomas Chisholm of Milton—a judgment he would soon have cause to reconsider. The men paraded through Philadelphia to cheers. "The streets were full of girles a shakeing hands and bidding us good buy," Wood wrote his wife. "I bet I shook hands with more than 500 girles. Some of the boys would stop and kiss them. I was in to big a hurry." In Washington, officers checked into the National Hotel while the men crowded into a stifling hall. Sergeant Robinson awoke in the night and ran outside retching. The men were so new to soldiering that when they marched past the Capitol and White House and across the Potomac, some had to be lifted into baggage wagons. "I have trudged along with my gun and pack and seen many a stout built rugged farmers boy fall out," Corporal Elmer Bragg wrote his mother. Corporal Wood found it "a pretty hard tramp. It was just like walking in ashes and we was covered all over with dust and dirt. . . . I stuck to it like a tiger."

The men pitched tents on Arlington Heights and went to sleep, planning to tidy up in the morning. At three o'clock they were ordered out under arms. With no ammunition in their cartridge boxes, they guessed their mission must be a bayonet charge. They marched half a mile and waited an hour, many of them falling asleep. They returned to camp, picked up their knapsacks and a day's rations, and marched to the Chain Bridge, which connected Arlington to the capital. "We thought it was quite a recommend to be called out the first morning after arriving in Virginia, while other regiments have usually lain still for months after arriving here, or rather done nothing but drill," Robinson wrote.

They moved near Fort Woodbury, part of the capital's defenses, and took up picks and shovels to build more works. "Families are every day ordered to take what they can with them and move to Washington," wrote Bragg. "Their houses are blown up and their places converted into entrenchments, Rifle Pits and Forts." Robinson found it "almost incredible that our army is now throwing up entrenchments under cover of which to fight on the defensive on the same ground over which it was driving the enemy a year ago."

It was in this camp that the men watched veteran regiments march past. "My God!" said one soldier, "shall we ever look like that?" Corporal Wood clung to one claim the passing veterans made. "They say the worst of it is over, that we shall not have such a time as they have," he wrote Julia. The men saw Major General George B. McClellan and assumed his army, back from the Peninsula campaign, was rushing to Bull Run. "There is a great battle now going on somewhere near Manassas," Chisholm wrote on August 29. "There has been a heavy cannonade going on ever since this morning. . . . The boys want to go, and no doubt if we were well drilled we should be there." As smoke drifted into camp, Wood wrote: "I should not think it strange if we were in battle before many days."

One evening Colonel Cross and Major Edward E. Sturtevant of the Fifth New Hampshire visited the Ninth. Their hosts knew Sturtevant as the state's first volunteer; he knew some of them from service in the three-month First New Hampshire. Cross chatted with Adjutant George H. Chandler of Concord, who noticed many "pretty hard looking fellows" in the Fifth's ranks. Chandler had already decided the war was "quite different from having regular and profitable business" back home, "but it is nothing more than what I made up my mind to before coming." Nevertheless, he was already convinced that it was "more of a task by ten times to subdue this rebellion than most people suppose."

The ground where the Ninth camped was as hard-bitten as the old soldiers they saw. It was "almost a waste," wrote George W. Barber, a private from Plainfield in Robinson and Bragg's company. "Fences have been carried away for fuel, fruit trees destroyed and everything eatable appropriated by the soldiers." Robinson thought the regiment was adapting well to army life. Digging rifle pits didn't bother him, and he claimed to enjoy eating hardtack and bacon, cooked or raw, as much as he liked dining at a ladies' boarding house back home. "I do miss the ladies, though," he wrote. Soldiers prepared for battle all around him. "From our camp ground I can behold no less than four forts, all mounted with dark, deep mouthed, murderous cannon. . . . . On the bank just opposite, across a little ravine, the band has been playing, and the mingled sounds of the soldiers' talking, laughing, hallooing and singing forms a strange and 'harmonious discord' to one unaccustomed to such scenes and sounds." He fretted that the enemy would simply bypass the capital. "We have fortified the heights till they are impregnable against any foe," he wrote, "but while we are doing this the rebels are crossing the Potomac in another place."

When the Ninth moved, its direction was not south toward Richmond, as many men had hoped, but north. The first night out, they camped in a grove near a tumble-down tavern in Leesboro. They marched further into Maryland the next two days. "The probability is, that we are now on the eve of a great and fearful struggle," Corporal Bragg wrote. "God alone knows who will here be called to sacrifice their lives to their country's cause. It may be one; it may be another. But can we not meet all this with firmness, if we put our confidence in an Almighty Arm; and go forward under the convictions of duty. I think we can." Corporal Wood had darker thoughts, writing his wife: "It is not likely that we all shall come home. And I am just as likely to be one of the number as any one else. But dear one my prayer to the Heavenly Father is that my life may be spared to see you once more and it seems just as though he would and I trust he will if I am faithfull to him." After another day's march, they spread their blankets on damp brier bushes and fell asleep. By morning many men were soaked.

On September 12, they received orders to lighten their load "to the smallest possible compass." They put overcoats, dress coats, and more into boxes with their names on them and loaded the boxes into wagons headed for Washington. Wood had found his things "so heavy it is enough to kill a fellow to carry them round, we have so much marching to do." Robinson gave up his backpack, Lieutenant Chisholm his books. "As I had them out one by one, and gave them a parting look," Chisholm wrote, "I came to

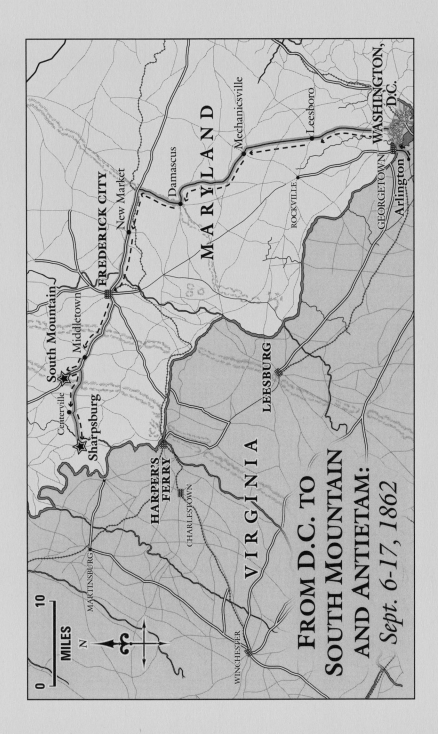

FROM D.C. TO
SOUTH MOUNTAIN
AND ANTIETAM:
Sept. 6-17, 1862

MARYLAND

VIRGINIA

WASHINGTON, D.C.

Georgetown

Arlington

Leesboro

Mechanicsville

ROCKVILLE

Damascus

New Market

FREDERICK CITY

Middletown

South Mountain

Centerville

Sharpsburg

Harper's Ferry

CHARLESTOWN

LEESBURG

MARTINSBURG

WINCHESTER

N

MILES

0   10

a prayer book from which myself or wife was wont to read a prayer each night when I was home. I had taken it with me thinking to do the same while away but now it must go." The rebels had recently fired a shell into the house where Chisholm wrote. "They appear to be skedaddling as fast as possible; whether they will keep on or turn and fight when they get a good place is impossible to tell."

The men awoke on a hill overlooking the Monocacy River and joined the Ninth Army Corps under Jesse L. Reno, a career military officer recently promoted to major general. Their brigade commander, James Nagle, had just won his first general's star. Robinson washed his shirt and bathed in the river before the men moved out. Townspeople in Frederick seemed pleased to see them. Windows and balconies on the main street were "all crowded with fair ones waving snow white handkerchiefs & miniature flags," Robinson wrote. People set pails of cold water and lemonade on their doorsteps. At Middletown on September 14, the men ate fresh beef and hardtack to the sound of gunfire from the long mountain ridge across their path. Just as Robinson began a letter, they were ordered to fall in. Heading toward South Mountain with "the mingled feelings of hope, fear and curiosity common to new troops," they marched past ambulances and stretcher-bearers carrying wounded men from the battlefield.

After they left the road, their colonel stopped them for an overdue lesson. He was Enoch Q. Fellows, the former Third New Hampshire commander, who was nearly deaf, disliked crowds, and wore a straw hat. Now he wanted to make sure his men could load their rifles. Some could, some couldn't. Several soldiers, uncertain they had loaded properly, pulled their triggers. Fortunately no one was hurt, but the test-firing "so enraged Col. Fellows that he whispered some pretty hard words," Robinson wrote.

The rebels held a commanding position atop South Mountain.

ENOCH Q. FELLOWS

When the Ninth reached its base, a breathless aide told Fellows to "hurry up those men, they are wanted immediately." The colonel ordered them to march double-time, but the incline was too steep and rugged for green soldiers to climb so fast. It didn't help that many had kept too much gear. They littered the slope behind them with blankets, canteens, and haversacks. Robinson refused to thrown away his writing tools, which he had wrapped in his "housewife," a soldier's sewing kit, and rolled into his blanket. He unbuckled his blanket strap on the run, "gave my 'roll' a shake and caught the article in question from the inner contents and let go all the rest." "All the rest" included his food.

As officers shouted orders and shells plowed the ground and smashed trees, the men marched into a field. After halting and turning, they wound up facing downhill with their backs to the enemy. "There was no little confusion," Robinson wrote, and the men "very naturally suspected something was wrong." The officers turned the Ninth toward the enemy, but the rear rank was now in front. In a battle line two men deep and 450 men long, the regiment was ordered forward with bayonets fixed. It lost cohesion climbing over a wall. When the men paused to regroup at a rail fence, some saw rebels before them and opened fire without orders. The rebels turned out to be soldiers of two Union regiments. The men of the Forty-sixth New York "only saved themselves by throwing themselves down on the ground," their colonel wrote.

At last in position with their bayonets winking in the sunlight, the Ninth charged headlong through the tall cornstalks. For some reason, when their line reached the woods beyond the corn, the rebels retreated. "Whether it was the noise or the long line of glistening bayonets or the random shots fired on reaching the woods, *something* drove the enemy from his strong position before us," Robinson wrote. The Ninth began to pull back in good order, but then some men heard a volley from the woods and broke and ran. When their officers at last stopped them, their enraged lieutenant colonel, Herbert B. Titus, walked along the re-formed line lecturing each company. He knew they were green, he said, but they had to follow orders. "Don't you ever fire a gun again, nor change your position, without orders," he told one company.

The regiment's fight over, the men pulled back to act as reserves. "It was a strange Sunday evening to us," Robinson wrote to his hometown paper. "At the very hour when the church bells were summoning our friends at home to the evening meeting, we were lying close to the ground to escape the bullets, which whistled over our heads in volleys, while the whole forest was lighted with the flash and resounded with the roll of musketry." Gradually the firing died away. Despite the mistakes, the bayonet charge was what the men remembered from their first fight. General Reno called it "a gallant charge," and Nagle praised them for "good cheer and true courage." They suffered twenty-three casualties, including two dead. Bragg learned on South Mountain what veteran warriors knew: "excitement" carried a man through the fight, but when the last shot was fired, exhaustion was sudden and total. "I have nothing but the clothes on my back," he wrote home. "My blanket and overcoat, shirts and stockings are all left on the Battlefield. Life you know is worth more than all else." It was cold and foggy, and many men shivered without blankets. Unlike Robinson, Bragg had also lost his stationery and had to write on a used memo.

Exploring the battlefield at daybreak, Robinson saw "ghastly corpses everywhere" amid blasted trees in littered fields. Most of the Union dead were gone, but the rebels had left theirs. In one patch Robinson saw eighteen men, most of them shot in the head. He counted fifty on less than half an acre. They were dirty, shoeless, and dressed in rags. Prisoners detailed to bury them found little of value in their pockets. Robinson pulled coarse bread from their haversacks and learned from their diaries that, like the men of his own regiment, some had only recently enlisted. "Swift but merited retribution for their treason," he wrote. Robinson had one last encounter with the dead that day. Leaving South Mountain in pursuit of the rebels, the Ninth passed through a cut where the fighting had been severe. As Robinson marched at the side of the regiment, he couldn't help stepping on corpses.

The pursuit was slow enough to give General Robert E. Lee time to consolidate his forces around Antietam Creek near Sharpsburg. When the Ninth made camp late on September 16, the men heard cannons ahead, a sign that another battle loomed. As the sun burned the fog away the next morning, "the grandeur and magnificence of the scene were apparent," wrote Lieutenant John E. Mason of Manchester. Looking down the battle line along the Antietam and in the surrounding hills, he declared it "a splendid picture."

Reno, the Ninth Corps commander, had been killed at South Mountain and replaced by Major General Ambrose Burnside, whom Mason praised as "the hero who *never lost a battle*." At mid-morning Burnside deployed his corps near a 125-foot stone bridge over the Antietam on the Union left. His men outnumbered the rebels but held a weak position. Only by crossing the bridge could they reach the narrow wagon path up the steep and rugged opposite bank. The rebels lay concealed on wooded table lands with a clear view of both Union troops and the bridge. As the Ninth New Hampshire moved in with its brigade, "our men were obliged to fall flat on their faces on a plowed field in fair sight, directly on the opposite bank of the river," wrote Mason. For four hours they had little chance to shoot back or advance. "The thundering of the cannons and the roar of musketry was a continual clang all day," wrote Bragg.

An incident at noon startled the men. Ignoring the manual for field officers, Titus, their tough but genial lieutenant colonel, borrowed a rifle "and used it, like any soldier." "Across the creek in the woods were posted the sharpshooters of the enemy in the trees, behind them, and in any other place that could afford concealment & protection," Titus wrote a comrade. "Now I am somewhat accustomed to looking for game in the woods: so when I got my eye on one of the scoundrels, I of course could do no less than make him agree not to shoot any more—a bargain they'll be likely to keep for a long time I'm thinking. But a sharpshooter in a tree fixed me at least temporarily. Well, the idea of dying for one's country may be all very fine, patriotic & poetical, but to be shot by one of those infernal, hang dog, vagabond, butternut skinned scoundrels is not so decidedly funny." The ball hit Titus's right shoulder below the joint and penetrated to his ribs. As he was carried off, he "held up his mangled arm . . . and bade us stand at our post," Bragg wrote. "We needed nothing else, but we had more work before us."

At two o'clock the brigade "stormed the bridge amid the most terrific volleys of musketry that ever came from Springfield muskets," Lieutenant Mason wrote with exaggeration. After a struggle in which hundreds of soldiers were killed, two other Union regiments had taken the bridge well before the Ninth advanced. "As we crossed over, the dead and the dying lay thick on either end of the bridge, some who had fallen earliest in the strife, cold and rigid in death, and some just breathing their last," wrote Robinson. Mason described "a promiscuous pile" of soldiers of both armies "massed together—often clenched in each others arms in their death struggles." The men ran up the bank on the other side and planted their flags. " 'Old

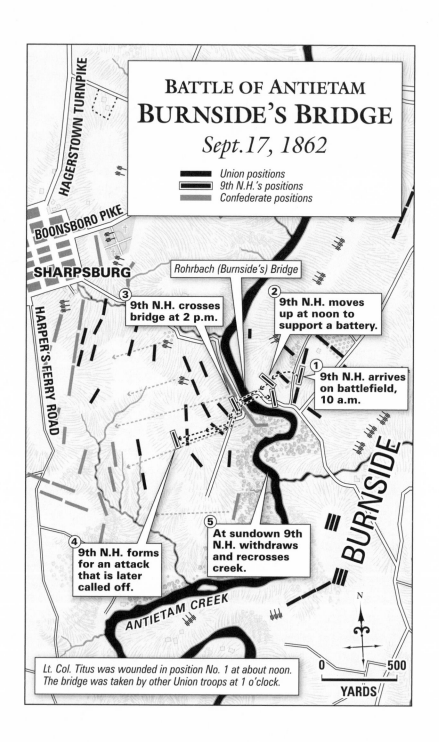

BATTLE OF ANTIETAM
BURNSIDE'S BRIDGE
Sept.17, 1862

▬▬▬ Union positions
▭▭▭ 9th N.H.'s positions
▬▬▬ Confederate positions

HAGERSTOWN TURNPIKE

BOONSBORO PIKE

SHARPSBURG

HARPER'S FERRY ROAD

Rohrbach (Burnside's) Bridge

③ 9th N.H. crosses bridge at 2 p.m.

② 9th N.H. moves up at noon to support a battery.

① 9th N.H. arrives on battlefield, 10 a.m.

BURNSIDE

⑤ At sundown 9th N.H. withdraws and recrosses creek.

④ 9th N.H. forms for an attack that is later called off.

ANTIETAM CREEK

N

Lt. Col. Titus was wounded in position No. 1 at about noon.
The bridge was taken by other Union troops at 1 o'clock.

0 _____ 500

YARDS

Glory' never seemed to look so finely and was never cheered so loudly," Mason wrote. Then enemy artillery stopped them cold. A shell exploded near Robinson and Bragg's company, wounding several men and covering Bragg with dirt. Late in the day, the men formed at the edge of a cornfield for a charge like the one they had made at South Mountain. This time it didn't happen. At sunset, after a half hour's wait, they rushed back toward the creek while rebel artillery pelted them with grape and canister. "Before we reached the ford each one of us was looking out for himself, and few of us came over 'dry shod,'" Robinson wrote.

Because of poor leadership, the Ninth Corps had failed at the bridge. By the time the fighting there began in earnest, McClellan, cautious to a fault, had already decided his challenge was to save his army rather than destroy Lee's. His orders to Burnside were testy and confused. For his part, Burnside showed no initiative when the battle plan failed. As a result, Lee held off the Yankees at the bridge for hours with a small force. The men of the Ninth New Hampshire knew none of this. They had helped secure the bridge and suffered eight deaths. They awoke the next day expecting the battle to resume. There was skirmishing but no attack, and Lee's army disappeared. "The enemy have again slipped away and we are now in pursuit," Bragg wrote, misreading McClellan's intentions. In words straight from McClellan's lexicon, Mason blamed politicians for Lee's escape, writing: "If we had been supplied with an army in reserve, we could have outflanked and captured the whole rebel army next morning, but for want of the troops now loafing around Washington, this glorious achievement could not be performed."

The Ninth had slept on the field amid groans and gasps. As "the crimsoned waters of the Antietam flow silently by our camp, war's sad requiem was sounding in our ears from the lips of the wounded and dying," Mason wrote. Yet he sensed that the men had taken part in "a glorious victory." In the worst single day of the war so far, McClellan's army had checked Lee's invasion of the North. Bragg credited divine providence for seeing the Ninth New Hampshire through. "For a new Regiment we have seen very hard times," he wrote. Mason paid homage to the Union dead: "Will it not be, then, a *pleasure* for any father or mother to say in future, 'my son died on the battle-field of Antietam, to preserve the blessings of a free government, we now all enjoy?'"

September 25, 1862

A MOTHER'S LOVE

THE ROMANCE BEGAN BY THE THINNEST OF CHANCES. George Ladd was twenty-two years old and lived with his mother and stepfather in West Concord. After his cousin, Luther Ladd, was killed in the streets of Baltimore in the first fatal fight of the war, George joined the Second New Hampshire Volunteers. Heading south, his train stopped at Lebanon, Pennsylvania, where Carrie Deppen, the sixteen-year-old daughter of a judge from nearby Myerstown, stood in the crowd waving. Private Ladd waved back and tossed something out the window. Carrie picked up a card on which he had scrawled his name and regiment and a note saying he was an eligible bachelor. She wrote to him two and a half weeks later, saying she was "too young for any person."

CARRIE DEPPEN

Undaunted, he was soon addressing her as "Dearest Carrie" or "Darling Carrie." "I agree with you in your idea of love," he wrote her in September 1861. He hoped his dreams would not turn out to be "mere air castles but may be realities if they should be in union with the object of my affection and love. Every day you grow nearer and dearer to me." He believed a higher power had inspired him to throw the note from the train and her to find it. She wrote to him out of curiosity at first, he knew, but the pace of their letters quickened. "I believe that we are inevitably drawn to love each other, don't you Carrie?" he wrote. "You asked me if the little winged messenger of love, the little blind boy Cupid, had ever made my heart his target. I plead 'guilty,' but I never felt more than mere friendship for those I associated with. . . . I was a wild sort of a boy, but now it is different altogether." Carrie sent George her picture and her encouragement.

Perhaps an enduring love would have bloomed from the youthful infatuation that kept the couple writing to each other. They filled their letters with promises as they faced a world of peril and possibility. It was the peril that settled the question. George's letters stopped after the second battle of Bull Run. Wounded there, he lost a leg to the surgeon's saw and died of infection four weeks later, on September 25, 1862. All that was left to Carrie were the letters in which he had shared his experiences, thoughts, and feelings. They had never even met.

George's death created a second bond for Carrie, a bond of grief. The army sent his things to his mother, Susan Abbott. Among them were Carrie's letters and the tattered picture of her that he had carried. George's father had died when he was a boy, and his mother had married Rufus Abbott, a farm laborer in West Concord. Susan Abbott appreciated the yearning in the girl's heart and the ardor in her letters to George. Nearly five months after her son's death, she wrote Carrie:

"Dear Beloved Daughter,

"Again I am permitted to take my pen in hand to answer your kind, interesting, and respectful letter that came to hand in due time. I am always glad to hear from you. I am always glad to hear from those I love, and God knows, my dear Carrie, that I do love you. And I have no reason to think but that I have your love in return. Although a few months ago we were strangers to each other, yet it was but a very short time before I began to feel as if you were not a stranger to me. That dear one that has gone from you and me provided a way for you and me that we might become acquainted with each other. If it had not been for those letters from you that he sent home, I suppose that I never should have known that such a girl in this world was living by that lovely name of Carrie C. Deppen. . . .

"You speak of favors and kindnesses that you receive from me, Carrie. Do I not receive more from you than you from me? I think I do. That last letter of yours was such a nice long letter. I will bet, Carrie, that I read your letters more times and oftener than you do mine. That beautiful little Valentine that I found enclosed, why, I think a great deal of it, and I will send something sometime in return. . . .

"No, Carrie, you did not write a foolish letter to George, that last one. I thought when I read it that you were very thoughtful and careful in writing to him. You wrote very cheerful and that is what the poor soldiers want, long, cheerful, and loving letters. I have the one you wrote George about your picture. Carrie, your picture, or your shadow, as our pictures are called, shows as if you stuck by George and he by you. It looks as if it had been through some hard battles, poor thing. He kept you with him through all his weary marches and on the battlefields, then you were with him when he fell, went with him to the hospital, was there when his thigh was amputated, then when the cold death sweat began to gather on his lovely face. You were there, but your hands were not able to render him any assistance (that is, your picture) that picture that he looked at so many times. He was taken away from it. You were left there alone. They took your lover away from you. Then, by chance, you came to see George's Mother. I will ever keep it, thinking how it went with George. And I think that with the picture he had your heart too.

"But, dear Carrie, I am so glad you have given your heart to that blessed Savior who has promised to never leave or forsake those that trust in Him. How kind He is to us. He has afflicted us, but He does not afflict willingly nor grieve the children of men. God has a right to His own. He has a right to take His own when He pleases. The blow is hard, oh so hard, dear Carrie, that at times it does seem as if it will crush me down, but then those words, "be still and know that I am God," will calm my troubled mind. I do feel Carrie dear, that God is my refuge and though He slay me, yet will I trust in Him. Let us be faithful until death and then we will go to be united in that land where sickness will never come.

"I hope this will find you and all your dear friends well. So, good night, sweet one. Much love to you, I am

"Your dearest Mother Abbott"

October 25, 1862

JUST A BOY

IN AUGUST 1862, SARAH LOW WROTE Hannah Stevenson to ask for a nursing job. "Crowded with work, come at once," Stevenson replied from Union Hospital in the Georgetown neighborhood of Washington.

But Dorothea Dix, the nurse super-intendent, wanted only homely married women over thirty. Low was thirty-one but single. Only through guile did she foil Dix's effort to send her home to Dover, New Hampshire.

The hospital, a three-story former hotel, was dingy and dirty. Latrines adjoined the kitchen, and the wards were crowded and air-less. Early in the war, an army inspector lamented the hospital's "narrow halls and tortuous pas-sages" and worried that when the doors and windows were shut in winter, typhus, gangrene, and dys-entery would become epidemic. "A

SARAH LOW

more perfect pestilence-box than this house I never saw," the nurse and future novelist Louisa May Alcott observed. Some of the staff abused patients. The head surgeon, A. M. Clark, "is very brutal in his manner to the patients," Low wrote. "He is a strong pro-slavery man & seems to think they are to be treated as slaves." She also believed Henry Perkins, a steward, starved them and sold their food for profit.

LOUISA MAY ALCOTT

Hannah Ropes, an older nurse who took a liking to Low, crusaded for better care, food, and sanitation. By going directly to Secretary of War Edwin M. Stanton, she suc-ceeded in having both Clark and Perkins jailed at the Old Capitol Prison. Ropes accused Perkins of beating a patient with a chisel and confining him in the cellar. Clark, she alleged, had tolerated this cruelty. As Ropes endured the fuss caused by her charges, Low became a quiet ally whose companionship took Ropes's mind off the struggle. She loved Low's gentle nature and became so close to her that they once sat by the fire in Ropes's room sharing a breakfast of corncakes and beefsteak from the same plate.

Low found it easy to care for men with infected stumps, punctured lungs, and fatal fevers. Almost from the start she viewed battlefield carnage with professional detachment. A man with bullet holes perforating every part of his body except his

HANNAH ROPES

face—fifteen wounds in all—struck her as "one very interesting case." She kept her ward clean and pleasant despite the deficiencies of her soldier-helpers, who shirked their chores, and her "colored man," who slept when he should have swept. Low devoted herself to the patients. One of the first was a young Michigan soldier whose leg amputation healed poorly. The bullet had passed through one leg, shattered the bone, and lodged in his other foot. An attendant held up his good leg to allow Low to clean and bandage the foot. "In dressing the wounds in the afternoon, we often have a pleasant time," she wrote, although her shifts were so tiring she often lost track of time. "Each days work is so absorbing that it is difficult to recall the events of the days that I neglect," she wrote.

Low had been on the job just over a month when she encountered a patient she identified only as Johnny. From speaking with Johnny and his regular nurse, Low knew his story. He had been sent to an orphanage on Randall's Island in the East River off Manhattan after his parents died of cholera. A farmer hired him but proved to be a cruel employer. The boy bore scars from the farmer's blows. When war came and boys at the orphanage began joining the army, Johnny signed up, too. He was barely a teenager. On the way to Bull Run in August 1862, he filled his knapsack with green corn and left it under a tree, expecting to reclaim it on the way back. After he was shot in battle, his first thought was that now he could not roast his corn. He arrived at the hospital wrapped in a blanket and so lonely he wished he had been killed outright. Everyone could see his wound was mortal. "But it was not his fate to die friendless and unmourned," Low wrote. His male nurse "could not have been more devoted to him if he had been his own father." Johnny called the man "Uncle." A woman visiting her son began stopping at Johnny's bed, and the hospital chaplain found a pastor to baptize him. Possibly sent by the pastor, young people visited the boy.

As Johnny's body withered, "Uncle" sat by his bedside eleven straight nights. Low cared for him by day. "He is so weak that his head has to be held like a very young baby's," she wrote on October 23. "He takes great pleasure in having his friends around him. The chaplain came to see him this evening, & he asked him to make a prayer for him." Two days later, when Johnny died, his empty bed moved Low to scribble well into the night to tell her mother all about him.

Knowing his young friends would return, the nurses decided to spare them a trip to the dead house. They brought Johnny's body back to the ward and washed and dressed it for burial as the other patients watched. At the foot of Johnny's bed they covered a table for a bier and laid the body on it. Johnny was so thin he seemed "hardly more than a shadow," Low wrote. The other patients cried—"these strong men weeping for a young boy." Across Johnny's heart the mother who had visited him laid a bouquet of white rosebuds in the shape of a cross. Low paid her last respects that night at the dead house, where the flowers were still lovely and Johnny "looked very calm & peaceful."

"Uncle," the boy's nurse, chose a plot in the congressional cemetery, took the body there, and stayed until the grave was filled. He placed the cross of rosebuds on the newly turned earth. Losing Johnny, Low wrote, was like "losing a child from a family."

December 13, 1862

FEET TO THE FOE

IT WAS FRIDAY NIGHT IN FREDERICKSBURG, and Colonel Edward E. Cross felt ill. His men were in the streets blowing off steam. They had, in Cross's words, "lost nothing of their gaiety or fun." Like nearly everyone in Major General Ambrose Burnside's army, the colonel had had ample time to look over rebel positions on the heights above the city. Either the rebels would charge down that night or the Yankees would march up the next morning into a storm of fire. Pick your poison, Cross thought. If it were up to him, he would have crossed farther down the Rappahannock River, where the ground was flatter and Union gunboats could support the infantry. Too ill to hold down food, he nevertheless prepared for battle. "I had the impression I was to be killed or badly wounded," he wrote in his journal, "so I made my will, and an inventory of my property, packed everything in my trunk, and gave my key to the chaplain." As his soldiers smashed furniture and fine china and warmed themselves over bonfires stoked with books and chair legs, Cross and two of his officers, Major Edward E. Sturtevant and Adjutant Charles F. Dodd, found a house to sleep in.

EDWARD E. CROSS

Cross rose early but was so dizzy and weak from old wounds that he could barely sit on his horse. He saw strength in the faces of the men of the Fifth New Hampshire. "I was among my brave boys," he wrote. "I found them cheerful & full of hope."

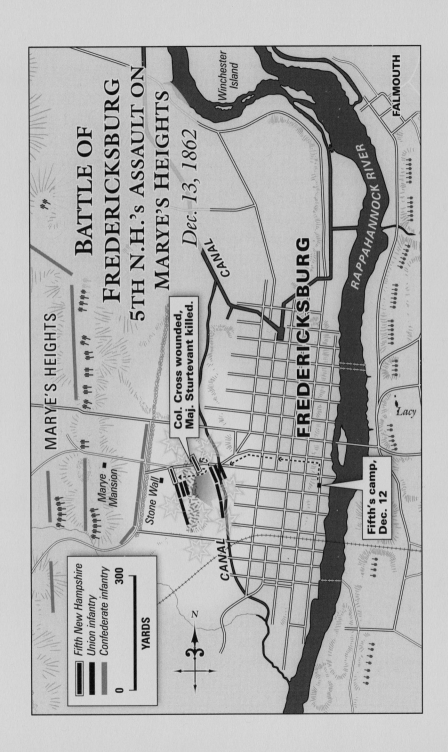

BATTLE OF
FREDERICKSBURG
5TH N.H.'s ASSAULT ON
MARYE'S HEIGHTS
Dec. 13, 1862

MARYE'S HEIGHTS

Winchester Island

FALMOUTH

RAPPAHANNOCK RIVER

CANAL

FREDERICKSBURG

Lacy

Col. Cross wounded,
Maj. Sturtevant killed.

Marye
Mansion

Stone Wall

Fifth's camp,
Dec. 12

CANAL

N

Fifth New Hampshire
Union infantry
Confederate infantry

0   300
YARDS

Six hours later, after watching other colonels march troops toward Marye's Heights with heavy losses, it was Cross's turn. He counted his men—249 rifles and 19 officers, a quarter of the Fifth's original number—and walked among them. Stay steady, close on the colors, do your duty, he told them. As they marched through town, artillery shells disrupted their ranks. They crossed a narrow canal and paused in a ravine to re-form. They moved out on the right end of their brigade, pushing slightly ahead of the other regiments into the cannon fire. Above the din Cross shouted, "Forward, men! Forward!" About halfway up the hill, as he marched on foot near the regimental flags, a shell exploded six feet off the ground right in his face. "I saw him fall & thought he was all stove in pieces," wrote Captain James E. Larkin. Cross tumbled face-first into the cold mud. The same barrage killed Major Sturtevant, depriving the Fifth of its leaders at a crucial moment.

Cross felt nothing until a shell fragment struck his left leg and woke him. He checked himself over. A piece of shell had gashed him just below his heart and nearly cracked his breastbone. His hat was gone, his face bruised everywhere. He had lost three teeth, and bits of gravel, tooth, and steel filled his mouth. He tasted blood. Hearing a gasp, he turned and saw an officer dying a foot away, his intestines spilled on the ground. Cross rose to his hands and knees and looked for the Fifth's flag. "Thank God, there it fluttered right amid the smoke and fire of the front line," he later wrote to a friend. He could hear his men cheer and saw the colors fall twice only to rise again. "My brave boys had gone along," he wrote. "I always told them never to stop for me."

First one captain and then another were killed leading the Fifth toward the rebel line behind the stone wall on Marye's Heights. Typical of Cross's soldiers was

GEORGE S. GOVE

Sergeant George S. Gove of Raymond, who had defied an order to sit out the fight because of boils on his legs. He decided "to go with the regt & the boys and share the charge with them." After the formation finally broke, Gove saw Frank Swift, a private in his company, grab the state flag and run toward the stone wall waving it. Gove ran ahead, too, and when Swift was shot down, he took the flag. Several men rushed to his side, but the rebel line was too strong to charge. Gove held the flag aloft until a shell fragment knocked him down thirty yards from the wall. "It was horrible," he wrote his mother. "The bullets flew over me like swarms of bees." One hit him in the leg, another in the back. "I felt that any moment might be my last," he wrote. He lay still, waiting for night.

Farther down the hill, Colonel Cross tried to crawl through the bodies, but a piece of shell split his scabbard, flattening him again. He could barely move, but he wriggled until his head pointed to town and his feet to the foe. Two more Union lines moved over him, "but soon they swayed back, trampling on the dead and dying." Another line lay down before it reached him, and Cross found himself between opposing infantry forces with artillery shells falling around him. Union guns placed across the Rappahannock often fired short, hitting their own men. Cross described his four hours lying on the field as "the most awful moments of my life." Minie balls fired by comrades zipped within a foot of his head. Trying to blot out the present, "I covered my face with both hands, and counted rapidly from one to one hundred, expecting every moment my brains would spatter the ground," he wrote. Later he suggested that "guardian angels" had watched over him, but a secular explanation suited him better: "My destiny saved me. The end of my days was reserved for another, and I hope, more fortunate occasion. For if I am to die on the battlefield, I pray that it may be with the cheers of victory in my ears."

It was December 13, one of the shortest days of the year, and night fell early. Daniel Cross, a Hanover man unrelated to the colonel, had been the Fifth's sergeant major but now worked on the division staff. Walking up the hill near dark, he found the colonel and called for a stretcher. Colonel Cross spent the night in the mayor's house and crossed the river to the Fifth's camp next morning. "I am not half as badly hurt as the papers say," he wrote his father. "You must not be in any apprehension about me." The colonel "stands higher with the regiment now than he ever did before," Larkin wrote his wife. Recalling Cross's wounds at Fair Oaks and Antietam, Lieutenant Gus Sanborn of Franklin said that if he had been hurt as often as the colonel, he would leave the army. "I do not know what we should do with out him to look out for us," he wrote.

Three veterans back in Concord reeled at the news from Fredericksburg and wrote the *Independent Democrat* to share their thoughts. Charles H. Smart, William C. Silver, and Walter S. Drew had all joined Sturtevant's company in 1861 and served until wounds disabled them. Sturtevant's death hit them hard. "His rank never placed him above the reach of his men," they wrote of the state's first volunteer. He had shared his blanket and food with men who had none. He had made time to "cheer up the drooping spirits of the men with some anecdote of by-gone days." The previous summer, while Cross was home recuperating, Sturtevant had led the Fifth during the retreat of McClellan's army across the Virginia Peninsula. The three veterans wrote that he had died "in the full vigor of manhood," just thirty-six years old. "A braver man never lived; a truer man never drew blade for his imperilled country."

The Fifth lost 157 men at Fredericksburg, including 57 dead. Sergeant Gove crawled away from the wall at Marye's Heights after dark and soon returned to soldiering. But in the face of the losses, Smart, Silver, and Drew worried how few men would be left to tell the Fifth's story. While trusting that "the renown of the 5th will ever be green in the memory of the people of New Hampshire," they added: "Let anyone look into the history of the 5th, and they will exclaim, 'The half has not been told.'"

Living in the capital, they especially resented people who criticized Cross. Men the colonel had forced out of the regiment accused him of unfairness, but Smart, Silver, and Drew didn't buy it. "Whatever charges his enemies may bring against him they cannot bring that of *cowardice*," they wrote. They lauded Cross's "intrepidity, celerity of movement, coolness under the most trying circumstances, and . . . indomitable bravery." They told how Cross sometimes carried medicine for ailing men in his saddlebags and always gave the next promotion to the most deserving soldier. "A better man to look after the welfare of his men never wore the eagles," they wrote. "Were we to enlist for a score of times, we should go under Col. Cross each time."

SLAVES, SOLDIERS, AND COTTON AT HILTON HEAD,
SOUTH CAROLINA (HENRY P. MOORE PHOTO).

Part II

TO SET MEN FREE

"There has been no mental food for them
any more than for the swine and cattle with
whom their lives are shared. The wonder
is that we find them so nearly human."

—Esther Hill Hawks, January 1863

January 1, 1863

JUBILEE?

AFTER THE THIRD NEW HAMPSHIRE VOLUNTEERS occupied Port Royal, South Carolina, Sergeant John M. Head toured the islands to check on former slaves farming plantations without white supervision. He found them "working faithfully and well, and that too without pay, and without, in many instances, even the promise of pay, other than clothes and food." He blamed the popular refrain that black people were lazy on prejudices repeated for years in the press. "The white man has always written the history of the black man," he wrote. "Things are changing. Justice does not sleep forever."

The Emancipation Proclamation took effect on January 1, 1863. A bold stroke justifying Head's optimism, it was also a half-measure tossed into the mighty wind of ignorance. Union soldiers viewed it through the lens of old opinions and new experience. To most, the war had made the fate of slavery a crucial practical question. Northern politicians, meanwhile, still discussed the issue in time-tested terms, but the question for them had also become practical: How would voters react to emancipation as a war aim?

Private John Burrill of the Second New Hampshire lay in a Philadelphia hospital on January 1. He expected the war to end with "no great difference in the nigger question from what there was when we commenced." He did not oppose slavery but was willing to see it abolished. "I believe in putting away any institution if by so doing it will help put down the rebellion," he wrote, "for I hold that nothing should stand in the way of the Union—niggers, or anything else." A Fourth New Hampshire sergeant reached the same conclusion for different reasons. "We all believe we are trying to restore the Union instead of freeing the negroes, and we hope we are not deceived," he wrote his local newspaper. He found South Carolina black people useful for labor but was sure his white comrades would never fight beside them. "If you should place a company of negroes into a white regiment," he wrote, "the first volley would be fired at them, and the second at the rebels." Yet for the sake of his children, he wanted slavery to end with the war.

The previous summer Captain Tileston A. Barker of the Second New Hampshire told a crowd at a Concord recruiting meeting that McClellan's army on the Peninsula "had to dig trenches and throw up breastworks when hundreds and thousands of negroes were hovering around our lines, but not one of them put into work to relieve our soldiers from the drudgery of the spade." He was "satisfied that this style of warfare is at an end, and that hereafter our government will use every means that God has put into our hands to put down this rebellion—niggers or anything else." At another war meeting Brigadier General Oliver O. Howard, a pious Mainer who had lost an arm on the Peninsula, called for raising and arming black regiments and "employing negroes in all places and in all times when they could be of service to the government."

One soldier who had carefully considered these issues was Private Edward F. Hall of the Third New Hampshire, a shoemaker from Exeter whose wife Susan sent him both Democratic and Republican newspapers. "There is two sides to every question—and I like to see both sides shown up plain and then judge for myself," he wrote her. Hall was thirty-eight, and "the Negro question" had troubled the nation all his adult life. "Now I don't believe in 'abolition' but in the progress of the war," he wrote Susan and his fifteen-year-old son Eddy from Hilton Head. He knew that as Union armies moved deeper into the South, more slaves would either flee their masters or be abandoned by them. "Now *something* must be done with them," he wrote. "What shall it be?" They "are robust and healthy—used to work—and are perfectly at home in the climate." They could build roads, load ships, gather wood, and do any other "hard and disagreeable work," but he opposed arming them. "They have been educated to fear the white man from their earliest infancy—and if they were to be brought up face to face with their former white masters, they would . . . run like sheep—they might do to shoot if they could be hid where the enemy couldn't see them perhaps—but we don't *want such* soldiers in this war—we want men who will face anything."

Charles E. Hurd, a Fourth New Hampshire private from Gilmanton

Iron Works, respected the former slaves he met. Many defied the common slur that they were "dumb beasts," he wrote. Some were smart and informed "considering how they have been bound under the tyranicle chanes of slavery during all their existence." They were "not half as bad as many of our soldiers who have had the privillage of a free school while the poor colored man has been deprived of it." John L. Kelly, the Fourth's quartermaster, knew most soldiers "exhibited an inordinate hatred toward the black man" at first. Now he sensed—or wanted to sense—"a silent, yet sure change" in favor of the proclamation. He assured readers of the *Daily American* in working-class Manchester that, contrary to Democratic claims, they needn't fear an invasion of former slaves inflicting "great injury to free white labor, by working cheaper." They disliked rocky soil and frigid weather, and even black northerners might "seek new homes in the congenial South" once slavery was gone, Kelly wrote. Lieutenant Edmund Dascomb of the Second New Hampshire blamed newspapers for racism in the ranks. "Is it strange when a portion of our press tell us that we are 'fighting for a pack of niggers' that many are found to believe it?" he asked. Captain Freedom Rhodes of the Fourteenth New Hampshire believed the army was warming to emancipation and would vote accordingly if given the chance.

Yet racial hostility still ran deep in the Union army. Lincoln's proclamation would only make the rebels fight harder, wrote Levi Miller of Strafford, a corporal in the Seventh New Hampshire. "If I should ever return north again I don't want to see a nigger every step I take for I have seen enough of them already," he wrote. Fourteenth New Hampshire Private Christopher Hoyt of Washington found former slaves "beter off than the poor folks are at home and a great deal beter than the soldiers are that is fighting for the black divels and they have more liberty." His comrade, Private William J. Combs of Winchester, liked a rumor that the Fourteenth might soon go home. "The soldiers think different of the war than thay did when they inlisted," he wrote. "The niggers do not want to bee free no more then we want to bee slaves." Lincoln had put forth the proclamation after a victory at Antietam, but Corporal Miles Peabody's regiment, the Fifth New Hampshire, had since marched to slaughter at Fredericksburg. He expected the war to be lost by summer. "When I enlisted I supposed that I was to fight to restore the Constitution and the Laws," he wrote his family in Antrim, "but I found out that I was mistaken for it has been all nigger nigger. As for me I did not come out here to shed my blood for the sake of raising niggers on an equal footing with whites, and if there be anyone left in your vicinity who want to fight for that purpose, jest send them out here and I will let them have my chance." Freeman E. Colby, a Henniker man who enlisted in 1862, had yet to face battle. If the South was going to win the war, he wrote his brother, he hoped it would happen "before I am matched against them myself. My patriotism, Newton, sunk into Chaos when I read the Nigger proclamation & I am afraid that it will never rise again."

Private Albert T. Austin of Mason wrote home from Louisiana that "the darkeys are As thick here as polleywags In a mud puddle and As black." Runaway slaves crowded around the camp of the Eighth New Hampshire near New Orleans. "If I thought we were fighting to free them I would throw my musket to the devil and leave," Private Charles Goings wrote his sister-in-law, Mary, in New London. Her husband Claude blamed "Old Abe and His gang of cutthroats [for] their Hellish Scheme of Emancipation and mismanagement of our Armies." They were "ready to Sacrefice us all in their attempt to Free the *Nigger*." Had he known this beforehand, he wrote, "it would have required force to have got me to Shoulder a musket." Private Enos G. Drew of Concord wrote that despite kind masters many slaves hated work so much they stole away from plantations "with a lie in their mouths," hoping that "if they get into camp they will have nothing to do but eat, drink, and sleep." Captain George Flanders of Sanbornton scoffed at arming former slaves and believed the white privates training them had "secured the post of drill master for the sport of the thing." They lashed unruly recruits to trees.

To many soldiers, abolitionists who flocked south to Union-occupied territory were less popular than freed slaves. Their mission was to help black people now fending for themselves without means, institutions, or education. "The Abolitionists have sent down some men & women, who have been in a measure recognized by the government to take charge of the plantations & negroes & raise cotton & corn," Colonel Haldimand Putnam of the Seventh New Hampshire wrote his father in Cornish. "They devote themselves mostly to instructing the negroes that all men were born free & equal except negroes who were born a great deal better than white folks. The consequence is that the amount of work done by them is small." When George Towle of the Fourth New Hampshire saw former slaves working plantations after their masters had fled, he interpreted this as a sign that they feared freedom. The soldiers hated them, he wrote, and felt the same about the abolitionists "sent down here to civilize the nigger."

One such volunteer was Daniel M. Robertson of Manchester, who managed the harvest and sale of cotton at Port Royal. He struggled at first to convince former slaves to pick, finding them "shrewd, cunning and inclined to dishonesty" in avoiding work. After the first payday the good pickers worked harder and the shirkers realized they must pick if they wanted money. Robertson had less cause to "appeal to their fears." He even found skilled workers among them—mechanics, carpenters, and a man to supervise the wood-cutters. Robertson warned against snap judgments about black people. "Being naturally timid and suspicious, they will not manifest their better qualities to a stranger," he wrote. "They know they have been wronged most outrageously by the white race."

Esther Hill Hawks, a Manchester doctor, spent much of the war on the south Atlantic coast. After two seventeen-week terms, she had graduated in the six-member class of 1857 from New England Female Medical College. Her husband Milton, also a doctor, wrote the governor three weeks into the war offering their services "in any of the hospitals or sick rooms connected with the U.S. Service during the war." When Esther volunteered as a nurse, Dorothea Dix, the supervisor, rejected her as too young and pretty. Back home, she bottled the elixir Milton had concocted from rum, bitters, crushed seed, and sugar water, and he made good money retailing it to soldiers. A tall woman at five-foot-seven with hazel eyes and black hair, Esther was twenty-eight years old when she went south again to join Milton in furthering the abolition cause. His antislavery views were so extreme that just before the cautious Lincoln announced his proclamation, he wrote her: "The greatest kindness that a man could do his government today would be to assassinate Pres. Lincoln—he stands directly in the way."

After the National Freedmen's Relief Association hired Milton to help Robertson supervise plantations seized in South Carolina, Esther began teaching black children and adults at Beaufort. Her students struck her as oddly ungrateful. Christianity was a force in their lives, but the Golden Rule seemed alien. One congregation denied care to a sick member but, when he died, devoted half a day to "lamenting and singing in a manner to convince one that their community had met with a very calamitous bereavement." Church members helped Hawks only if she watched them closely or if they liked her. She concluded that Sea Island black people were "the lowest type—the flattest nosed and thickest lipped—accompanied by the numbest sculls anywhere to be met in America." She blamed their isolation, writing: "There has been no mental food for them any more than for the swine and cattle with whom their lives are shared. The wonder is that we find them so nearly human."

January 1, 1863, found Hawks at Hilton Head, where the chaplain of the army's first black regiment, the First South Carolina, put on a celebration. Black civilians were wary of the event because white soldiers had told them General Rufus Saxton would return them to their masters if they came. The few black civilians present heard speeches from Saxton and Colonel Thomas W. Higginson of the First South Carolina. The regiment received a new stand of colors, and the soldiers and their guests ate beef cooked in a pit—"a *bar-becue*," Hawks heard it called. There was no food for the white guests. Hawks rode home hungry and weary but knew she would one day cherish the memory of "the first celebration of the indipendence of the freedmen in South Carolina."

Also at the celebration was Liberty Billings, Higginson's second in command. Strapped around Billings's ample waist was a sword and sash sent by friends in Concord. He considered the gift a token of support for "the grand experiment . . . of teaching the art of war to that unfortunate race who have been the innocent occasion of this most terrible conflict." Billings was clear about his war aims. "Only the sword can now carve a pathway to true peace by loosing the iron manacles that bind the limbs of the slave," he wrote. Slavery was "the ulcer that has for years been eating out the life of the real Union." He saw it as God's will that the black man be armed and white officers "guide him to the promised land of manhood."

In Concord that day, there was another meeting—to nominate a Republican for governor. The March election would be the proclamation's first test at the polls since its enactment. Feeding on military setbacks and damning the idea of a war to free the slaves, Democrats campaigned for peace. Colonel Cross was in town, and Republicans offered him a deal: Work for their nominee and they would help him get a brigadier general's star. Cross was a staunch Democrat. "I hope God has caused this war to kill off the Abolition Party," he had written to a friend. But he had bled so much for the Union and seen so many good men die that he could not abide the thought of losing the war. He rejected the deal but agreed to speak at the Republican convention.

When Cross rose to the platform, every listener knew he was in the presence of a hero. Cross had been hit nine times at Fair Oaks, including a gunshot wound in the thigh that, in his words, "tore the flesh in the most shocking style." Shell fragments had cut his face and head at Antietam. Eighteen days before the convention, an artillery round had exploded in his face at Fredericksburg. Cross accepted a thunderous ovation on behalf of the Fifth New Hampshire, "the men I have the honor to command, that is, the shattered remnants of that regiment of men who are left after ten bloody battles." Pointing to the tattered regimental colors, he said, "Those flags have never been trailed in dishonor." Someone waved them above Cross's head, and the crowd cheered again. He paused, perhaps choking up, and apologized that his chest wound made it hard for him to speak. He told of the six men who had been shot carrying the colors toward the stone wall on Marye's Heights. He closed with a wish that whoever the people elected in March would bring honor to the state, and the crowd burst into applause.

Franklin Pierce, whom Cross sometimes informed of Washington intrigues, was out of town when the colonel spoke. Pierce had been a partisan in the nation's slavery debate for thirty years as a state Democratic leader and as president, appeasing the South at every turn. The proclamation infuriated him. Although he had vowed to stay out of the public debate, as was the custom for ex-presidents, he often wrote political rants to his right-hand man, John H. George. George passed the letters on to William Butterfield, editor of the Democratic *Patriot*, who printed them unsigned but nearly verbatim.

On January 2, Pierce wrote George a letter that appeared anonymously in the *Patriot* a week later. One of its central claims—that the proclamation would lead to an uprising in which slaves would rape white women and kill like beasts—was a scare tactic southerners and their sympathizers had peddled for decades. The letter called the proclamation "the climax of folly and wickedness" and said any real patriot must reject Lincoln and his war because of it. The proclamation had tipped the administration's hand. "We know what Mr. Lincoln means, so far as he can be said to have a meaning of his own," Pierce wrote. The president, a man of "limited ability and narrow intelligence," was the abolitionists' "willing instrument for all the woe which has thus far been brought upon the country and for all the degradation, all the atrocity, all the dessolation and ruin which is only too palpably before us." To Pierce, it was bad enough that Lincoln had deliberately violated the Constitution. It was bad enough that 100,000 men had already died for abolition. Now Lincoln's proclamation invited slaves "to slay & devastate without regard to age or sex." Pierce prayed the public would wake up to this fanaticism while there was still time "to stay the restless march of barbarism."

In the months after Lincoln announced his proclamation and Pierce predicted plunder, rape, and ruin, some things changed and some didn't. The slaves did not revolt, and relations between northern soldiers and former slaves often defied Lincoln's hopes.

An incident in Carrollton, Louisiana, during the proclamation winter showed how far northerners still had to come. Two companies of the Fifteenth New Hampshire were assigned to enforce order in occupied territory. A local plantation owner complained that his Negroes refused to work. The provost marshal sent the soldiers to the plantation with orders to whip them "till they promised obedience." Men of the Fifteenth flogged the Negroes, and the Negroes went back to work.

Months later, when the *Boston Traveller* reported this incident, Edwin M. Wheelock, chaplain of the Fifteenth, felt compelled to explain the circumstances behind it. Wheelock, the former Unitarian minister in Dover, had volunteered as chaplain in part because of Lincoln's preliminary proclamation in September. He began working with freedmen after the Fifteenth arrived in New Orleans and became deputy superintendent of black labor in the Department of the Gulf. Wheelock assured *Traveller* readers that using northern troops as plantation overseers was not the policy of Major General Nathaniel Banks, the department's commander. Rather it was "the unlawful and wrongful action of a subordinate, illustrating that mean, hound-like, slavery-loving spirit, for which neither the army nor the nation is yet sufficiently purged." Had Banks heard of the incident when it occurred, Wheelock had no doubt he would have punished the offending officer. For anyone to blame Banks for "a petty act of tyranny" that he had neither sanctioned nor known about would be unjust, Wheelock wrote.

The Negroes on the plantation in Carrollton were the intended beneficiaries of Lincoln's proclamation. What they knew about that, and what they thought of being flogged by Union soldiers, went unrecorded.

BROTHERS

THE RHODES BOYS WERE FROM THE STATE'S FAR NORTH, born in Northumberland and living in Lancaster when war came. Freedom, the older brother at twenty-two, enlisted right away, becoming a sergeant in the Second regiment. Eldad, two years younger, joined the Fifth in December and soon won his sergeant's stripes. They saw each other often in Virginia in 1862 before both were wounded during the Seven Days fighting.

Eldad's wound was worse. After a shell fragment hit his foot at Malvern Hill, he walked eight miles through mud and rain with two men propping him up. "Kind friends alone prevented me from falling into the hands of the Enemy," he wrote in his diary. He disliked Union Hospital in Washington, D.C., and grew even crankier at the Soldiers' Rest, a way station for men preparing to return to their regiments. "A miserable lousy place," he called it at first, and thereafter "the Hog Pen." In late August he returned to Alexandria, where the food was as bad as the days were hot. "We are growing dainty on hard bread and tainted pork," he wrote his parents. The Union cause was "*lost, lost hopelessly lost forever.*" The rebels, fighting for a united South behind good generals, "have driven us from the Peninsula, have defeated us in the recent desperate conflicts at Manassas, and now our whole proud Armys are compelled to hover about within sight of the Dome of the Capitol for its defence," he wrote. His parents told him reinforcements were coming, but Eldad knew it would take "another weary winter" for new troops to drill and train. And why would they do any better than the enormous army that had already dwindled away? Eldad asked his parents to keep his opinions

FREEDOM RHODES

to themselves. The good news was that his foot had healed and he was about to rejoin his regiment.

He caught up with the Fifth New Hampshire on its march into Maryland. People in Frederick cheered the men on their way toward South Mountain, where a battle was under way. After sleeping at the mountain's base, they marched up to where the "dead lay thick among the rocks." Ordered to lead the entire army onward, the Fifth double-timed down the mountain and reached Antietam Creek before nightfall. On September 17, "We were hurried into the deadly fire and fought like men," Eldad wrote. When shell fragments bloodied the forehead of Colonel Cross, the Fifth's leader, he streaked his cheeks with gunpowder and blood, his war paint, and burst into war whoops as the bullets flew. One of those bullets hit Eldad in the chest and went through his lung. Cutler Edson, a forty-two-year-old bugler from Enfield doubling as a nurse, helped him to his tent in the Pry house yard, where the Fifth had camped the night before. Edson cut off Eldad's bloody shirt and moved him to the Prys' barn, part of a makeshift hospital.

Eldad slept poorly and awoke spitting blood. His right arm lay useless at his side. The good news was that his chest did not hurt much. Nor had the rebel bullet broken his habit of "croaking," as the soldiers liked to say. "Poor arrangements these for wounded men—an old barn with nothing to

ELDAD RHODES KEPT THE SHIRT
HE WAS WEARING WHEN HE
WAS SHOT AT ANTIETAM.

ELDAD RHODES DREW THE LEAN-TO HIS COMRADE CUTLER
EDSON MADE FOR HIM NEAR THE PRY HOUSE. SERGEANT
RHODES IS ON THE LEFT, EDSON ON THE RIGHT.

eat," he wrote. Thirteen days later, he ended his diary entry: "May God take vengeance on those who will abuse wounded soldiers like this." Edson stayed with him, shopped for him in Sharpsburg, and attached his tent to a fence. Out her window Elizabeth Pry often saw Eldad struggling to get up and around. When winter set in, Edson moved him to the hospital in Frederick.

Freedom Rhodes, meanwhile, had transferred to the Fourteenth New Hampshire as a captain. He was stationed near Washington when word of his brother's wound came from Eldad's captain, Welcome A. Crafts. The prognosis was grim. "A traitor's bullet had pierced his lung, and though living, the chances of his recovery were small," Freedom wrote. He expected news of Eldad's death any day. Instead, he received a letter from Eldad saying he was on the mend. Freedom was skeptical, noting that Eldad's once-bold handwriting looked as "tremulous as that of Stephen Hopkins to the Declaration of Independence." He got a pass and went looking for his little brother.

Just after New Year's Day, John Adams, a black coachman, drove Freedom to catch a train in Maryland. On the way they saw traces of Robert E. Lee's retreating army—footprints, half-burned fences, charred spots where the rebels had cooked, and hundreds of corncobs strewn beside the road. At the military hospital in Frederick, a twenty-acre complex of seven wooden barracks with a capacity of a hundred patients each, Freedom heard Eldad before he saw him. Someone was playing "The Battle Hymn of the Republic," and Eldad was singing along: "John Brown's body lies a mouldering in the grave . . ." The brothers had sung the song together on the Peninsula.

Whose idea it was to return to the scene of Eldad's shooting is unclear, but Eldad must have wanted it. It was winter, travel might be difficult, and he had done nothing strenuous for months. Yet the Antietam campaign had been a rare and historic success: Eldad and his comrades had chased the rebels from northern soil. The brothers set out from Frederick on January 6 so that one could show the other this place of triumph and suffering. They left by carriage, "jogging along over the magnificent macadamized turnpike" that ran twenty-two miles to Sharpsburg. Rounding a pass, they caught their first glimpse of South Mountain. At Middletown, they admired the fertile valley with hills and mountains all around. They saw "hundreds of comfort-breathing farmhouses standing out front of the patchwork of forest and field, and a tortuous little stream that would have reflected sunbeams just as poetically as any other, had the clouds above permitted," Freedom wrote. The town's church spires pointed toward snow-capped mountains, a scene "that transplanted our fancies to New England."

The view made it hard to believe two great armies had passed through so recently, although there were signs of this as well: fire-spots, more corncobs, decomposing horse carcasses, a burned bridge. As the brothers climbed South Mountain, Freedom admired the strength of the rebel position. They stopped at the summit to eat at the country inn where Confederate General Samuel Garland had stayed before the battle and where his corpse had been laid the next night. The proprietor's wife, daughter, and servants had been inside the inn during the battle. It had stood between dueling cannons, and one of many musket balls that struck it shattered a window and dropped to the floor.

When the brothers left at four o'clock, falling temperatures had frozen the mud. "Our nag was smooth-shod and descended with great difficulty,"

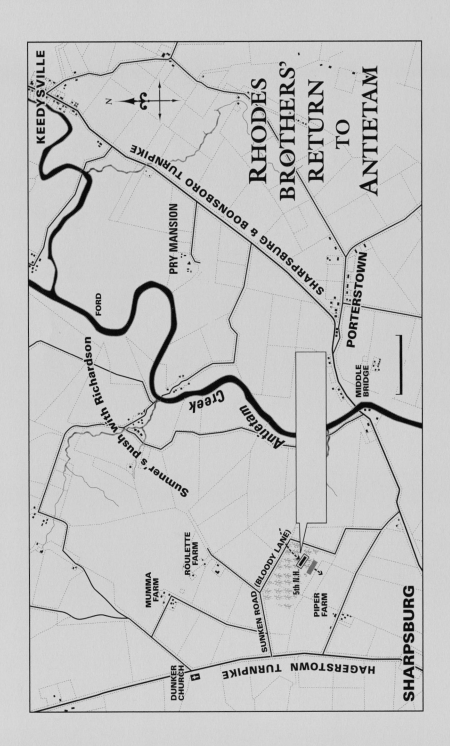

RHODES BROTHERS' RETURN TO ANTIETAM

KEEDYSVILLE

SHARPSBURG & BOONSBORO TURNPIKE

PRY MANSION

FORD

Sumner's push with Richardson

Antietam Creek

PORTERSTOWN

MIDDLE BRIDGE

MUMMA FARM

ROULETTE FARM

SUNKEN ROAD (BLOODY LANE)

5th N.H.

PIPER FARM

DUNKER CHURCH

HAGERSTOWN TURNPIKE

SHARPSBURG

wrote Freedom. The horse slid twenty feet at a time, stiffening its legs to stay afoot and taking nearly an hour to cover a mile. As they skidded and halted, Eldad recalled his regiment's brisk, steady pace over the same ground nearly four months before. The carriage reached Boonsboro, where the Fifth had saved a bridge, and Keedysville, where the Union army had passed smoldering rebel campfires in the woods. Then a large brick mansion came in view. This was the Pry house, McClellan's headquarters above Antietam Creek and the place where Eldad had begun his recovery. Major General Israel Richardson, the Fifth's division commander, had also been carried there. Wounded in the abdomen by a shell fragment but expected to recover, the general had died of infection at the house.

Elizabeth Pry and her children recognized Eldad and greeted the brothers as though they were long-lost family. She recalled how Eldad "would totter down to the house for milk. . . . How I pitied you." George Washington George, a lieutenant in Eldad's company who had lost a leg in the battle, was still at a nearby farm. The brothers found him resting with his wife at his side. Indeed, George would soon return to Amherst, where he would be hailed in print as "defooted but not defeated." From the farmhouse Eldad retrieved the scabbard that Captain Crafts had left behind. A ball had bent it at a right angle. The farmer had liked Crafts and wanted to keep the sword, but Eldad told him Crafts wanted it. Back at the Pry house, where the brothers spent the night, they were shown the room where Richardson died and the bed McClellan and Major General Joseph Hooker shared before and after the battle.

The Rhodeses arose early on January 7 and went first to a grassy strip above a sweet potato patch between two elms. There, by the garden fence, Eldad had slept the night before the battle and recuperated afterward, taking honey from a beehive and using a rise in the garden for a pillow. Next they visited the spot where McClellan had watched the fighting unfold on what Freedom called "the mightiest battle-field of America." Phillip Pry pointed to where he had seen Hooker's men put the rebels to "pell-mell flight." He showed the brothers one of the now-famous cornfields and the place between two sycamores where Richardson was hit. He took them to the cemetery where wounded men who died in his house and barn were buried. Pry had supervised their arrangement in rows with headboards identifying those whose names were known. The brothers found the graves of William Yates, a Fifth New Hampshire private from Milan, and, a few steps away, an unknown soldier of the Fifth Georgia. "Had they met three years ago they would have known each other as citizens of the same great Republic," Freedom wrote.

Across Antietam Creek a man gave the brothers wrong directions to Bloody Lane, where Eldad had been wounded. They found themselves wandering through "a great cemetery" where unmarked mounds and bullet-pocked tree trunks abounded. Freedom counted a hundred holes in one tree. Since the battle souvenir hunters "had gathered the most desirable relics" but left the unexploded shells. Still seeking Bloody Lane, Freedom drove the carriage across fields covered with coats, hats, boots, shoes, knapsacks, and cartridge boxes. The brothers reached the Dunker Church, a brick building badly damaged by bullets and shells. They saw broken trees, fences reduced to splinters, and fields as flat as forest paths. They met a boy and asked again about Bloody Lane, and this time they found it. What had confused Eldad, he now realized, was that they had been driving through the fields the rebels crossed to attack the Fifth New Hampshire. During the battle he had approached the lane over hills and fields from the opposite direction.

The brothers looked down and saw that they were riding over a "rag carpet"—uniforms and scraps of cloth left on the field. Then, near Bloody Lane, they made an even more startling discovery. It had rained during the night, and in a small basin created by horse hooves,

ELDAD RHODES IN
LATER LIFE

the water was the color of brick. Nearby a mound had settled into a large pit—a charnel house on the battlefield. Looking more closely into the water, exactly sixteen weeks after the battle, the brothers saw human gore and blood. Out of the carriage now, they walked to where the Fifth New Hampshire had captured the colors of the Fourth North Carolina. Moments later, they stood where Eldad had been shot. He had lain an hour, his blood running into the ground. Freedom chose these words to describe the return to this place with Eldad: "As we turned to the carriage again how fervently we thanked Heaven that the dark angel passed him thus over in his carnival."

Now it was time to go. They gathered shell fragments as souvenirs and stopped to retrieve a rifle Eldad had taken from a rebel prisoner on the way to battle and left with a farmer on the Old Sharpsburg Road. It is hard to imagine these relics would ever mean as much to them as the memory of their journey together.

March 10, 1863

DOWN TO THE WIRE

THE GUBERNATORIAL ELECTION OF 1863 could hardly have come at a worse time for Republicans. The slaughter at Fredericksburg was fresh in voters' minds. Congress was on the verge of passing a draft. The election would be the first test for the Emancipation Proclamation since its enactment. All in all, it seemed likely that when the new governor was inaugurated in June, New Hampshire would be led by a Peace Democrat—a Copperhead. As Franklin Pierce, the former president, worked behind the scenes to bring about such a result, he confided to his friend John H. George that if Democrats could not win this election, "we must regard the state as irredeemable."

The Republicans, who had held the governor's office for nearly five years, faced two immediate questions: Did they have a political operative who could beat the odds against them? And how would they handle the Emancipation Proclamation during the ten-week campaign? For answers they turned to youth. The man who stepped forward to run the campaign was William E. Chandler, a twenty-seven-year-old lawyer from a well-heeled Concord family. And the person who became the face and voice of the party's antislavery position was the twenty-year-old Quaker Anna E. Dickinson.

The proclamation pushed the Republicans into a major strategic shift. After years of resisting the abolitionist label, they embraced it. Benjamin F.

Prescott, secretary of the party's state committee, invited abolitionists of national stature to barnstorm the state to get out the vote. His star orator turned out to be the little-known Dickinson. In a stream of letters during the campaign, Prescott cheered her on and assured her theirs was a winning cause, all evidence to the contrary.

Governor Nathaniel Berry was leaving office after two one-year terms, and his successor was to be chosen on town meeting day in March. Chandler put forth his father-in-law, the Concord railroad man Joseph A. Gilmore, for the nomination. The convention that chose Gilmore on January 1 resembled a war rally, with a speech by Colonel Cross and a platform centered on sustaining the war. The proclamation took effect that very day, but no one mentioned it. That night, Prescott visited the home of philanthropists Nathaniel and Armenia White, which "was crowded till midnight with friends of emancipation," he wrote Dickinson. He wished she had come, but she was celebrating with Frederick Douglass and others in Boston. "The contest can have but one ending—no com-

ANNA E. DICKINSON

promise, no conciliation—but either the Palmetto or the Stars and Stripes from one end of the country to the other," she said there.

Dickinson had begun speaking for women's rights and abolition at the age of seventeen in and around her native Philadelphia, where she eventually found work as a clerk at the U.S. Mint. She borrowed money to tour New England in late 1862, but military setbacks shrank the crowds for her anti-slavery lectures. Her last appearance was in December in Concord, where she gave a talk called "The Nation's Peril" and received just ten dollars. "I would have gone home, but had not the means," she told a friend afterward. "Beyond my Concord meeting all was darkness; I had no further plans."

Prescott was in the audience that night, and Dickinson's lecture captivated him. When he heard afterward that she was considering a career in theater, he advised her to stick with politics. "I believe you can exert a better influence, and be more useful in society in the position you now occupy," he wrote. "The stage I know is fascinating, but one must incessantly be surrounded by those whose characters are of a doubtful nature." He recommended that the state Republican committee hire her, and almost immediately she was invited to Keene. After she spoke there, a *New Hampshire Sentinel* reporter portrayed her as a puppet of the antislavery *New York Tribune*. "The abolitionists opened the campaign on Friday evening last at the Town Hall, with a scold after the most approved *Tribune* pattern, by Miss Dickinson of Philadelphia—one of the 'strong-minded' class," the *Sentinel* reported. "It is thought that the lady did much good." This review from "a *rebel paper*" pleased Prescott.

To oppose Gilmore, the Democrats nominated Ira Eastman of Gilmanton, a former congressman and judge, on a peace platform. The party saw the proclamation as an unconstitutional act that ended any hope of reconciliation with the South. Democrats also scorned the draft and the army's ineptitude. The *Patriot* denounced black recruitment as "a pitiful confession of weakness on the part of the Government. It is virtually saying to the world that they cannot raise more white troops to fight for the abolition of slavery and the destruction of the Constitution and Union. . . . Make it truly a white man's war, and there will be no need to call upon negroes to join the army." John H. George, who was running for Congress on a promise to obstruct the war in any way he could, called Lincoln "a knave, an imbecile, a usurper and a tyrant." Another Democratic candidate, William Burns, said that rather than see the slaves freed, he "would prefer that the government be destroyed."

The *Patriot* ran a withering campaign against Gilmore. In an appeal to farmers, a writer who signed himself "Langdon" accused Gilmore of ruthlessness in seizing land for his railroad. He reminded working men of the nominee's order that they work on Sunday. He thus portrayed Gilmore as not only "the 'dummy' on the abolition kite" but also the "Railroad King and Sabbath breaker." If elected, he would support the draft, crushing "the last vestige of constitutional liberty," "Langdon" wrote. To illustrate the army's sunken morale, the *Patriot* published letters from unnamed soldiers. "I sometimes think the time has passed when we can *conquer* the South," wrote a former teacher from Loudon serving in the Twelfth New Hampshire. Union generals "don't think any more of having a soldier killed than you would of losing a sheep," wrote another soldier. A Sixth New Hampshire man put it simply: " 'On to Richmond' is played out among us soldiers."

Despite such dissent in the ranks, most soldiers liked the policies of Major General Joseph Hooker, the new leader of the Army of the Potomac. Thomas C. Cheney, an artilleryman from Derry, wrote home: "The Spirets of the Armey under Hooker are improving daily, confidence is being restored, and there is less fault finding, as we get rid of fault finding Generals. . . . Factionests are being cleaned out of the Armey, and I hope you will clean them out in NH next March." Private Lauren Elmer Bent of the Fourteenth New Hampshire assured his family in Winchester that soldiers who wrote defeatist letters to newspapers were in the minority. "No patriot will growl about the Governments freeing the slaves," he wrote. "It is a means, not an end. . . . We have as good a right to confiscate the slaves of rebels as any other property as a means of putting down this rebellion." Those who disagreed were "rebels themselves," Bent believed.

The slavery issue still divided more than it united, but antislavery speakers flocked to the state on Gilmore's behalf. Dickinson became Prescott's favorite, preferable even to the famed Theodore Dwight Weld. "I will risk you anywhere," he wrote her. "I think you will get good audiences wherever you go." By contrast, Weld was a good man and fine scholar but "too high above his audience for immediate effect." Prescott also brought in Andrew Jackson Hamilton, a Texan with Union sympathies. Lincoln had given him a brigadier's star, and Hamilton spoke in full uniform in Concord. "He looked like a hero, or he is, though he has not fought many battles," Prescott wrote Dickinson. He was equally pleased with Moncure D. Conway, who had broken with his Virginia family and led thirty-two of his father's slaves to freedom in Ohio.

To townspeople who flocked to see Dickinson during her twenty-speech tour, she was as much a phenomenon for her appearance and demeanor as for her words. Reporters invariably wrote detailed, subjective descriptions of her. A composite looks something like this: Dickinson was slight, average in height, and graceful. Her face was pleasant with thick dark hair and deep gray eyes, but a long square jaw kept her from being a true beauty. She wore modest Quaker dress. Her voice was strong but not loud, "as clear as the tone of metal, and yet with a reed-like softness." In manner she was confident without being bold. Her simple words, often spoken with passion, painted clear pictures. Having grown up in a large, poor family, she connected with working-class people.

Dickinson's message was typical of antislavery speeches of the day. She had long argued that without emancipation, "we have no war-cry—no noble motive. Where the flag of freedom waves merely for the white man, God will be against us." She wanted slavery treated as the moral evil it was. White people could form an intelligent view of the fitness of black people for freedom only if they gave them a chance to show what they could do, she said. As proof that slaves yearned for freedom, she cited the thousands who were risking their lives to escape to Union lines. Dickinson advocated recruitment of black soldiers and criticized General McClellan and other Democratic military leaders for their soft-glove approach to slavery and slaveholders. She said the war would be shorter if abolition were its explicit aim.

Soon Dickinson was in demand all over the state, her gender an asset. Early in the war, with many young men gone, the once-bustling streets of New Hampshire towns had fallen still. Now many women in black trod those streets. "The women in the State who have sons in the war are considerably nervous and want the war closed . . . at almost any sacrifice," Prescott wrote Dickinson. "Please encourage them in all possible ways, and in this way you can do much good." He knew from her fan mail that she was also drawing men of all political parties. Jacob H. Ela, who had once bankrolled the abolitionist *Herald of Freedom*, heard her speak in Tamworth. She drew a huge crowd, including many Democrats. "They were as uncomfortable a sett as you ever saw," Ela wrote Prescott. "Old Sam Emerson writhed and twisted and Dr Mason & Ben his brother couldn't keep still." A woman identified several "*minions of satan*" in Dickinson's Moultonborough audience and "saw the big tears roll down some of their cheeks."

While acting as Dickinson's scheduler, adviser, and paymaster, Prescott also offered her his sunny perspective. "Everything now is working in our favor," he wrote her in late February. "I have always felt confident and cheerful. I believe we shall succeed in this state at the coming election. I believe we shall succeed in our struggle with the rebellion. I have faith that this country is to be purified, and that it will stand before the world ere long a truly *free* country. My prayer is that I may be permitted to see the joyful day when every man can stand up and say that I am free."

Chandler, Gilmore's campaign director, saw little reason for such optimism. He knew Gilmore was far short of the majority he needed to win a popular election. The only hope was to deny Eastman a majority and throw the election into the Republican-controlled Legislature. Chandler went looking for a third-party candidate to siphon votes away from Eastman. He asked Secretary of War Stanton to press Colonel Walter Harriman to run, and pro-war Democrats obligingly nominated him. Harriman, who commanded the Eleventh New Hampshire, lived in Warner. Colonel Cross thought he had sold out for a brigadier's star, but the evidence does not support this. "Everything we hold dear on earth is involved in this great contest," Harriman said in his acceptance letter. He implored voters to ignore "those who go about preaching discontent and thus encouraging desertions from the army . . . and holding out promises of Peace without present-

WALTER HARRIMAN

ing any reasonable grounds in which to anchor the hope of peace." Prescott explained the value of the three-man field to Dickinson. "Many votes will be taken from the Democratic Party for they do not want to vote for Eastman," he wrote. "Some few who do not want to vote for Gilmore will also find a refuge. . . . We think we know how to play our cards as well as the 'Copperheads.'"

Chandler played another card, arranging a furlough for the Second New Hampshire before the election. Soldiers could vote only if they were at home. The stated purpose of the Second's return was to recruit, not vote, but William Butterfield, the *Patriot's* editor, protested that the men of this regiment were "almost unanimous for Gilmore." Butterfield would have had no complaint had the Seventh New Hampshire been sent home. Caleb Dodge wrote his sister Sophia in Plymouth that when his company took a mock vote, it was 36-6 in favor of the Democrats. "When we left

WILLIAM E. CHANDLER

Manchester it was the other way but the Negro question has changed them," he wrote.

Chandler faced one more crisis. He had touted his fifty-one-year-old father-in-law as a tireless campaigner, but eight days before the vote Gilmore threatened to quit. "I find my health is such that I must not undertake to have anything more to do with political matters and you will excuse me from anything of the kind," he wrote Chandler. "I am going to take it fair & easy . . . and if elected well and good and if not just as well." Chandler was livid. "If you propose to stop working I do not," he fired back. "You *shall* be elected Governor and the State saved." He insisted Gilmore raise $5,000 immediately or risk seeing his daughter Ann—Chandler's wife—lose her home. If Gilmore didn't get the money, Chandler vowed to sell the house on Merrimack Street along with his bank stock, furniture, and library. "I will either die, leave the state or bankrupt myself to elect you governor," he wrote. Gilmore raised the money.

The campaign's climax occurred in Bradford, a town of 1,200 people, the Friday before the election. William A. Howard, chairman of the Michigan Republican Party, and George, the Democratic congressional candidate from Concord, engaged in a four-hour debate on the Emancipation Proclamation. A railroad building was cleared and both parties sponsored free rides from neighboring towns in an effort to pack it. Concord Republicans reserved a twelve-car train for Bradford at half past five. Hearing of this, George hired a five o'clock train. Two thousand people crammed the hall, including 300 women. By the time the last train arrived, spectators had filled even the standing space and hundreds of people lingered outside hoping to replace anyone who left early. George argued that if Lincoln had been more conciliatory, every state but South Carolina would have remained in the Union. For soldiers and their families, a prolonged war to free the slaves "presents no picture of future hope or promise," he said. He called for ending the war "at the earliest moment consistent with national salvation" and for stopping "the fanatical and farcical attempt to elevate four million of negroes by the ruin of twenty-six million of the white race." Howard defended the proclamation, saying its constitutionality rested firmly on the president's war powers. By freeing and enlisting slaves, he said, the president deprived the rebellion of their labor. George responded that the proclamation had in fact strengthened the South "by arousing the jealousies of the Union white man who hated the idea of negro equality with all the ardor that belonged to the Caucasian man."

Judge William D. Kelley, a Philadelphia abolitionist, spoke the next night in Concord. Prescott assured Dickinson he had "listened to *more eloquent representatives* from the city of brotherly love"—meaning her— and added: "Just before elections a little more fire and energy is better." He wrote this letter on Sunday morning. "Only this sanctified day and Monday remain before the battle will be fought, the result of which will be eagerly looked for by every patriot in the country," he wrote. "Traitors too are interested, and desire to see the rebels triumph in this State. I have the fullest confidence that their hopes will be blasted." The campaign had been all uphill. "Apparently the Administration have been slow, too conciliatory, too lenient to the rebels in arms and their apologists and sympathizers at home; unwilling to grapple with the great questions involved in this struggle, and which underlie the whole matter," Prescott wrote. "We have not had any victories either by sea or by land to encourage us, but continued defeats, and unpleasant delays. But notwithstanding all this, we shall triumph in this State if I am not greatly mistaken."

On March 10, men trooped to town halls to vote. In East Washington, a sliver of a village in a rich but rocky valley, Julia Jones, a young woman with Republican leanings, looked out her window and wished she could join them. "All morning long I've been watching them pass—the voters—traitors and loyalists, 'Publicans and sinners, for this never-to-be-forgotten Town Meeting Day," she wrote Major Samuel Duncan. She expected Gilmore to carry East Washington but lose the state. "Being a woman," she wrote, "I must quietly fold my hands & wait the issue." If women could have voted, Eleanor Noyes's vote would have canceled Jones's. She believed the country was at last awakening to the administration's single fixation. "The 'nigger on the brain' malady is being understood," she wrote from Hanover. Only a reversal of Lincoln's policies could "save the country from utter ruin and shame."

By nightfall all that remained was to count the votes. Chandler had tilted the odds toward Gilmore in every way he could and Prescott had pushed the abolition message to the limit. Now the idea of fighting a brutal war for the sake of freeing the slaves came down to the numbers. In all, 66,250 voters turned out—32,833 for Eastman, 29,045 for Gilmore, 4,372 for Harriman. Eastman won 49.6 percent, 293 votes shy of a popular majority. Democrats howled, but the Legislature elected Gilmore, sparing Lincoln a rebuke and the challenge of dealing with an antiwar governor in New Hampshire.

JOSEPH A. GILMORE

Prescott's optimism thus rewarded, he sent Dickinson's mother a thank-you gift—several items made by the local Shakers, "a sect possessing many peculiarities which your daughter can better explain." He had visited the Canterbury village with Anna. The gifts were typical of Shaker practicality. "I hope you will find them useful," Prescott wrote Mary Dickinson, "for they are certainly not ornamental." To Anna, Prescott sent a glowing compliment: "I regret that Providence has furnished only one woman for such a crisis as this. I wish we had 50 Anna E. Dickinsons scattered all over the country telling people the truth." Connecticut Republicans hired Dickinson for their spring election, and she soon won national renown. On January 16, 1864, she spoke to Lincoln, his Cabinet, and Congress for more than an hour in the U.S. House of Representatives. Reporting on her talk, Whitelaw Reid of the *Cincinnati Gazette* called her "the bravest advocate for the integrity of the Republic and the demand for universal liberty throughout it." New Hampshire had started her on this journey, and in return she had helped state Republicans win a victory far more decisive than the vote count. When the Legislature met in June just before the third summer of the war, Joseph Gilmore gave the inaugural address while his son-in-law, William E. Chandler, looked on from the House speaker's chair.

March 27, 1863

DAMNED ABOLITIONIST

LIBERTY BILLINGS HAD A FIRST NAME TO MATCH his politics. A hulk of a man who had pastored in Concord's Unitarian Church for a year and a half without winning a call from the congregation, he joined the Fourth New Hampshire Infantry as its chaplain in 1862. Billings was an outspoken abolitionist, and when the regiment reached St. Augustine, he rejoiced to see a group of slaves more promising than those he had encountered in the South Carolina Sea Islands. There were 500 "good-looking specimens of their race," he wrote. "In some flows the blood of the Spaniard, and in others the fair skin of the Saxon struggles with the swarthy color of the African."

The day after his arrival, Rufus Saxton, military governor of the Department of the South, gathered the slaves together and declared them free. To Billings, their wild joy laid to rest claims that they did not want their freedom. "The fire of Liberty had burned in their hearts as well as in those of prouder and more beautiful races," he wrote. "As I mingled in the sea of black and yellow faces, it seemed the Day of Jubilee had come to them." Their owners had often rented them out by the day, and soon former slaves were doing the same work for pay, earning a living by cooking, washing, and fishing. Their former owners, women without skills and men with "hardly the genius to open a jackknife," lined up at the military commissary. Billings saw irony in women begging for handouts from "a government their husbands and brothers are fighting to destroy."

In relating these events to a newspaper back home, Billings did not sound like a chaplain. His letters contained no news of the Fourth's welfare or his attention to his flock. Indeed, he had been assigned to a regiment that even freedmen saw as one of the most racist in the department. Its officers "dislike the colored man as intensely as any slave owner," Billings wrote. Saxton's freeing of the slaves enraged them. "There are some in the Regiment, and not entirely confined to privates, who can scarcely pass a colored person without a curse." In their "negro-hating spirit" some taunted and struck black men, hurled bricks through their windows, and insulted black women. "There are some good officers; men who can spell negro with one g—who can say abolitionist without the prefix *damned*; men who see a greater work for the Northern soldier than to protect a rebel hen-coop," Billings wrote. He chastised the rest for an inclination to "trample upon the rights of a race that has few advocates and few friends. What have these people 'guilty of a skin not colored like our own' done that they should be thus cruelly treated by us?—*They* are not in arms against the government." Nor were they "the originators of this unholy war, but only the innocent occasion of it. The slave masters made this war upon the government, and they have been our masters as well as the slave's for the last fifty years."

Not surprisingly, this public berating brought the men of the Fourth down on their chaplain. George Towle, a captain from Portsmouth, considered Billings "probably as big a rascal as ever took refuge under the clerical cloth. . . . What such fellows are ever allowed to be born for. But I suppose they are produced in the same inexplicable way that other pests of mankind—yellow fever, cholera, plagues, &c.—are started to prey upon our race." Officers told their girlfriends in St. Augustine that Billings was an abolitionist. When he passed their doors, they spat upon him "cat-like." He took this as a compliment, writing for the newspaper: "The whole delicate proceeding is much to my credit, and I offer it as a testimony to my fidelity to my principles." After the Fourth returned to Hilton Head, he wrote that its officers' southern principles were hurting the army. "The advocate of human slavery is the advocate of that for which Jeff Davis is fighting; and if all slaves are the property of their masters Jeff Davis has the *right* to take them into Kansas or New Hampshire." He believed that many of his comrades wanted the slave power "restored to its former rule of this country with only a change of leaders."

This turned out to be a parting shot. Although his abolitionist fervor exceeded his military skill, Chaplain Billings had landed a new job, and he loved it. He was lieutenant colonel of the First South Carolina Volunteers, the Union army's first black regiment. Its commander was the Massachusetts antislavery leader Thomas W. Higginson. At the age of forty, Billings set out to fight the war in a new way, one that punished the South through plunder and destruction. While raiding settlements and plantations to carry off anything of use to the Union army, the soldiers sought out slaves to press into military service. If on his expeditions Billings could also enrich himself, all the better: anything that hurt a southerner helped the northern cause.

Billings dismissed reports that the First South Carolina would be assigned mainly to fatigue and guard duty. He promised readers that he and the other white officers would "make it one of the most efficient regiments in the field. . . . That the colored race will fight resolutely and firmly, and that they can be most thoroughly drilled and disciplined, admits of no question here." The soldiers were "of every shade of color, from the complexion of the late Daniel Webster to a deep black." Some could read, some had no schooling at all. They had worked as pilots, mechanics, farmers, servants, and field hands. Billings wrote this letter on the desk of T. Butler King. His men had seized it during an expedition to St. Simons Island, where they also took away slaves, horses, cattle, rice, and corn and ransacked Retreat Mansion, King's plantation house. "We stripped it of everything," wrote Billings. He had no sympathy for the absent King, a state senator who had led the Georgia legislature's committee on secession and later served as the state's trade minister to Europe. After the *Ben De Ford* delivered the raiders back to Camp Saxton at Beaufort, Billings was "presented with" King's piano and desk. Fellow abolitionist Charlotte Forten saw the desk in Billings's tent after he insisted she come in. "I did not want to go at all, but he was so persistent we had to," she wrote in her diary. "I fear he is a somewhat vain person."

General Saxton sent the First and Second South Carolina regiments to Jacksonville. Their mission was to raid communities along the St. Johns River to recruit black soldiers and laborers and "to carry the proclamation of freedom to the enslaved." They were to occupy as much of Florida as possible and use all means consistent with "civilized warfare to weaken, harass, and annoy" the rebels.

Billings joined a raiding party under Colonel James Montgomery of the Second South Carolina. The 125 raiders were mostly Montgomery's men, but Higginson gladly lent his lieutenant colonel to the mission. He described Billings as "a large, soft, amiable man with long curly black hair & blue spectacles, thoroughly well-meaning, & unmilitary to the last degree." Though "touchy," Billings might be useful as a speaker and recruiter, Higginson wrote. Before boarding the *General Meigs*, the raiders packed only hardtack, as Montgomery wanted them to live off the land. Along the river's east bank they stopped at settlements and confiscated food, horses, and a few black people. A woman later told a rebel picket soldiers had stolen what they wanted from her trunk and destroyed the rest. Montgomery bragged to a local man that he would capture and occupy Palatka, the last upriver landing on the St. Johns that large vessels could reach. After a raiding party returned with fine furniture and oranges, Montgomery's whole

JAMES MONTGOMERY

force rendezvoused across from the town. He planned to take Palatka in the morning.

The resourceful Florida cavalry captain James Jackson Dickison had other ideas. Kept apprised of the Yankees' movements, he ordered his men to tie up their horses and steal into Palatka on foot. With fifty of them Dickison moved into a garden behind a plank fence a hundred yards from the river. He could see the wharf where he expected the invaders to land. Soon black soldiers from the *General Meigs* were climbing down onto the wharf. When several had gathered, Dickison's men opened fire.

Liberty Billings was on the ship's ladder, his feet about to touch down, at just that moment. A ball went through both his hands without breaking a bone. As he started back up, another ball struck his hip but caused only a bruise. Not so fortunate was a black private in his mid-forties named John Quincy, who had begged to come on the expedition to retrieve his family in Palatka. Shot just above the ankle, Quincy crumpled to the wharf. Billings made it back aboard on his own, but comrades had to drag Quincy in. The *General Meigs* fired its light cannons at the rebels as it escaped downriver, but the skirmish was over. Dickison and his men ran down to check the damage. "Among the trophies on the wharf was a considerable quantity of blood in several places and also many fragments of bone, pronounced by

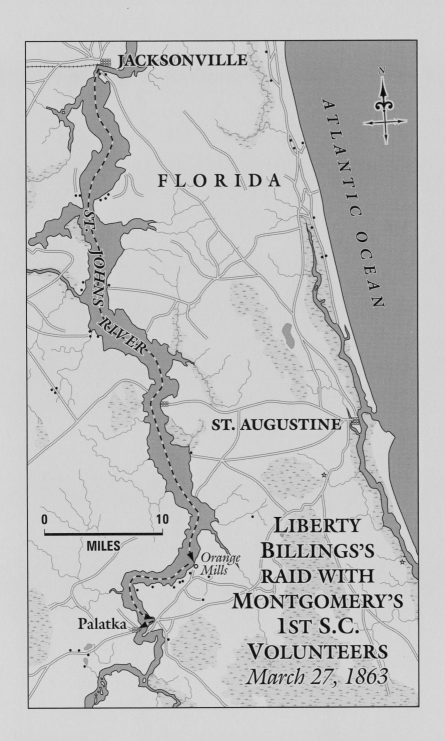

March 27, 1863 ▪ *Damned abolitionist*

the surgeon of the post here pieces of cranium," Dickison reported. In fact, only Billings and Quincy had been wounded. Any bone Dickison's men found came from Quincy's leg.

Back in Jacksonville, Surgeon Seth Rogers treated Billings for "a ball through the fleshy margin of each hand" between the thumb and index finger. He decided not to amputate Quincy's leg and worried more about his patient's spirits than his body. He did not see how Quincy would reconcile his wound "with the theory he so often preaches to the men, that when one trusts in God and is not a coward, he will be protected against the bullets of his enemies." Infection set in three days later and Rogers amputated after all. Quincy developed lockjaw and died.

By then Union forces had been ordered to abandon the mission of plundering and repatriating Florida. News of the Palatka skirmish filtered through Saxton's command. Doctor Esther Hawks, whom Higginson described as "a tall, good-natured rather girlish young woman," lamented Billings's misfortune and Quincy's death and called the expedition "a miserable failure productive of nothing but evil." Higginson made light of Billings's suffering. "He brought home three slight wounds, two of which clearly belong to the Major & me, both of whom have been exposed much more than the Lt. Col & feel a little envious," he wrote. "Such *little* wounds, & yet they are wounds and save the necessity of any larger one. We try to treat him pleasantly, but we think it rather grasping in him." Higginson wrote his wife that Billings "all but cried to go home & show his martyred hands to the Concord ladies who had previously planned a festival for him at City Hall! Heaven forgive me if I wrong him, but he is an uncommon baby, for his size."

Higginson wanted Billings gone. "A wound is a wound no matter if one stumbles into it, as was undeniably the case with him," he wrote. "For myself I could spare him forever; he is absolutely worthless to me." If only an heiress "would fall in love with his mild beauties, & induce him to resign," he wrote. "Wouldn't I endorse it?" Weary of waiting for such luck, Higginson reported Billings's ineptitude to higher-ups. When Billings could not answer even simple questions about military practices, an inquiry board decided he lacked leadership skills and sent him home. Higginson felt guilty about the outcome. "It is humiliating & you mustn't worry if some of his tears turn to ink, though he can hardly be so foolish," he wrote his mother. "I pity him a good deal."

May 23, 1863

THE AMPUTATION

WHEN PRIVATE NAPOLEON B. PERKINS SAW the surgeons walk into his ward and turn toward his bed, he knew the time had come. His wounded leg had kept him awake all night. The day before, the surgeon had explained his case: "Mortification had taken place in the foot and when it reached my vitals I knew what the result would be." Though just nineteen years old, Perkins had seen men die under the knife and did not wish to face his fate alone. The surgeons had given him till morning to summon friends or family, but his brother's train came too late and his brother-in-law could not bring himself to be present. Now he lay alone, far from the family home on Beech Hill in Stark.

Perkins most longed to have his mother at his side, even though she had done her best to keep him home. When war came, he was like any boy of seventeen living in a far corner of the nation. The seventh of ten children, he saw the young men of northern New Hampshire rush to join the fight, and he wanted to go, too. He signed up for the Third New Hampshire, then the Fifth, but because of his age, he needed parental permission. His mother convinced his father to withhold it. Perkins heard that a regiment across the border required no permission. On October 23, 1861, two months shy of his eighteenth birthday, he joined the Fifth Maine Light Artillery. On the day the men were mustered in and given uniforms, he later wrote, "most of us felt as proud as we ever did in our lives."

The first winter Perkins came home on furlough after three of his sisters died of diphtheria, a virulent upper respiratory infection. He and three other siblings survived the disease. Camped near Fredericksburg the next December, he again fell ill. As he recovered at Seminary Hospital in Georgetown, he accepted the head surgeon's offer of a job as a hospital steward but reconsidered the next day and returned to his regiment.

By May 1863, Perkins had survived two battles and made a bosom buddy of Dixie Warren. They were tent-mates, along with Corporal Frank Grover, sharing whatever good came their way. Perkins and Warren planned adventures after the war, if they survived it, and each vowed to notify the other's family if one of them did not. On May 3, their battery of five cannons was called into the fight at Chancellorsville, Virginia, where General Hooker hoped his army could defeat Lee's and advance on Richmond. The Maine battery was setting up in an apple orchard near the Chancellor House when rebel artillery found them. Apple blossoms and leaves filled the air, men fell at their guns, and an ammunition chest exploded. Wounded horses shrieked. As Perkins watched Corporal Grover sight his cannon, a shell hit Grover in the chest. Closer by, blood poured from the leg of one of Perkins's horses. The animal struggled to break free, and Perkins called to his sergeant, Anson Loomis of Colebrook. Loomis told him to unhitch the horse and replace it with a spare.

Just then a ball struck Perkins above the right knee. He started toward the woods but had to hop on his left leg because his right could bear no weight. Forty yards along, he stumbled, tried to catch himself with his right foot, and crashed face-first in a road. Woozy from blood loss and still in pain, he heard horses race toward him and feared being trampled. Loomis tried to lift him onto a horse, but it hurt too much. The sergeant helped him to the roadside and left him a canteen and blanket but could find no stretcher-bearers. Later Loomis returned and tied a cord around Perkins's thigh above the wound. A shell struck an ammunition box, killing six horses and covering Perkins with dirt. "For a moment I thought it killed me," he wrote. Shells ignited the woods he had failed to reach. Whipped by the wind, the fire suffocated men who thought they had found refuge there. Perkins heard their screams for help.

The Fifth Maine Light Battery's horses were all dead or dying, and the men had to retreat. Irish Brigade infantrymen helped drag their guns off the field. Fearing he might be left, Perkins shouted and Loomis came running. He and three other men lifted Perkins onto a blanket and took him away. They passed a group carrying the battery commander, Captain George F. Leppien, who raised his head to ask who was on the other blanket. "Perkins," the men shouted. "Poor fellow," said Leppien. A short time later Leppien's leg was amputated and he died. The men carrying Perkins overtook a cannon attached to its two-wheel limber and lifted him onto an ammunition box, but the bumpy ride hurt his leg. His tent-mate, Dixie Warren, found him beside the road and rolled him onto a stretcher. Warren and three comrades carried him three miles to a plantation where wounded men filled the main house, yard, and outbuildings. The surgeons were German, but when Perkins was laid on their table, he could see they were about to take his leg off. He passed out protesting. When he awoke, he still had his leg, but he lay on a hearth with his head in the fireplace and soot drifting down the chimney into his eyes. Warren pulled him out onto the crowded floor.

It was a hideous night, one repeated often in Perkins's dreams. The pain in his leg kept him awake. Other wounded men moaned, cursed, and prayed. Near him a rebel with a head wound babbled nonsense and tried again and again to rise, tumbling onto Perkins when he could not. Warren lifted the rebel each time, calmed him, and laid him down. When morning finally came, many of the wounded were dead, including the rebel. "Poor fellow, I was glad when he died, he suffered so much," Perkins wrote.

As the Army of the Potomac began its retreat across the Rappahannock River on May 5, Warren had to go along. For a day and a half he had provided his friend with water, coffee, hardtack, and hope. After he left, Perkins found the ten-dollar bill he had stuck in his wallet. The retreat worried Perkins, especially as death and recovery emptied the room that had become his universe. Would he fall into enemy hands? Fortune again smiled on him. "Can't you help me?" he shouted to Austin Marshall, a comrade in the next room. Marshall removed a door from its hinges, spread a blanket on it, and rolled Perkins onto the blanket. A doctor hailed four Pennsylvanians, who placed a stick under each end of the door and carried Perkins on their shoulders. Across the river they left him under an apple tree near another Union field hospital.

From there to St. Aloysius General Hospital in Washington, Perkins traveled by ambulance, boxcar, and steamer. President Lincoln boarded the steamer and shook every man's hand, including that of a wounded rebel prisoner. "Who was that man?" the prisoner asked. Aboard the steamer Perkins saw Edwin Stewart, a soldier from his battery whose leg had been amputated above the knee. "He was crazy as could be," wrote Perkins. "It kept a man beside him all the time to prevent him tearing the bandage from his stump." Stewart died two days later.

Perkins's own leg sometimes swelled so much he worried the skin would burst. A bag of chipped ice failed to reduce the swelling, and doctors at St. Aloysius could find no shell fragment in the wound. Finally, Doctor Alexander Ingram told him amputation was necessary. When Perkins asked if there was a chance of survival, Ingram told him it was his only chance. "Take it off," Perkins said. He had gangrene, an infection that often killed. This is what Ingram meant when he told Perkins "mortification" had set in. The standard treatment was to remove the affected limb by one of two methods. During or after a battle, when surgeons had to amputate many limbs under duress, they left a flap of skin and muscle to fold and sew over the point of amputation. Infection often set in under the flap. Patients were more likely to survive a circular amputation, where surgeons first cut the skin above the wound all the way around the limb. This is the method Ingram and his assistants used on Perkins.

When they arrived at his bedside on May 23, they placed a table beside him and screened it off for privacy. He asked them to wait until he was unconscious before lifting him onto the table, but even after inhaling ether and chloroform he objected when they moved him. They gave him more ether. He felt Ingram's knife cutting his flesh and asked for more. The next thing he knew, hands were busy on his wet stump. He asked if the moisture was blood. No, water, he was told. By then, Ingram and his assistants had cut around the thigh in a relatively even line, sliced through the muscle, sawed the bone and filed it smooth, and pulled skin over the bone. As they tied the major blood vessels off and sewed up the wound, Perkins stirred again. "That was the time I thought they would kill me," he wrote. The amputation took less than half an hour.

The pain returned two months later. The surgeons took a new interest in Perkins's stump but kept their findings to themselves. One day he convinced a nurse to bring him a mirror. The problem was obvious. The swelling had receded, but the skin around the stump contracted. The bone protruded an inch. The only solution was to cut it off, but it took weeks for Ingram to convince Perkins the operation was necessary. After he did, a surgeon grasped the bone and moved it from side to side until it snapped off at the flesh. Another surgeon snipped off the splinters and re-stitched the stump.

Perkins's war was over, but his ordeal had just begun. Maggots infested the wound, and bedsores riddled his back. Learning to use crutches was painful, but when he and another amputee made a joint purchase of a pair of shoes, they laughed about it. Deciding his mother would be less shocked to see him again on an artificial leg, he went through the falls and other agonies of learning to use one.

On December 7, 1863, Perkins received his discharge and headed north toward home. His twentieth birthday was just days away. He missed his comrades-in-arms, but he was alive and determined and proud to have been a soldier. "If permitted, and occasion required," he wrote in his account of his travails, "I would go through the same experience again. Our country is worth thousands of lives such as mine."

June 28, 1863

THE CAUSE DEFINED

THE POSTMARKS ON THE ENVELOPES Lucien Smith sent to his sister, Mary Corning, tracked his regiment's movements along the Atlantic coast. The letters inside chronicled a more important journey, the one in Lucien's mind as he considered why he was fighting and where the many black people he encountered fit into the Union cause.

LUCIEN B. SMITH

Lucien was a twenty-four-year-old bachelor from Woodstock when he joined the Fourth New Hampshire Volunteers in August 1861. Like most of his comrades he clung to the prejudices he brought south with him. Other than his fellow soldiers, nearly everyone he encountered in South Carolina was a former slave. Smith's first impressions confirmed what he had read before the war. They were "as layzy as can be," he wrote Corning in 1861. He resented stories in the northern press claiming that black men were helping to build fortifications. It just wasn't so. "I have herd fellows say they had some sympathy for them till they came out here but have none now," he wrote. In St. Augustine he saw black residents as prey. He suggested his brother join him so they could take advantage of their ignorance. "We would have a good time and live fat—take oysters and corn bread away from the Negroes. I do that now when I am on picket Guard. Three men got into the Guard house today for stealing things from the Negroes. I am care full that the officers are some where else when I trade with them."

In 1863, with the Union war effort sagging and the Emancipation Proclamation in effect, Corning wondered if Lucien did not regret having gone to war while others stayed home. The best girls, she wrote her brother, were finding their way into the arms of young men who had been wise enough to avoid serving. Didn't Lucien want to come home and take advantage of a situation where girls greatly outnumbered boys?

Lucien answered on June 28 from Folly Island, where the Fourth was preparing for an assault on Fort Wagner, a stronghold on Charleston Bay. He told Corning it did not bother him that the boys back home were getting the best girls. "Girls and nothing else could keep me home while there is a Traitor in arms against my Country," he wrote. "The boys at home are having good times I have no doubt. They enjoy Freedom and are as well off as though there was no war, but if peace should ever be restored I can come back to N.H. with a clear conscience thinking that I had done all required of me." The war would teach him "to prize peace and not get in another war unless absolutely necessary." But even if war came again, "I could come out again and conquer or perish. . . . Better die a free man than live a Slave. When I am not willing to help maintain the laws of the United States, I will not ask to be protected by them."

While still dubious of the abilities of black people, he now saw them as deprived of opportunity, not doomed by race to inferiority. In a year and a half in the South, he had never seen a school for black children or for white. "The Negroes were all about ragged and dirty and the Southern Whites as a mass have but little Education if any," he wrote. The result was a society in which the landed aristocracy flourished by consigning the masses to ignorance and poverty. Optimistic by nature, he believed the death and destruction brought on by war would strengthen the whole country. "I think this war will be a good thing for the South in the end," he wrote. "It will be a death blow to the aristocracy. I believe that the poor class will be raised to their proper position and I hope it will [be] down with the aristocracy, let the people rule, let the majority rule and not the minority." Even with the war going badly, he decried those who called for peace on any terms. "The man who goes for that at this time is no better than a traitor," he wrote. "It is now that we want a United North & evry effort should be used to whip these rebels."

Smith now saw humanity in those "layzy" Negroes all around him. If they wanted freedom enough to fight for it, he believed they deserved to have it. He had heard that his regiment might be called upon to help the new black regiments in Florida. "We are the boys that are not afraid to help them, even if they are Negroes," he wrote. "I like the idea of making Negroes fight if they will put them into the fights and make them earn their Liberty. I am willing to help Free them. . . . If a man deserves Liberty, he will fight for it. If he will not fight he does not deserve it and a man does not deserve to be protected by the Flagg which if he is needed he will not help sustain.

"That is my belief and you can tell anyone."

July 2, 1863

THREE SOLDIERS AT GETTYSBURG

IT BEGAN AS A NIGHT MARCH IN JUNE. In the darkness Private Martin Haynes heard what he could not see, the "unceasing tramp, tramp, tramp of thousands of feet, and the monotonous clatter of tin dippers ticking against bayonets and canteens." The Second New Hampshire regiment was on the move again, chasing the army of Robert E. Lee. Marching in the same division of the Third Corps, Sergeant Richard Musgrove of the Twelfth New Hampshire discarded his cherished blanket during a hot day's haul of twenty-six miles. The soldiers' feet turned the dry roads into dust-beds "while every twig and leaf was laden with dust, and the air was so thick with the flying particles that one could see but a little way ahead," Musgrove wrote. Before the Fifth New Hampshire joined the northward advance, Colonel Edward E. Cross watched the Third Corps pass. Once under way, Cross rode with two young protégés, reminiscing about his days in the West and daydreaming aloud about life after the war. Occasionally he turned solemn, insisting that the coming battle would be his last.

Haynes, Musgrove, and Cross, all veterans of hard fighting, were heading toward more of the same. Late on July 2, 1863, within a few hundred yards of each other on the vast battlefield at Gettysburg, Pennsylvania, their regiments would face furious rebel attacks as they strove to turn back Lee's second invasion of the North. Their fates would intertwine during those hours, as the travails of one regiment imperiled another, and the predicament of those two regiments decided the fortunes of the third.

The twenty-one-year-old Private Haynes had the eyes and ears of the reporter he had been before the war. In two years of soldiering, he had experienced long marches, both Bull Run battles, and his regiment's fights

MARTIN A. HAYNES AND CORNELIA LANE HAYNES

on the Peninsula. He described these events in letters to Cornelia Lane, his sweetheart back in Manchester. Then, when the regiment was sent home to vote in March 1863, he married Cornelia and sought an officer's commission. This quest failed despite help from prominent politicians.

At dawn on June 30 near Taneytown, Maryland, twenty-five miles from Gettysburg, Haynes wrote Cornelia about his week on the march. Foragers found a store of bacon the first day out and paid for it even though they suspected its keepers had intended it for rebel guerrillas. "I not only gorged at supper, but had my haversack loaded," Haynes wrote. The men crossed the Potomac on pontoon bridges at Edwards Ferry thirty miles north of

Washington. Night was falling, but instead of making camp or moving on to the broad turnpike, they took the narrow towpath alongside the Ohio and Chesapeake Canal. Rain muddied the trail. "By ten o'clock there was no organization left," Haynes wrote. "The division was a straggling, swearing, disgusted mob." He and two comrades slid down the bank into the bushes. Corporal Jess Dewey of Haynes's Manchester company had been carrying the regimental colors. "Anybody that wants to carry the flag can have it," he said, "but I won't lug it another inch." Haynes had lost his rubber poncho and had only a piece of shelter tent to keep the rain off.

After another day's march the men camped and dried out. "I had a share in a big fire of fence rails," Haynes wrote. He hung his boots before it, put on dry socks, and got a good night's sleep. The regiment marched all the next day with South Mountain in view. That night Haynes was detailed as a camp guard, a job "about as much use as a second tail for a cat." Not a man to abide pointless duty, he nodded off at his post and slept until his relief woke him. "I was greatly relieved, on looking around, to find that nobody had run away with the camp in my absence," he wrote. Marching through Frederick, the men cheered Gilman Marston, their first colonel and now a brigadier general. The next day they camped outside Taneytown near the Pennsylvania line. They relished being in country "where the people are our friends, and where the Old Flag and cheers for the Union are the rule and not the exception." Here they could buy what they needed, "as the country has not been ravaged and plundered by the armies." A woman peddling butter from her stone spring-house made sure Haynes got her last pat. He spread it on fresh bread and shared the treat with a friend.

Rumors circulated that the regiment would rest here, and Haynes decided to tend to personal matters. He had nearly lost his knapsack during the march and worried that Cornelia's letters might fall into the hands of a stranger. He dropped the letters in the fire. He found someone to pull an aching tooth. Then Major General Daniel Sickles arrived, and things changed. Sickles, the corps commander, had a reputation for being "careful of the men." They credited him for the rest they expected. After sharing this view with Cornelia, Haynes wrote: "The sun is out and we have orders to pack for a march."

Sergeant Richard Musgrove's Twelfth New Hampshire regiment, also in Sickles's corps, was newer than Haynes's but knew the horrors of battle. Men from central New Hampshire had formed the Twelfth in August

1862. Twenty-one years old at the time, Musgrove lived in Bristol, a mill town, and was prepping at nearby Tilton Academy for college. His parents were English-born, his father having been a cabin boy on a British fighting ship during the War of 1812. Musgrove received a $200 bonus to enlist, but he joined for the cause and his community as well. In early May at Chancellorsville the Twelfth lost nearly half its men— 72 killed and 253 wounded. All three staff officers were wounded, and Colonel Robert Potter, a West Pointer and Mexican War hero, was

RICHARD W. MUSGROVE

captured. This left a captain, John Langley of Nottingham, in charge of the regiment. At Chancellorsville a rebel ball knocked Musgrove's musket out of his hand, Captain Orlando W. Keyes of Holderness was shot dead at his feet, and a wounded man near him hobbled along with "the flesh so torn away from his hips that I could see the joints."

On the way to Gettysburg, Musgrove, like Haynes, fell out of the muddy slog along the canal but, unlike Haynes, was chagrined to be a straggler. Only when he caught up with the regiment and heard how few men had stayed with the colors did his guilt lift. From Frederick to Taneytown, the Twelfth marched at the head of the corps, and the men did not have to suck dust. At the edge of one village, women brought them milk, pies, and doughnuts. "These women poured out such love for the Union that we retired not only refreshed, but with a fresh inspiration for the cause," Musgrove wrote. The regiment pulled guard duty in Taneytown as the Twelfth Corps moved through on its northward journey and then camped three miles from town on the Emmitsburg Road.

In a heavy rain on July 1 the men marched west to Emmitsburg, where a fire had burned half the town the week before. Turning north, they heard the sound of battle in the distance. It lasted until sundown, but the regiment marched on. When it halted at midnight, orders passed through the ranks to lie still beside the road. Correctly guessing the enemy was near, the men gripped their tin dippers to prevent rattling and lay down. They had marched to within a few hundred yards of rebel pickets near the Black Horse Tavern. Brigadier General Joseph Carr, their brigade commander, moved back through them with his staff officers and servants. A man near Musgrove whispered, "Officers and niggers to the rear, march," and the men stifled their laughter. Soon they rose and moved out of danger, looping around the vague contours of hills they would soon know as the Round Tops. By the time they bedded down in a field northwest of these hills, the calendar had turned to July 2.

Colonel Cross and the Fifth New Hampshire reached Gettysburg that morning. Cross had led his men into four major battles, been shot through the thigh at Fair Oaks, and survived a shell explosion in his face at Fredericksburg. For months he had lobbied for a brigadier general's star,

COLONEL CROSS

even pleading his case to President Lincoln. He wrote Franklin Pierce that the president had promised him the promotion, but as much as he deserved it, his politics and outspokenness stymied him. Even without the star, Cross, like other senior colonels, was given a general's job for this campaign, leading a brigade of four infantry regiments in Major General Winfield Scott Hancock's Second Corps. With 780 muskets in all, the brigade was smaller than the single regiment Cross had brought south from Concord twenty months earlier.

Cross had ridden his horse Jack toward Gettysburg between two young officers who had flourished under his command. On his right was Frank Butler, a captain three inches taller than the six-foot-three Cross. Butler had left the Fifth for the Signal Corps but been lured back as a company commander. On Cross's left was Charles Hale, a studious lieutenant whom Cross had plucked from the Fifth for his brigade staff. When they spoke of the fight ahead, the colonel said, "It will be my last battle." He had packed his papers in a box in the headquarters wagon, and he asked Hale to give them to his brother Richard, the Fifth New Hampshire's major, after the battle. Cross also said how touched he was by his officers' gift of a sword, watch, and spurs. On the last night of the march he told Butler the story of his life, interrupting the narrative to complain of pain from his wounds. He spoke of the future, asking Butler to be his adjutant once he got his promotion. He also asked him to bring Julia Jones to his hometown of Lancaster after the war and promised to lead them on a tour of the White Mountains if they came. Jones was a

CHARLES HALE

vivacious, tart-humored young woman from East Washington who counted Butler among her many admirers. The colonel "had a high opinion of her," Butler wrote.

After the brigade reached Gettysburg at six in the morning, Cross led it to the left end of Hancock's line on Cemetery Ridge. There, looking west out over the Emmitsburg Road to the rebel line on Seminary Ridge, the men waited in a rising heat. Curious about the men camped in the fields below and to his brigade's left, Cross rode out to investigate. In the woods near a wheatfield west of Little Round Top, Cross found the camp of the Second New Hampshire and visited friends there. He returned brimming with information, briefing Hale on the previous day's fighting, identifying their neighbors as Third Corps soldiers, and pointing down to the camp of the Second New Hampshire. As soldiers of both armies had arrived throughout the previous day, they fought a running battle that ended with a Union retreat through the town and into the hills the soldiers now occupied. "Gentlemen," Cross said, "it looks as though the whole of Lee's army is right here in Pennsylvania. There will be a great battle fought here today." Expecting orders to advance at any moment, the officers soon tired of standing beside their horses. At noon they unbridled and fed them. Soldiers who had drawn the short straws strung canteens around their necks and walked down the ridge to Plum Run to fill them. Men smoked, ate, wrote letters, played cards, "all as indifferent to the sun as salamanders," Hale observed. Cross paced away the hours, his hands clasped behind him.

At about four o'clock, sporadic cannon fire became a roar and musket smoke rose from the Third Corps lines. Sickles had been ordered to extend the Union line from Cross's position on the ridge to Little Round Top, but he had decided on his own to push his corps forward to higher ground along the Emmitsburg Road. Rebel General James Longstreet's divisions were now attacking them there. Cross stopped pacing and began a ritual which veterans like Hale knew from past battles. He pulled a new silk bandana from an inside pocket, draped it over his lifted knee, and folded it. He handed his hat to Hale and tied the bandana around his head. The difference this day was that the bandana was black, not red. The ritual had amused Hale in the past, but the change of color upset him. His hands shook as he tightened the knot at the back of Cross's head. General Hancock rode up with his staff and shouted, "Colonel Cross, today will bring you a star." Cross shook his head and replied, "No, general, this is my last battle."

WINFIELD SCOTT HANCOCK

Private Haynes's regiment was engaged in the fight that had set Cross in motion. When the Second New Hampshire left the woods behind John Rose's wheatfield at quick time, rebel artillery fired on it. A shell knocked a flag out of its bearer's hands and broke the staff in three pieces. The Second, along with the Seventh New Jersey, was pulled out of line and sent to a peach orchard on the Emmitsburg Road. Brigadier General Charles K. Graham deployed them to support the six twelve-pound cannons of the First New York Light Artillery. The Second numbered 24 officers and 330 rifles. At first its line formed an elbow bend with some companies facing the road and the rest perpendicular to it. Then, because the men along the road were too exposed, they joined their comrades. Graham sent Company B, the Goodwin Rifles, to serve as sharpshooters in a one-story wooden farmhouse with outbuildings just north of the orchard on the Emmitsburg Road.

A shell exploded in Private Haynes's company just as the men tried to settle in. Pieces of it sliced away the thigh of Private Jonathan Merrill of Canaan on Haynes's right and wounded the two men on his left. "And I never had a scratch," he wrote Cornelia. "Talk about luck!" Leaves and twigs blown from the peach trees rained down on the men, and geysers of dirt erupted where shells struck the earth. Some shells skipped along the ground killing and maiming as they flew. Corporal Johnny Barker of Manchester was leaning on a peach tree when a shell burst to his left. A fragment hit the top of his skull, cracking it open and knocking him senseless. Carried back and left on the ground, he awoke but could not see. He crawled aimlessly about, stopping to ask directions of a man who turned out to be a corpse, before he was picked up and taken to the Third Corps hospital. Another shell fragment struck the cartridge box of Corporal Thomas Bignall of Gilsum. The cartridges exploded one by one, driving balls into "his quivering form" like a string of firecrackers, Haynes wrote. "I never was under such an artillery fire," he added—no idle comment given how often the Second had supported batteries, beginning with the first major battle of the war.

Lying for two hours before Ames's battery, the men could see nothing beyond the smoke from the guns. From time to time an officer moved out to survey the front. Enemy fire intensified when the battery ran out of ammunition at about five o'clock and another battery moved in. From where they lay, the men could see Little Round Top, where fighting was so hot that Haynes described it as a "rocky pinnacle belching flames like a volcano." Their commander, Colonel Edwin Bailey of Manchester, spied two infantry regiments advancing on their front and threatening the battery they were supporting. Graham granted Bailey's request to charge. His thinned line ran out of the orchard "with a yell and such impetuosity" that the rebels fell back. "A wild time," Haynes called the charge. Another man wrote: "It seemed as if every man was fighting in his own dooryard, and bound to win or die in the attempt." The Second and other regiments briefly held their ground, but Longstreet's brigades came on in overwhelming force. Rebel artillery opened from several directions until "the peach orchard seemed to be almost moving in the windage of hurtling metal," Haynes wrote. Enemy

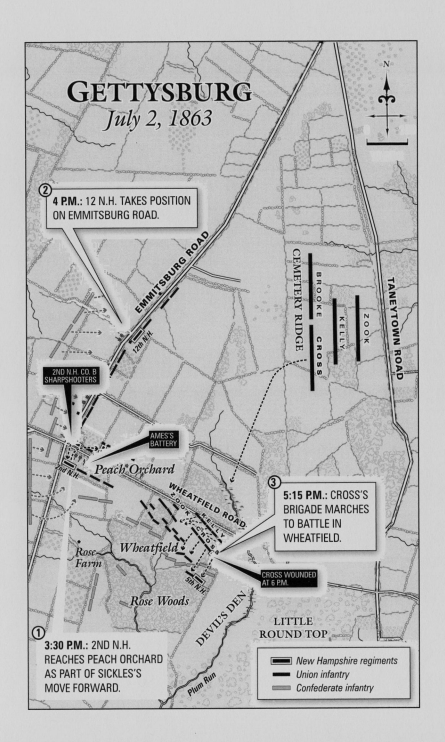

GETTYSBURG
July 2, 1863

N

② **4 P.M.:** 12 N.H. TAKES POSITION ON EMMITSBURG ROAD.

EMMITSBURG ROAD

CEMETERY RIDGE

BROOKE

KELLY

ZOOK

CROSS

TANEYTOWN ROAD

12th N.H.

2ND N.H. CO. B SHARPSHOOTERS

AMES'S BATTERY

2nd N.H.

Peach Orchard

WHEATFIELD ROAD

ZOOK KELLY

CROSS

③ **5:15 P.M.:** CROSS'S BRIGADE MARCHES TO BATTLE IN WHEATFIELD.

Wheatfield

Rose Farm

5th N.H.

CROSS WOUNDED AT 6 P.M.

Rose Woods

DEVIL'S DEN

LITTLE ROUND TOP

① **3:30 P.M.:** 2ND N.H. REACHES PEACH ORCHARD AS PART OF SICKLES'S MOVE FORWARD.

Plum Run

New Hampshire regiments
Union infantry
Confederate infantry

infantry used the cover of this fire to sweep forward and drive Graham's men before it. Private Wyman Holden of Concord, a sharpshooter in the barn across the road, described the attack. "When their infantry advanced, the constant crowding toward the center kept the ranks full and well closed up, our fire making apparently little or no impression upon them," he wrote. "They were reinforced from right and left at every step." The only thing wrong with the Second's shooting, Holden observed, was that "there was not enough of it." A soldier using the pen name "Darnard" wrote that the attack "caused us to show them our backs and let them see how fast we could walk a short distance." Some men could not get out. Among those captured were a sergeant and three privates. "Travel, you damned Yankees, you had ought to be shot," their lead captor shouted, waving a pistol. "I am a Mississippian, by God." The regiment left so many wounded men behind that when it reached safety it was difficult to count its losses. Shot through the lung, Edmund Dascomb of Greenfield, a lieutenant who had sheathed his sword to take up the rifle of one of his fallen men, lay on the field for three days before being found alive. He soon died. Writing to Cornelia, Haynes listed five dead men he knew, including Barker, who actually survived despite the gaping hole in his skull.

About half a mile away, Sergeant Musgrove and the rest of the Twelfth New Hampshire experienced the fighting in the peach orchard as "a deafening roar, one continuous crash." It was so loud Musgrove could see but not hear the shells passing over his own regiment from both Union and Confederate guns. Originally deployed in an apple orchard on the Third Corps line, the Twelfth lay there for more than an hour before it was ordered to advance. The men charged beyond the Emmitsburg Road but could not stay long. Rebel infantry counterattacked from their front just as artillery and infantry moving out of the peach orchard opened on the left flank of the Twelfth's brigade. The crossfire "rendered our position such as no troops could withstand," Musgrove wrote.

Staying put meant death or capture, and retreat wasn't much better. When the order came, the men didn't know which way to go. As they tried to figure it out, men fell all around Musgrove. He heard Corporal Frank Knowlton of Sanbornton cry out as a shell blew away his hip. Knowlton reached out a hand for help and died. The color guard was a target, as usual. Minie balls slew Sergeant William Howe of Holderness carrying the state flag and Corporal Samuel Brown of Hebron trying to pick it up. Grasping

Old Glory, Sergeant Luther Parker of Hill collapsed with a shattered leg. After nearly every color bearer was killed or wounded, Corporal Edward L. Shepard of Holderness and Private George E. Worthen of Plymouth took up the flags and brought them to safety. A ball hit Private Asa O. Carr of Pittsfield in the chest, puncturing a lung, but he later had the presence of mind to collect shards of his breastbone as souvenirs. Grapeshot tore into the leg of Musgrove's Bristol friend Charles N. Drake, who crawled a hundred yards toward Cemetery Ridge and hid behind a boulder. It did him little good. By mistake an advancing Union soldier shot him through the left lung. Musgrove found the retreat galling. "Troops can take hard blows when like blows can be given in return, but here in making this movement no reply could be made to the enemy though our men were still falling," he wrote. The remnant of the Twelfth finally scrambled to the safety of the Sixth Corps lines, but the rebels were winning the day. "The line of the 3d Corps was rolled back upon itself and the safety of the entire army threatened," Musgrove wrote.

When Colonel Cross saw a messenger riding up to Major General John Caldwell, his division commander, he knew his brigade's long wait was over. The division was about to be ordered in to check the damage to Sickles's crumbling corps. "Mount, gentlemen," Cross shouted to his staff, swinging his long, lean body into the saddle. Hale admired how the colonel rode Jack, "tall in the saddle, straight as an arrow, lithe like an Indian, with a head on his shoulders that was poised with grace like a woman's, and those sharp eyes that noted everything in the range of vision." The brigade hastened toward John Rose's twenty-acre wheatfield and the woods south of it just after five o'clock. As the men reached the Middletown Road, which ran past the wheatfield, an aide to Caldwell shouted, "The enemy is breaking in directly on your right! Strike him quick!" Cross maneuvered his veterans into line, and off they went. Rebels behind the stone wall ahead fired on them, but Cross's men covered the first 200 yards so quickly they overran and captured the rebel skirmishers lying in the wheatfield. The brigade formed a firing line behind a rise. Cross dismounted, walked among his men, and scanned the field as the battle raged. The men were hitting their targets but "catching it hot also, for wounded men were staggering back to the rear, and the dead were getting thick along the ground," Lieutenant Hale observed. Cross's instinct in a jam was always to go forward, never back. He ordered his commanders to prepare for a charge. His old regiment, the

Fifth New Hampshire, was on the far left in Rose's woods, and he decided to deliver the attack order himself. He left word for the rest of the brigade to charge when the Fifth's bugles sounded. Hale, who was guarding rebel prisoners, saw Cross disappear into the trees.

As their comrades fought in the wheatfield, the men of the Fifth had marched a hundred yards into the woods without seeing anyone to shoot at. Then rebels lying behind oak trees and boulders began to pick the men off one by one. Lieutenant Colonel Charles Hapgood, commanding the regiment, marched it through this fire to a small crest, where the men sought cover and aligned their right with the left of the 148th Pennsylvania.

CHARLES PHELPS

The men carried eighty rounds each, split between their cartridge boxes and their pockets, and were exchanging fire with the enemy when Cross reached Hapgood. Forty yards away, a rebel rifleman lay concealed atop a boulder with a forked tree protruding from it. Before Cross finished a sentence, Hapgood saw a muzzle flash above the boulder. The marksman's ball hit Cross in the navel and exited near his spine. Hapgood called for an ambulance and ordered Charles Phelps, a sergeant from Amherst who had served with him since his company's muster nearly two years before, to shoot the man who had shot Cross. Phelps did as he was told.

The Fifth fought on without Cross, as he had trained it to do and as it had done at Fair Oaks and Fredericksburg. "The work became hot," wrote Sergeant George S. Gove. "We drove them at first but they had the advantage of position & we had to pull back some. They picked off our men very fast from behind trees & rocks." Clark Cragin, a private from Jaffrey who had just turned nineteen, went down early with a wound that made every man wince—especially in a regiment whose favorite bawdy camp tune was an Irish ditty called "One-Ball Riley." As the Fifth moved forward, a rebel minie ball destroyed Cragin's left testicle and ricocheted off his pocketknife. The regiment fought for so long that most of the men ran out of ammunition and had to raid the cartridge boxes of fallen comrades. Hapgood appealed in vain for more ammunition. As the Fifth's relief approached from the rear, Sergeant Gove was shot in the same shoulder that had been hit at Fair Oaks and Antietam—"the old place," he called it. The ball broke no bones. When replacements arrived, Hapgood warned their colonel that his regiment would never reach the Fifth's position if the Fifth pulled out first. If the rebels saw the Fifth leaving, he said, they would stand, fire, and advance. But the colonel insisted. Hapgood later said that when his prophecy proved true, the relieving regiment made it out of the woods faster than his did. The Fifth had lost heavily. "When I went into that position with the regiment, there were two lines, one man standing behind the other," Hapgood wrote. "When I came out of it, there was only one line, and the men were several paces apart." Twenty-seven men were killed, fifty-three wounded. In the darkness and confusion the retreat was as brutal as any the regiment had ever faced. On his way out Sergeant Phelps was mortally wounded.

Because the enemy overran the Fifth's position, the regiment left many casualties on the field. Among them was George Bucknam, the Concord man who had spent months trapped on Davids' Island near New York after being shot at Fair Oaks. He had returned to the Fifth in time to fight at Chancellorsville. When his brother Warren asked about that battle, he wrote: "I have come pretty near to death's back door two or three times since I have been in the service, but he seems to say that he will let me know when it is time for him to call on me." He compared the sound of flying bullets to bagpipes: "their music is more charming the farther they are off." His treatment after the Fair Oaks wound had embittered him. "Did you ever imagine what a beautiful thing it was to be killed for a great country's sake?" he asked Warren. "Well, I don't see it!"

It took more than a month for Warren to learn the details of his brother's death at Gettysburg. Silas G. Sylvester, a Concord merchant who sold picture frames and Boston friction matches, learned from returning soldiers that his own son George, a private in the Fifth, had been shot in the neck, the ball severing an artery. "I am wounded," George said, and fell dead. The same soldiers told Silas of George Bucknam's fate, and he wrote Warren a note about it. If death warned George Bucknam his time was coming, he had no chance to say so. Shot in the head, he died in minutes, "or perhaps moments."

As night pulled its curtain over the long day, a familiar gloom settled on the men of the three New Hampshire regiments. They had fought bravely but suffered heavy losses and had reason to fear the battle was lost. They had taken ground only to give it up and retreated before rebel advances. The way back was treacherous, and many wandered aimlessly in the sultry, starless night. The only good news was that the enemy had not punched through their porous line to attack from the rear. As they waited for what tomorrow might bring, they worried about their friends. Some mounted parties to search for their wounded while others watched by firelight to see who straggled in.

From the Second New Hampshire's bivouac, Private Haynes went looking for men from his company. The regiment's losses were severe—47 killed and more than 100 wounded. One man Haynes found was Ed Kenaston, a thirty-five-year-old private from Manchester. "I blundered onto him in the field hospital," Haynes wrote. "He was lying by a stone wall, in a field packed with wounded men. He had lost everything but the bloody clothes he wore." Haynes gave Kenaston a full canteen and all the food in his haversack. Rain was coming, and Kenaston wanted something more than his blood-soaked trousers to shield him from it. Haynes found him an overcoat. "I loathe a thief, but I am glad I stole that overcoat," he wrote. Haynes asked Cornelia to pass along a message. Though shot through both legs, Kenaston wanted his family told that "it is only a flesh wound, and with a little assistance he will be able to stand on his feet."

Sergeant Musgrove's search for missing comrades lasted days. Luther Parker, the wounded flag-bearer, bled to death after an operation. Private Charles Drake, whose leg had been shattered by grapeshot before he was shot by a fellow Union soldier, survived an amputation. Musgrove asked what became of the amputated leg. "The hogs ate it up," Drake said, telling Musgrove it hurt his absent limb to see the animals tear flesh from the bone. A stranger visited the Twelfth's camp with a message for Musgrove: a friend of his was in the Sixth Corps hospital. The friend turned out to be Private Jonathan Leavitt of Sanbornton, who had shared a tent with Musgrove. While relieving Sickles's men, Sixth Corps soldiers had rescued Leavitt. Musgrove found him lying on a stretcher. "Both feet and ankles had been crushed by a cannon ball or shell," he wrote. While Leavitt awaited medical attention under an apple tree, "his feet had turned black and were fast becoming a mass of corruption." Musgrove suspected he had received no care because of the Third Corps diamond emblem on his cap. He gave Leavitt water and went looking for a surgeon. Finally he rounded up three comrades from his own regiment, and together they carried Leavitt two miles to the Third Corps hospital. After telling the twenty-five-year-old Leavitt he had a good chance of survival, the surgeon flicked away his blackened feet and ankles with a knife and amputated farther up. Musgrove was standing at Leavitt's side when he died on the operating table.

An ambulance carried Colonel Cross from John Rose's woods to a rocky dell between the Taneytown and Baltimore roads. Shielded by boulders, many of the dead and wounded lay on the ground with blankets thrown over them. Campfires flickered and shadows danced across the faces of the men gathered around Cross. "All faces were sad, all hearts were sorrowful," wrote William Child of Bath, the Fifth's assistant surgeon. John Bucknam, the surgeon, had been Cross's childhood friend in Lancaster. He told the colonel his gut wound was mortal and gave him morphine. Cross, still in pain, asked to see various officers of the Fifth. One was Lieutenant Hale, who had ridden beside him into Gettysburg less than twenty-four hours before. On his way back to the brigade's original position on Cemetery Ridge, Hale encountered the wounded Sergeant Gove, his uniform dripping blood. When Hale reached the ridge, the men there were disheartened. "We had held our own, but the loss had been frightful, and we had gained no ground," Hale wrote. Learning of Cross's wound, he "sat right down on the ground, feeling that hope was dead." Duty and distance kept him from going to the colonel, but Captains Butler and James E. Larkin and a few other officers found Cross. As Bucknam called out the visitors' names, Cross shook each by the hand. "Goodbye, Larkin, goodbye, Butler," he said. "Be all good soldiers. I've met a soldier's death." He lamented not living to see the country at peace again and told the officers, "I think the boys will miss me." Talking took his mind off the pain only briefly, and he begged for chloroform. "Blow my brains out," he screamed. "Shoot me. How long must I live in such pain?" He died half an hour after midnight. Captain Thomas Livermore of Milford, whom Cross had asked for, was occupied as chief of ambulances for the Second Corps. When he finally reached the field hospital, Cross was dead. Livermore lifted the blanket from the colonel's face and studied his features in the eerie light. "They were placid and exceedingly lifelike, and it was hard to persuade myself that the flush of life had gone from them," Livermore wrote. "His lofty forehead was smooth, his long, silky beard lay on his chest undisheveled, and he looked more as he would if he slept than seemed possible."

July 4, 1863

GLORIOUS FOURTH

PEOPLE CAME ON FOOT, ON HORSEBACK, AND IN CARRIAGES drawn by two, four, and six horses. Extra trains delivered passengers at half fare from points around the state and Boston. By the time Franklin Pierce rose to state his case against President Lincoln and the war, the crowd had filled the State House yard and spilled onto Concord's Main Street. Even in spots where Pierce would be impossible to hear, people stood on fences and buildings to see him. Women lined the windows inside the State House to witness the proceedings, twenty men sat on the branches of one sprawling maple, and every climbable tree in the yard held its fill. The *Patriot*, which had promoted the rally for weeks, estimated the crowd at more than twenty-five thousand people.

FRANKLIN PIERCE

Much of the public was sick of the war, and not just because of its human cost. Union armies seemed unable to win a battle under any general. As far as Pierce's audience knew, at this moment Lee's army was running loose in Pennsylvania and the rebels were holding on at Vicksburg. Democrats hated the Emancipation Proclamation, the draft, the enlistment of black soldiers, and the administration's crackdown on dissent. As they had predicted, the war had become an abolition war.

Six years beyond his term in the White House, Pierce remained a powerful symbol of this Democratic point of view. He seldom spoke publicly, but when Democrats in both Boston and New Hampshire invited him to preside at their Independence Day rallies, he could not resist the temptation. Clement Vallandigham, an Ohio congressman, had been jailed in May for damning the war and calling for the ouster of "King Lincoln." Sidney Webster, Pierce's former secretary, knew his old boss was steaming over this but urged him not to speak. "Can you not, in a letter declining to preside, say all you w'd say as presiding officer?" Webster wrote him. Pierce said no to Boston, yes to Concord, and the New Hampshire Democratic Party seized the moment. In trumpeting "The Mass Meeting of the Democracy," the *Patriot* declared: "Never have we known our people so emphatically wide awake and enthusiastic in any movement." The party hired Colonel William Beals of Boston, the premier patriotic decorator in the East, to adorn the capital.

The Fourth was not quite the blue-sky day Democrats had hoped for, but visitors emerged from the trains that morning into an explosion of red, white, and blue. Beals and his crew had hung so many banners on Main Street that spectators walked into "a field of waving flags," the *Patriot* gushed. Banners carried the names of Washington, Jefferson, Webster, McClellan, Jackson, and Pierce. One read, "The Constitution as it is, the Union as it was." On a downtown building hung a large painting celebrating "The Uprising of the North." Banners, streamers, and tiny flags, all rippling in the breeze, draped the American House, home of the party's headquarters. The center of this festival of color was the State House yard, where workers had erected a huge speakers' platform. Those who stood facing it saw a backdrop of tricolored streamers wafting on the façade of the State House, a huge flag waving from the dome, and signal flags flying from the cupola. At the front of the yard on Main Street, Beals had installed a grand arch emblazoned in silver with the motto "Constitutional Liberty." An eagle atop the arch held an array of American flags, and a red liberty cap, a national symbol since the Revolution, sat on a 200-foot pole. The crowd in the yard would welcome the speakers as they passed through the silver-spangled damask curtain hung from the arch.

There was no question why so many people had come or so much money had been spent on decorations. The *Patriot* attributed the size of the crowd to the "peculiar circumstances" of the day. "Many years have passed since the people of this State have had the opportunity . . . to hear the voice of Gen. Pierce, once so familiar to them, on a public occasion of such a character." The holiday gave him a chance to "show where the Democracy of New Hampshire stand and intend to remain." He had not been entirely silent. He had advised state Democratic leaders throughout the war, and the *Patriot* often printed his views anonymously. A few days after the Confederate attack on Fort Sumter, he had spoken to a gathering of Concord residents from the balcony of the Eagle Hotel opposite the State House. If war came, he said then, all people of the North must stand together. He closed that day with these words: "I would not live in a state the right and honor of which I was not prepared to defend at all hazards and at all extremities."

If he had felt the need to stand for unity in 1861, by 1863 he had lost patience with the Lincoln administration and its policies. He had come to the State House yard on the Fourth of July to vent his frustrations. It wasn't only Sidney Webster, his former secretary, who worried that speaking in anger could hurt Pierce's reputation or subject him to scorn. Pierce's loyal friend Nathaniel Hawthorne also understood the danger. That is why Hawthorne, his Bowdoin College classmate and author of his 1852 campaign biography, came to Concord to be with Pierce on this important day.

By half past eleven, when Pierce, Hawthorne, and the rest of the official party left the Eagle Hotel, passed under the arch, and mounted the speakers' platform, the crowd was alive. Men surged forward for a better view and a better listen. Brass bands were everywhere—at least twenty of them. William Butterfield, editor of the *Patriot*, had been at every major political gathering in Concord since 1840 and proclaimed Pierce's audience the largest by thousands. This was partisan one-upmanship, not reliable witness. A big crowd had gathered in the yard two weeks earlier for a Republican rally. John C. Frémont, the main speaker, and his wife Jessie failed to show up for some reason, but the crowd heard Postmaster General Montgomery Blair and Major General Benjamin F. Butler praise the war effort. The abolitionist

Hutchinson family sang, and Henry P. Rolfe, a lawyer and former Douglas Democrat, read resolutions supporting the Union cause.

When Pierce reached the platform, a thunderous ovation swept up toward him. The crowd saw before it a familiar figure, a wiry man five feet nine inches tall, narrow in the shoulders, a bit hollow in the chest. He had lived in Concord since 1838, when he was the thirty-three-year-old boy wonder of state politics. His neighbors knew him as personable, dignified, and authoritative. The former president acknowledged the long applause as an expression of "the great aggregation of personal relations which thirty years of manhood-life have formed between us." He told his listeners he felt the same respect and affection toward them that they had always bestowed on him.

Pierce read his speech from a printed text, speaking in a strong, clear voice. He began by invoking the founding fathers. This was obligatory in a Fourth of July oration, but it came naturally to Pierce. His father had fought in the Revolution. His political philosophy was rooted in anti-federalism. To him, the founders had struck a sacrosanct compromise when they gave states the power to decide for themselves whether to allow slavery. Pierce used metaphor to describe what the founders had made. They were master builders, he said, and they had built "an august temple." They had "bowed with devout and grateful hearts" before this temple and fought to defend the Constitution that served as its supporting columns. The founders were no Utopians. They knew, Pierce said, that national power rested in reconciling diverse interests and that this diversity should be a source of strength, not a cause of conflict. Now the temple had been razed, and "evil times" darkened the land. The current generation had yielded to "the passionate emotions of narrow and aggressive sectionalism" and lost sight of the founders' genius. "The cause of our calamities," Pierce said, "is the vicious intermeddling of too many of the citizens of the northern states with the constitutional rights of the southern states." While waging a war so barbaric that it "makes the blood run cold," the Lincoln administration was also gulping up power and crushing civil liberties. "Who, I ask, has clothed the president with power to dictate to any one of us when we must or when we may speak or be silent upon any subject?" Pierce thundered. For similar words Vallandigham was about to be banished from the North, but Pierce wasn't finished. He demeaned the war effort, calling it "a national disaster, red with the best and bravest blood of the country, North and South." The sorrows the war had inflicted had brought no reward. "We have seen in the experience of the last two years how futile are all our efforts to maintain the Union by force of arms," he said. And now that Lincoln had proclaimed emancipation of the slaves in seceded states, the war "cannot fail to be fruitless in everything except the harvest of woe which it is ripening for what was once the peerless republic."

As subsequent speakers piled on, news that the Army of the Potomac had defeated Lee on the third day at Gettysburg reached Concord and drifted through the crowd. The telegraph office was at the Columbian Hotel, just south of the State House. To compensate for the absence of a regular daily newspaper in the capital, Colonel Joseph W. Robinson issued "The Telegraphic Bulletin" twice a day with the latest war dispatches. Many in the crowd doubted the news from Gettysburg. "It made them writhe in agony," the *Independent Democrat* reported. "They swore the official intelligence signed by President Lincoln and General Meade was a Black Republican lie, gotten up to injure the meeting." Worse news for the Democrats soon followed. On the very morning they met, Union forces under Ulysses S. Grant captured Vicksburg, Mississippi.

However justified Pierce might have been in defending free speech, his defeatist view of northern armies and call for peace could not have come at a less opportune time. Even if the Lincoln administration had wanted to punish him for his denunciations, there was no need. The Union armies had done Lincoln's talking for him. Their victories had refuted Pierce's argument and made him look the fool.

This awkward confluence of events did not faze either Pierce's friend Hawthorne or Butterfield. In a letter to his sister-in-law Elizabeth Peabody after the speech, Hawthorne saw strength in Pierce's position while recognizing the source of that strength as a vestige of the past. "A traitor!" he wrote her. "Why, he is the only loyal man in the country, North or South. Everybody else has outgrown the old faith in the Union, or got outside of it in one way or the other; but Pierce retains it in all the simplicity with which he inherited it from his father." Butterfield's spread in the *Patriot* about Pierce's speech and the Democratic meeting was long and fawning. Only after nearly two pages of it, including letters of regret from out-of-state bigwigs who could not attend, did readers find short articles about Gettysburg and Vicksburg.

By late in the day, the *Patriot* reported, even though thousands of people had left to catch their trains, the crowd "seemed not to have diminished in the least." In the yard 500 lanterns hung "as thickly as pearls upon the coronet of an Eastern queen." Above Railroad Square, C. E. Masten of Roxbury, Massachusetts, shot off fireworks. An hour before midnight, the last train left the station and the streets fell quiet.

July 4, 1863

'OUR HAPPINESS WAS COMPLETE'

AFTER MONTHS OF EASY WORK OCCUPYING KENTUCKY, the Ninth New Hampshire Volunteers suddenly found themselves sleeping in the woods with insects and reptiles and wielding axes and shovels in General Ulysses S. Grant's siege of Vicksburg. The city was a rebel stronghold, its high bluffs controlling traffic on the Mississippi River below, but its residents had been trapped for four weeks when the Ninth arrived in early June. Grant's line touched the river "above and below the town, thus giving them no chance of escape except by the river," George H. Chandler, the Ninth's adjutant, wrote his mother. The river "is commanded by our fixed batteries and gunboats, and moreover there is but one boat in the whole city and that a little skiff. The suffering of their situation must be horrible." The Union force simply dug in and waited. "With the certain prospect of a speedy and unconditional fall of the city, active offensive operations appear needless," Chandler wrote. "We can soon have the whole thing with no more loss of life." The Ninth supported batteries which lobbed shells into the city "every two or three minutes day and night." The pounding had "already forced the inhabitants to dig caves in the ground and hide there for security. It will avail them little however while they have nothing to eat."

The assignment was temporary, and the sooner the Ninth returned to Kentucky, the happier Chandler would be. "Here we have the gum tree, the magnolia, the cane brake and other southern trees, not to mention all kinds of uncongenial spirits in the shapes of animals," he wrote. "There are large snakes and lizards under foot all the time. I killed a striped snake day before yesterday nearly six feet long, and it was not an uncommon specimen." Flies, wood ticks, ants, and mosquitoes were plentiful, and men ate only hardtack and other things they could carry. "The water is very warm and brackish, and has no effect to quench thirst, no matter how freely one may drink," Chandler wrote. He also shared a complaint that applied to his brother. William Chandler, a Concord lawyer and Republican operative, had bought a substitute to avoid the draft. "We do the best we can and keep in good spirits," George wrote his mother. "I wish, however, that some of the rampant patriots at home were obliged to go just one day with us. All I care about is that the thing is not equal, but comes all the time upon the same ones."

Peering into Vicksburg through a glass, Chandler found the city smaller than he imagined. He planned to take a closer look on the Fourth of July. After the artillery barrage on the city that day, fireworks were scheduled. Chandler and three other officers decided to ride to the river to see the show. They got more than they bargained for. "When we reached our outer works we found a flag of truce flying and heard that there was a suspension and negotiations which might result in the capitulation of the place," Chandler wrote his brother. The officers visited the camp of the Eighth Illinois Infantry and learned that surrender was imminent and that the Eighth would soon enter Vicksburg. "We attached ourselves to the staff of that regt and had the high honor and extreme happiness of entering Vicksburg with the 1st brigade which passed in," Chandler wrote. "It was indeed a glorious 4th for us. We went in with the bands playing the Star Spangled banner and the drums & fifes playing Yankee Doodle & Dixie, with all the secesh looking at us with a stupid stare." Their joy would soon echo across the North as citizens learned that the Union army had regained control of the Mississippi River. The four officers watered their horses in the river in the middle of Vicksburg and saw Old Glory wave atop the courthouse. They watched rebel soldiers stack arms and march away and reveled in the capture of thirty thousand prisoners, cannons, and countless small arms. "You may suppose our happiness was complete," Chandler declared.

Neither his sentence nor his day ended with these words. The full sentence read: "You may suppose our happiness was complete—and here comes the other side of our experience." When Chandler's party returned

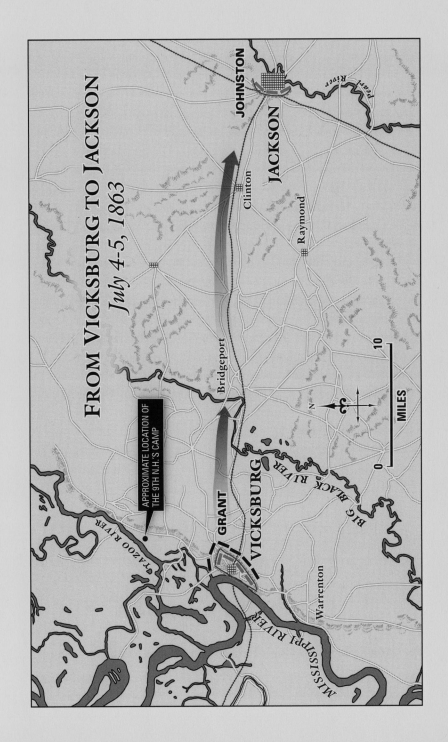

FROM VICKSBURG TO JACKSON
July 4-5, 1863

JOHNSTON

Pearl River

JACKSON

Clinton

Raymond

Bridgeport

APPROXIMATE LOCATION OF
THE 9TH N.H.'S CAMP

N

MILES

10

0

GRANT

VICKSBURG

BIG BLACK RIVER

YAZOO RIVER

Warrenton

MISSISSIPPI RIVER

to camp late that night, the Ninth New Hampshire was gone. It had moved on toward Jackson, the Mississippi capital. "More dead than alive from heat & fatigue," the four officers rested briefly and set out after their regiment. They overtook it at noon and rode on until dark, when they reached the Big Black River, a tributary of the Mississippi. Here they waited for a battery to cross, but the pontoon bridge collapsed and a caisson plunged into the river. Gun, driver, and horses were lost. Thinking their toil done, the men lay on the riverbank in a thunderstorm. As the river rose ominously, they awoke to orders to cross immediately. The Ninth had but one leaky scow to ferry men across eight at a time. "I was afraid we should all drown," wrote Chandler, "but we got across by daylight & resumed our hot and heavy march."

Forty-eight hours earlier, Chandler and his friends had stood on the bank of the Mississippi for a fireworks display. They had witnessed the fall of Vicksburg, an event far more significant, but they had also learned that in Grant's army rest was no priority. Before the month was out, the Ninth joined in taking Jackson. "All manner of things strewed the streets and every soldier sought to make himself ridiculous in appropriating some useless article," Chandler wrote his brother. After a raid on the city's apothecaries, he saw an entire squad newly armed with "female syringes," or douches. Having now been present for the vandalism that wrecked Fredericksburg on the eve of that battle, the capitulation of Vicksburg, and the looting of Jackson, he was weary of such triumphs. "I don't care if I never see another city sacked," he wrote.

July 15, 1863

RETURN TO ANTIETAM

FOR A DAY, CHARLES CARLETON COFFIN'S CURIOSITY led him on a detour. While the Union army moved south from Gettysburg, Carleton, the pen name by which his readers and the soldiers knew him, left it to visit the battlefield at Antietam. This had been the site of the deadliest day in American history. The death toll was 2,100 Union soldiers, 1,550 Confederate. There were nearly 23,000 casualties in all. Carleton, the *Boston Journal's* chief war correspondent, had witnessed the battle. John Cummings, a Sixth New Hampshire officer who fought at Burnside's Bridge, wrote afterward that Carleton's account was "as good a description of the battle as it is possible for one witness to give." Carleton's purpose in returning was to show the contrast between the chaos of battle and the peace that had reclaimed the rolling fields of western Maryland during the ten months since. "The leaves of autumn have fallen, the snows of winter, the rains of summer," he wrote. "It will be interesting to take a look at the field, to note how far time has repaired the desolation—how far nature, with its ceaseless round of change, its growth and decay of leaves, fruits, and flowers, has repaired the waste of war."

Carleton had traveled a winding road to the front lines of the Civil War. Born in Boscawen in 1823, he grew up with a keen interest in politics. He saw President Andrew Jackson in Concord as a nine-year-old, read the *Herald of Freedom*, the abolitionist paper of the day, and worked for William Henry Harrison in the campaign of 1840. He attended Pembroke Academy but jumped from job to job afterward, teaching, working on the family farm, clerking in a Boston store, and returning to New Hampshire as a chainman on a railroad survey crew. Then he became an independent contractor, selling lumber to the railroads, and bought a farm in West Boscawen. When the economy soured, he went to work for his brother-in-law, Moses Gerrish Farmer, who had invented an electrical fire alarm system. Carleton escaped the financial doldrums by negotiating a patent for one of Farmer's inventions. With the profit—$1,850—he again set out for Boston.

At the age of thirty, despite his business success, Carleton still loved to write. New Hampshire newspapers published his articles about agriculture, and he also wrote poetry. In Boston he took a reporting job at no pay to learn the trade. He read the speeches of people he admired and decided stories were best told in simple words, not flowery or starchy ones. He found his calling, although it was years before he made a decent living at it. In the months before the war he was night editor of the *Boston Herald*. Reports of the secession of southern states came one after another, and he later recalled the night shift with pleasure. "Through the live-long night, till nearly 3 a.m., I sat at my desk editing the exciting news," he wrote. "The reporters usually left the room about eleven, and from that time to the hour of going to press, I was alone—save the company of two mice that became so friendly that they would sit on my desk, and make a supper of crackers and cheese, which I doled out to them."

When war broke out, Carleton tried to join the Army, but he was thirty-seven years old and unhealthy. The Army rejected him. He went to Washington, D.C., where another New Hampshire native, Senator Henry Wilson of Massachusetts, advised him to become a war correspondent. Though not on the *Journal's* payroll, Carleton began sending letters to the paper about troops arriving and encamping around the capital. The *Journal* ran twenty-one of his letters in less than a month but did not hire Carleton.

His break came when the Union and Confederate armies clashed at Bull Run. His account was lucid, detailed, and accurate. The *Journal* hired him for twenty-five dollars a week plus getting-around money. His marching orders were to "keep the *Journal* at the front," he later remembered. "Use all means for obtaining and transmitting important information, regardless of expense." After Bull Run, he went west for the battles of Fort Donelson and Shiloh, which raised Grant to prominence. He was at Corinth and Fort Pillow before returning east to cover Antietam, Fredericksburg, and Gettysburg. On July 2, he rode from Cemetery Ridge, where Colonel Cross awaited battle, out to Abraham Trostle's barnyard, where the Twelfth New Hampshire would soon fight, and over to the Second New Hampshire's perilous position in the peach orchard. He spurred his horse past John Rose's barn, where he saw Union pickets in the doorways. He witnessed the movement in which Cross's brigade swept down into the wheatfield. He described the fighting from Little Round Top through the wheatfield out to the Emmitsburg Road as "the writhing of two wrestlers. Seventy thousand men were contending for the mastery of a territory scarcely a mile square!"

Carleton returned to Antietam thirteen days later. For once his purpose was not to turn the confusion of war into a coherent narrative but to remember and reflect. Two miles east of the battlefield, he paused at a cemetery for soldiers who had died in the hospital. "It is a small enclosure taken from a clover field," he wrote. "Between it and the road is a shady grove of oaks—old trees that have swayed in the winds of hundreds of winters. The shade on this summer morning is calm, deep and holy. From the field there is the odor of clover blossoms." The 159 graves each had "a rounded white headboard, and rude lettering, with name, regiment and company of the dead. A loving heart, a faithful hand has planted a rose bush above the dust of Prescott Remick of Co. G, 2d Mass. It is fresh and green; its roots are creeping down to the coffin lid and will draw its nourishment from the mouldering form beneath. Another year and the crimson flower will bloom with rarest beauty and richest fragrance."

As Carleton moved on to the battlefield, landmarks reminded him of the scenes he had witnessed on September 17. At Joseph Poffenberger's farm, where the center of the Union right wing had stood, two horses killed by cannon shot had lain in the doorway, dead Pennsylvania soldiers under the garden fence. "You could have driven a stage coach through the west gable of the house where a shell had ripped an opening," Carleton wrote. He recalled General O. O. Howard's order for cannon fire. "How those grey masses waved, reeled, staggered, swayed to and fro, and then fled!" he wrote. The Dunker church was now "simply a monument attesting to the fierceness of the fight." Bullets had pocked its walls, and shells had breached them. Its windows were gone. Ten months before, in the church doorway, he had come upon a rebel gun crew consisting of a major, a captain, and eleven soldiers. They were all dead.

Nearby, Carleton ran into Samuel Mumma, whose farm had stood between the two armies. A Union shell started a fire that consumed Mumma's barn, and the rebels burned his house. The contending armies destroyed his fences and ruined his fields. But Mumma had already rebuilt. In his field, a reaper was cutting the grain. At the Bloody Lane, Carleton recalled how the federals had rooted out General D. H. Hill's men and chased them off. "What a fearful slaughter of rebels," he wrote. "You could have walked up the hill stepping upon the dead all the way." Ten months later, Carleton picked through remnants of the fighting: moldy knapsacks, caps, cartridge boxes. The elements had erased their owners' names. His last stop was Burnside Bridge. "One must see the ground to appreciate the valor of the troops," he wrote. Union soldiers had forced their way across the bridge and up a hill, meeting heavy resistance. When the shooting stopped, the dead were buried where they fell. Now, the crude headboards that had marked the graves had been tossed aside for plowing.

What Carleton had seen on his first visit to Antietam would stay with him as long as he lived, but on this day he learned how quickly nature and human hands reclaim the land from the crash and carnage of battle. In the gentle breeze of a July morning, he wrote, there was "nothing to mark the places of burial but the deeper green of the growing corn."

July 18, 1863

DARK NIGHT

FERDINAND DAVIS LOVED HIS RIFLE as every good infantryman must. He had chosen it at the Seventh New Hampshire's first camp in Manchester and cared for it for nearly two years. He had polished its stock and brass and proudly held it ready for inspection. But now, at a crucial moment, his weapon failed him. From the darkness atop Fort Wagner at the mouth of Charleston Bay, he looked down at the bombproof structure that had shielded the rebel garrison from a day-long artillery and naval barrage. He saw soldiers emerge from it and fire. When he pulled the trigger to shoot one of them, nothing happened. He tried again. Nothing. By this point in the assault, Union regiments had lost cohesion and it was every man for himself. For a sergeant with a rifle that wouldn't shoot, there was only one thing to do: crawl back down the wall.

Davis had been clear about why he was fighting from the first shots of the war two years earlier. His mother had died in 1849, when he was nine, and his father, a ship captain, left him with an uncle and went on a voyage around the world with Ferdinand's two older brothers in his crew. In 1861 Ferdinand was twenty-one years old and learning the carpenter's trade in Lebanon. An older neighbor, the wheelwright Jerome B. House, set out to recruit a company for the Seventh New Hampshire. Seeing House as "a very fine man, one that I am willing to trust myself under," Davis enlisted. Andrew Lane, another neighbor, joined, too. The pay for a private was thirteen dollars a month, plus enlistment bounties totaling twenty dollars and a payment of one hundred dollars upon

FERDINAND DAVIS

mustering out. "The pay is inducement enough for some without any other," Ferdinand wrote his brother. "But I think it is my duty to go. I am a single man and can be spared better than men with families. This government must be sustained. I do not suspect my individual exertions will do it but I hope to do my part, and if every young man in the north that is capable of bearing arms would take the same stand, I think those southern traitors would soon get their due."

The Seventh was first deployed at Fort Jefferson in the Dry Tortugas, seventy miles west of Key West, Florida. Colonel Haldimand S. Putnam, a West Pointer from Cornish, kept the regiment busy drilling each day and mounting guns on the ramparts, and time passed quickly. Davis sometimes went sailing during off-duty hours. On one excursion he saw a cloud of gulls hovering above East Key six miles from the fort. His four-man party, which included Lieutenant House, landed and saw thousands of gulls nesting in the shrubs. They collected a hundred eggs, a prize much admired back at Fort Jefferson, and soon returned for more. While Davis was grateful for news from afar of Union victories, his view of war remained philosophical. He observed that even military victories brought sorrow to families. "What a strange way to settle disputes for men to come together and kill each other," he wrote his brother, "but so I suppose it has always been and so I suppose it will always be."

By the time the Seventh landed on Morris Island, the site of Fort Wagner, Davis was his company's first sergeant under Captain House and Lieutenant Lane. On July 10, 1863, the soldiers rowed from a nearby island to the landing beach, which had been secured earlier in the day by a Union assault force. During the march to their new camp an enemy shell bounded right at Davis, and he dived into the sand. "Tho scared about as badly as a man could be, I was enabled to exert control over myself that no man ever knew it," he wrote. The same could not be said for two other men in the shell's path. They went to Putnam and asked to go to the rear. "To one he gave a kick under the coat tail so vigorous as to nearly lift the fellow off his feet," Davis wrote. The regiment set to work with shovels and picks fortifying artillery positions and the parallel sand barriers that shielded the infantry from the guns of Fort Wagner and the other forts guarding Charleston harbor. They slept restlessly amid sea oats. The parallels blocked night sea breezes, and by day "a July sun gave full attention" as enemy shells whistled overhead.

CAMP OF THE SEVENTH NEW HAMPSHIRE ON
MORRIS ISLAND (HENRY P. MOORE PHOTO).

Fort Wagner, the Union objective, was made of sand and earth supported by logs and sandbags. It was protected by thirty-foot walls and a location that made it hard to reach. Its cannons guarded the southern entrance to the harbor. Because of its proximity to Fort Sumter, where the war began, and because northerners viewed Charleston as a flashpoint of the rebellion, Wagner was a symbolic as well as a military prize.

With the rest of the assault force the Seventh formed on the beach at nine o'clock on July 18. By then, dysentery had reduced the regiment's ranks to 480 officers and men. They were assigned to the right end of the Second Brigade, which Putnam commanded. The First Brigade included Colonel Robert Gould Shaw's Fifty-fourth Massachusetts, a black regiment, and the Third New Hampshire. As the men stood in the heat, Union guns boomed. Five federal monitors and the armored steamer *New Ironsides* joined the batteries on Morris Island in shelling Fort Wagner.

Davis saw Brigadier General Quincy A. Gillmore and his staff climb a lookout tower on a hill of sand. Gillmore commanded Union forces on Morris Island. A year earlier in Georgia, he had mounted the siege of Fort Pulaski, where rifled naval guns blew holes in the walls and forced a surrender without an infantry attack. Davis watched Gillmore ascend to the highest timber of the lookout perch, where he sat with his legs dangling

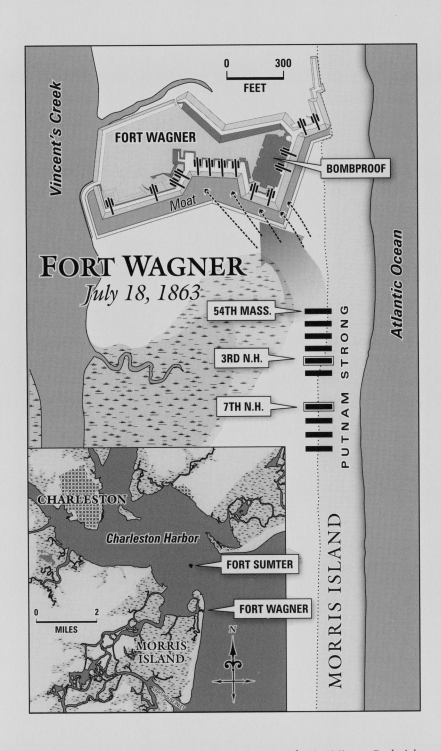

FORT WAGNER
July 18, 1863

FORT WAGNER

BOMBPROOF

Moat

54TH MASS.

3RD N.H.

7TH N.H.

0   300
FEET

Vincent's Creek

Atlantic Ocean

PUTNAM   STRONG

MORRIS ISLAND

CHARLESTON

Charleston Harbor

FORT SUMTER

FORT WAGNER

MORRIS ISLAND

0   2
MILES

N

July 18, 1863 ■ *Dark night*

over the side and a lorgnette pressed to his eyes to assess the shelling of Fort Wagner. Although the rebels had not fled, Davis and others on the beach took the sudden silencing of the fort's guns to mean the Union barrage had subdued it. They saw clouds of sand spray into the air from direct hits on the fort's walls. Twice Union gunners shot away the rebel flag, but twice rebel soldiers replaced it. Nevertheless, as Davis and his comrades lay in the stifling heat, they were sure the shelling would at least reduce the garrison. "We were soon undeceived," he wrote.

After Gillmore told his commanders the infantry must attack, Putnam called the Second Brigade into line and ordered the men to remove the firing caps from their weapons and fix bayonets. The First Brigade moved out, the Fifty-fourth Massachusetts leading the way across a narrow neck of sand toward Wagner. As the Seventh New Hampshire awaited Putnam's order to follow these men in, Union batteries and gunships ceased fire lest they endanger the spearhead of the assault force. The sudden quiet was eerie. "For a few minutes nothing broke the silence but the tramp of marching columns and the surf upon the sandy beach," Davis wrote. Then Wagner's guns opened and rebel infantrymen emerged from their bombproof shelter inside and fired away from the parapet. As grape, canister, and minie balls slowed the First Brigade's advance, Putnam ordered his men to lie down. Atop the fort's wall Davis saw sparks of rebel gunfire reflect like tiny lightning flashes against the dark clouds. Missiles passed over the men's heads and cut the grass around them. They heard shouts and cheers ahead, and soon First Brigade soldiers streamed toward them, escaping to the rear. They allowed the wounded to pass but tried to force men who were merely panicked back toward the fort.

At last the Seventh New Hampshire stood and prepared for its march across a strip of sand wide enough for just six of its ten companies. The other four were to follow. A rising tide was narrowing the approach from the right, and swamp bordered its left. As first sergeant of Company C, Davis took his place in the right rear of the formation behind Captain House just before a minie ball caromed off the butt of a musket and struck House in the hip. He staggered backward and collapsed. Later, reflecting on this moment, Davis wrote that "the most trying place for a soldier is to stand inactive under a withering fire." Seeing that House could not get up, Davis rushed to tell their mutual friend and neighbor, Lieutenant Lane, that he was now in charge.

Above the roar Putnam shouted, "Forward!" Lane waved his sword and cried, "Come on, boys!" The Seventh set off across sand hardened by the tramp of the men who had gone before. The regiment moved at quick-step, but its march seemed endless. "The air was filled with horrors, and the conviction that the damned had broken loose and were holding high carnival on that fated plain was forced upon us," Davis wrote. The horrors included solid shell, minie balls, grapeshot, canister, and the iron plates and bolts that had held the grapeshot. Soldiers dropped at every step. When shells blew gaps in the line, the men closed them. Davis heard Lane call him and shouted, "Here I am!" The only officer left in the company, Lane reminded Davis to take charge if he was hit.

The regiment reached the moat in front of the fort's southeast wall. Davis, Lane, and other men in the right companies were fortunate the water was just two feet deep at that point, but the brigade's coordinated effort ended here. Putnam's notion of a bayonet charge ended with it. Davis followed Lane across the moat, the water rising just above their knees. It was now dark, and as Davis looked up he again saw rifle flashes atop the wall, this time at close range. He shot at a cannon and paused to reload. As he drove the ball home, he saw Lane climbing the fort's sloping wall. For a moment the lieutenant's form stood in silhouette against the night sky, and then he was gone.

Davis began climbing, too. He heard someone shout, "Charge!" "Charge what?" he wondered. When he reached the fort's highest point, he found a hole in the wall and ducked in for cover. A soldier was already inside, and because the man had been drinking, Davis assumed he was from the First Brigade. Putnam had denied his men a whiskey ration before the battle. Hiding in a dark corner, Davis looked down and saw the shelter that had protected the rebels from Union shelling. Men in its doorway stood firing at attackers on the ramparts. Davis decided to shoot the next man who came into the opening. He raised his rifle, aimed, and pulled the trigger. Nothing happened.

Helpless without a functioning weapon, he looked for a place to scramble back down the wall. First he had to pass through cannon fire. He timed it and found shelter from the next shot inside a crease in the wall. He felt the wind from the big gun's next charge as it passed over him, but by now the night's exertion had dulled his fear. "What at other times would have produced a keen sense of horror did not affect me in the least," he wrote.

He ran along the parapet to where he had climbed the wall. Looking down, he saw a crowd of men who had stopped there after crossing the moat. He climbed down.

By chance Davis saw Fred Prescott, a sergeant from Bristol who carried a ball screw with him. Using it, Davis tried in vain to pull the charge out of his jammed rifle. The two sergeants scaled the wall again, dodged corpses along the parapet, and found the shelter Davis had first occupied. Prescott handed Davis a dead man's rifle. "Here's one that will shoot," he said. Davis knew his sentimental regard for the rifle he had carried for two years had no place here. "I threw down the gun that wouldn't shoot and took the one that would," he wrote. Only later did he lament having traded his "Enfield beauty" for "the hardest looking old Springfield shooting piece my eyes had ever beheld."

The two sergeants did not see Colonel Putnam, but they had been in the same area where Putnam made a stand. After Putnam's horse was shot out from under him on the beach, he gathered men from his regiments and climbed into the fort. In darkness he led this force across the roof of the bombproof toward a rebel gun, but it turned out a deep chasm separated his men from the gun. They retreated to a sheltered area, where Putnam called for reinforcements, but the division's Third Brigade was never sent forward. Now Prescott and Davis answered a call for men to attack the same gun, but their small force had to stop where Putnam's had.

Davis left Prescott and found shelter in a cannon chamber in the wall. It was too dark and chaotic even to inquire who his new comrades were. They lay on their bellies, watched for a flash from the opposite side, and fired toward the flash. Then they pulled back to reload, lay down again, and awaited the next flash. They had no idea whether they were hitting anyone, but sometimes they heard a thud in their ranks that "told too plainly of the success of the enemy's fire." Occasionally someone shouted that reinforcements were coming, but this call soon lost its power to encourage them.

Gradually the guns went still and Davis heard someone say softly, "Pass the word along." He guessed a retreat had been ordered. If so, it was either get out now or face capture. And once the retreat became general, men in its rear would be the most vulnerable. Davis walked the ramparts to a place where a drop of six feet brought him to a bench along the outer wall. The men crowded onto the bench made room for him but cried "Don't go out there!" and "You'll be shot!" as he continued down the wall. On a low roof he found bodies in heaps. He slid into the moat, which had risen to waist deep with the tide, and parted the bobbing corpses to make his way across.

Clear of the fort, Davis dimly perceived other men retreating on the bay side of the sandy neck. Deciding the enemy would concentrate its fire on them, he shouldered his Springfield and entered the marsh to the right. He was exhausted. He wanted to run but could manage only a fast walk. Shell holes pocked his path, and as he passed them, voices called to him. "For God's sake, help me!" a man shouted. Davis kept moving at first but then paused to give a wounded man his canteen and his regrets that he could do no more. When he thought he was out of range of the fort, he angled toward the beach and joined a retreating throng. He was helping a man with a leg wound when Wagner's big guns fired again. The man screeched, bolted, and ran off into the darkness. "Go to it, my wounded friend, you're a howling success on a retreat," Davis muttered to himself.

It was a sad regimental camp to which Davis at last returned. The Seventh had lost 41 killed, 119 wounded, and 56 missing, many of whom never returned. The casualties of the Fifty-fourth Massachusetts numbered 34 killed, 146 wounded, and 92 captured or missing. Eleven officers of the Seventh were killed or mortally wounded. Colonel Putnam had been shot in the head. The rebels buried him with the other dead, and when asked under a flag of truce to return his remains, they sent over the wrong body. Captain House and Lieutenant Lane, Davis's friends from Lebanon, were absent. After falling with his hip wound early in the march to the fort, House had crept on his hands and one knee until stretcher-bearers picked him up. He was in his tent

COL. HALDIMAND S. PUTNAM

being treated when Davis returned. Surgeons could not find the ball, and the wound was so painful that only while sitting in a chair could House bear it. He was taken home in the chair and died in it three months later. The coroner found the bullet wedged between his hip socket and the ball of his thigh bone. No one knew just what had happened to Lane. The morning after the battle, the rebels found Private Stephen D. Smith of Hanover alive in the moat. As they carried him to the top of the fort, Smith looked down from his stretcher and saw the lieutenant's face. Lane's legs were hanging over the edge of the parapet. Smith couldn't tell how he had died, but he saw no blood on Lane's head or face.

It fell to Davis, as first sergeant, to muster Company C on the beach the next morning. The only officers in the company were dead or badly wounded. To Davis, Colonel Putnam had been the epitome of a military man: tall, erect, decisive, and demanding. Whether it was true or not, Davis and many others in the Seventh believed their colonel had argued against the infantry assault on Fort Wagner. They also blamed the generals for ignoring Putnam's calls for reinforcements. Davis hoped the generals had learned something from the deadly repulse. If not, he believed, nothing at all had been gained for a great sacrifice of lives. The previous morning, fifty-one men in Company C had formed for battle. Now, as Davis called the roll, nineteen answered present.

July 20, 1863

TO GAIN A COUNTRY

THIRTY-SIX HOURS AFTER THEIR CHARGE ON FORT WAGNER, dozens of wounded men of the Fifty-fourth Massachusetts reached the docks in Beaufort, South Carolina. Esther Hawks, a doctor from Manchester, was ready for them. She had been working since April at the first hospital for black soldiers. She had come south with her husband Milton, also a doctor, who was now in Florida. In treating the men of Colonel Thomas W. Higginson's First South Carolina regiment, Esther had felt easy among these soldiers, finding "nothing repelant to my feelings about them any more than there is to all dirty people." In the hospital, "we could keep them as clean as we chose." The challenges now were the number of patients and the severity of their wounds. At Wagner, nearly 150 of the Fifty-fourth had been wounded. As Hawks, a second doctor, and a hospital steward made room for them, stretcher-bearers laid the bodies, "all mangled and ghastly," on blankets. None of the wounded had been treated, and the medical team had no time to feed them.

Help arrived like magic. Former slaves lugged in broth and gruel by the bucketful. They made lemonade and brought fruit, vegetables, and cakes. The U.S. Sanitary Commission, a precursor of the Red Cross, supplied clothes, bandages, bedding, and medical supplies. By the next day, all the wounds were dressed, and the men lay in clean beds wearing fresh clothes. Soldiers with infected wounds were moved to tents outside to spare others the odor.

ESTHER HILL HAWKS

Hawks, an ardent abolitionist, was curious about her patients' lives, families, and motives. She was used to dealing with uneducated former slaves, but many men in the Fifty-fourth had had some schooling and gained a measure of prosperity. They were farmers, laborers, harness-makers, seamen, and shoemakers from nearly every northern state. Hawks got to know and like them. She prayed for their recovery and mourned them when they died, as twenty-four of them did.

Charley Reason, a twenty-three-year-old laborer, had his arm amputated. Hawks washed his face afterward and held his remaining hand. She found him uncomplaining. When she asked why he had volunteered, he told her of his flight from his master in Maryland to a farm in Syracuse, New York, where he found a paying job. His mother was dead, and he had never known his father. Reason had jumped at the chance to oppose the system he was born into. He volunteered to fight "not for my country—I never had one—but to gain one." A few days later, Hawks watched as his eager expression faded. He whispered, "Pray with me," fell unconscious, and died. Another private with a shattered arm, Johnny Lott, had taught school before the war. Hawks asked if he wished he had been born white. He was satisfied to be black, he told her, especially now that he had an opportunity to fight for a better life. "I am ready to give my other arm, or my life if necessary, for my race," he said. Three severely wounded brothers named Krunkleton, farmers from Pennsylvania, lay side by side in the hospital. A fourth had been killed at Fort Wagner, and a fifth was serving in the Fifty-fifth Massachusetts. One of them told Hawks they had tried to volunteer when the war began and been rebuffed. Now, he said, they were fighting for a country that would give their race its rightful place.

First Sergeant John Morgan was a difficult patient. A twenty-four-year-old married man, he was a graduate of Oberlin College who had worked before the war as a barber, and he was ambitious. His men found him arbitrary and unlikable, but Hawks thought he would make a good officer if the ban on black officers was ever lifted. He told Hawks he was willing to die fighting for his rights, but he regretted being wounded in the spine. He had been knocked from the parapet at Wagner and then shot in the back as he lay on the ground. He worried about whispers that he had been wounded with his back to the enemy. He told Hawks he wished the bullet had killed him. During the men's first days at the hospital, they asked constantly about their colonel, Robert Gould Shaw. When his death became common knowledge, it was Sergeant Morgan who told her how the men felt. Shaw's friends might find it a disgrace for him to be buried with his soldiers, Morgan said, but if they understood how the soldiers loved him they would know he could have no more honorable grave.

After two months of caring for the men of the Fifty-fourth, Hawks was replaced by Charles Mead, an assistant surgeon from New York, whom she described as "a young, ineficient disipated negro-hating tyrant." Her husband returned with his regiment from Florida, and Hawks set about creating a school for the black soldiers of two hospitals. Those she taught and treated never forgot her. One found her Christ-like, writing that just as the disciples mourned Christ's death, the soldiers were sorry to see her go. "You lady's left your homes and come here to teach our lost and blind race [who] have bin [kept] from all larning and lost from all of the enjoyment of this life," he wrote. Another soldier called Hawks the only true friend of the black man in Beaufort. When his head ached, he recalled, she put her hand on his forehead and the pain disappeared.

August 14, 1863

THE CUP OF SORROW

A CROWD GATHERED AT THE CONCORD RAILROAD DEPOT at nine o'clock on a Friday morning to welcome the Sixteenth New Hampshire Volunteers home from Dixie. Covering the event, Amos Hadley of the *Independent Democrat* noted that "here and there we saw in the crowd of friends a weeping wife, mother, or sister, who had learned that the dear friend she had expected to meet, had been struck down by disease, or smitten by death, since the Regiment had been upon its homeward way." As the day wore on, it became clear that the Sixteenth, without losing a man in battle, had suffered a calamity. In nine months of service, disease had killed nearly 200 of its men, and more were dying. During the two-week trip home from Louisiana the regiment had left sick soldiers all along the Mississippi River: forty in Vicksburg, thirty-six between there and Cairo, Illinois. The trail of sickness and death continued east by rail through Indianapolis, Buffalo, Albany, and Worcester.

It was not only the bewilderment of women at the depot that alerted the crowd to the scope of the suffering. There were fifty-one sick men still aboard the train. Members of the Soldiers' Aid Society tended to these men and "assisted the feeble to carriages, and carts covered with mattresses," but would there be room for them all? An improvised clinic at city hall had sixty beds, and a hospital was being built nearby. During the next three weeks, doctors and nurses cared for a hundred soldiers from the Sixteenth and the Fifteenth, another nine-month regiment just returned. Eight died within two days of arriving, nine more by early September.

To ease the distress of the families of men left behind, Governor Gilmore, the railroad boss who had taken office in June, sent two men to retrace the Sixteenth's route and look after any New Hampshire soldiers they found. The two were his son, the Reverend Joseph H. Gilmore, an accomplished scholar who had written the hymn "He Leadeth Me" and recently become the Baptist pastor in Fisherville, and P. Brainard Cogswell, a journalist who lived in the household of the Concord abolitionist Parker Pillsbury. The governor told them to spare no expense in caring for the sick.

On August 16 the two shared news that the thirty men in Worcester were all well enough to start for home. At Albany, Miss Carey, a Quaker "who has abandoned the position which wealth and education assign her to become the head of a noble charity," was watching over five sick New Hampshire soldiers. Two Sixteenth men were in danger, Charles Thompson of Franklin, "quite sick with typhoid fever," and Isaac C. Drew of Portsmouth, "very low." Thompson lived, Drew died. At Albany Gilmore and Cogswell "stumbled on a car-load of sick soldiers, procured omnibuses, got them all (without distinction of State) up to hospital." Among them were George C. Andrews of New Boston and five other Sixteenth soldiers who had been left at Cairo. Gilmore helped Andrews to a comfortable bed, but he died two weeks later.

Although Gilmore and Cogswell had planned to travel only as far as Buffalo, they pushed on after hearing of sick men farther west. They helped men at Indianapolis and Mattoon, Illinois. They visited the "unpleasant and unhealthy" hospital at Mound City, where twenty-one New Hampshire men had died in seventeen days. The surgeon begged them to take away the New Hampshire soldiers as well as nineteen men from other New England states. If they didn't, he said, all would surely die. The same surgeon told them that when a boatload of ill New Hampshire men arrived earlier at Mound City, a decomposed corpse lay exposed on deck and a Concord man was carried to the hospital "in the last stages of typhoid fever and *without a single rag of clothing on his body*."

Cogswell and Gilmore started east with twenty-four soldiers in their care. Only eight could stand. Not one had changed clothes in weeks, nor could a single man lift his knapsack from one train to another. They collected more soldiers along the way, their hospital on wheels growing to forty patients. They acted as nurses and porters and ate and slept with the sick. The day they reached Buffalo, thirteen New Hampshire soldiers, including six from the Fifteenth and Sixteenth regiments, were buried in that city's Forest Lawn Cemetery. "Nowhere have our soldiers been so tenderly cared for as in the city of Buffalo," they wrote. The bodies were "interred in neat black walnut coffins in a private cemetery & followed to the grave by more than fifty private carriages." The *Buffalo Express* reported Governor Gilmore's offer to pay for the care of his state's soldiers, but the people of Buffalo wouldn't hear of it. Cogswell and Pastor Gilmore were exhausted when they reached Concord on August 26, but they cherished the soldiers they had helped. "I tell you, their eyes shine when they see us," Gilmore had written his father.

Yet not even these Good Samaritans could fully grasp the hell the Sixteenth New Hampshire had endured. Although the regiment lost its first man to illness in Louisiana in January, the devastation began in the spring, when it was sent to occupy Fort Burton at Butte a la Rose. On April 19, the men boarded four boats and steamed onto a lake unlike the clear ponds of New Hampshire. Along Lake Grand's shore, "thick underbrush admits only the slimy, sinuous windings of the moccasin or rattlesnake, or the furtive creeping of the alligator," a soldier wrote. The boats next entered a narrow stream where branches scraped their sides and they sometimes beached on sharp shallow turns. The men saw smoke rising above the trees ahead and knew their destination was near. A dead tree crashed across the bow of the *Clifton*, the convoy's most heavily armed ship. When the convoy reached Fort Burton, one shot from the *Clifton* persuaded the rebel garrison to run down its flag. Private James Richardson of Lebanon wished his nephew had been there to see it. "There was a Reb gun boat in front of the fort when we hove in sight," he wrote. "Our boats put it to them with all fury & they left for up river in all haste." The rebel boats escaped, but the soldiers in the fort did not. "In less time than it takes to write it, they were waving everything white they could lay their hands on," "Fred" wrote his hometown newspaper. Sixty officers and men were captured and sent back to Brashear City on one of the boats that had brought the Sixteenth to the fort. Their commander told Captain Daniel E. Howard of Hopkinton that although we were "doubtless glad to get there, we would be much more pleased when we left." Lieutenant Colonel Henry W. Fuller of Concord informed another officer that he was a prisoner. The officer was "damned glad of it," as were other captives. "They said they had staid there in the swamps as long as they desired to, and they thought when we had been there a few months we would be glad to surrender also."

The new barracks at the fort convinced many men that this prophecy was sour grapes. "It is a treat for the men and officers to have an opportunity once more to sleep on something besides the ground, and have a comfortable roof to shelter them from the inclemencies of the cold night dews," wrote "Fred." Another man called the new quarters "better barracks than we have seen since enlistment, not excepting those on the Pine Plains of Concord." Richardson wrote his brother that the men "lived high by

August 14, 1863 ▪ *The cup of sorrow*

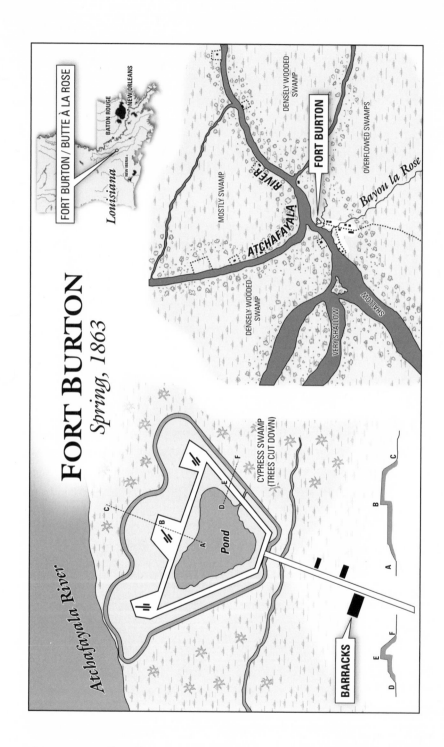

FORT BURTON
Spring, 1863

Atchafayala River

FORT BURTON / BUTTE À LA ROSE

BATON ROUGE

NEW ORLEANS

Louisiana

NEW IBERIA

MOSTLY SWAMP

DENSELY WOODED SWAMP

DENSELY WOODED SWAMP

ATCHAFAYALA RIVER

FORT BURTON

OVERFLOWED SWAMPS

Bayou la Rose

VERY SHALLOW

SHALLOW

Pond

C

B

A

F

E

D

CYPRESS SWAMP
(TREES CUT DOWN)

C

B

A

E

F

D

BARRACKS

foreaging" for two weeks, stealing cattle, sheep, eggs, poultry, sugar, and molasses. But then local people "complained so bitterly a stop has been put to it." Luther Townsend of Salem, the Sixteenth's adjutant, extolled the fort's "commanding view" of Atchafayala Bayou.

Not everyone was so smitten. "How long we're to stay in this place nobody knows, but I hope not long," Andrew Farnum wrote his father in West Concord. There was a morass on the parade ground. Even the man who praised the barracks called the place "execrable." Captain Howard found it "a fearful and pestilentive spot" with the only available drinking water coming from the overflow of Red River Valley swamps. The fort was a meeting place for mosquitoes, fleas, ticks, and lice, snakes, lizards, frogs, and germs that caused dysentery, yellow fever, malaria, and other diseases. A soldier described the mosquitoes as "comparatively civil and respectful during the day, but at the approach of night their scattered forces are heard returning from all quarters, and can be seen 'massing' their columns in the immediate vicinity of their intended point of attack, and piping up their accursed strains as a kind of prelude to combined assaults upon those whose blood they seek." The bedtime routine was to tuck mosquito netting under a blanket, undress quickly, wave a newspaper around the head, open the netting, dive into bed, and re-tuck the netting. The men fell asleep to a "continuous hum and buzz" while thanking "nature and art for gauze and muslin."

A regimental doctor died, another took a furlough, and the chaplain went home sick. Like most regiments, the Sixteenth relied on its sutler, an itinerant merchant, for goods not supplied by the government. After a train accident killed his son, the sutler left, depriving the men of lemons, oranges, and other fruit. The sick turned yellow. Sores erupted on their skin and they shook with fever. Many lost so much weight they looked skeletal. One soldier's diary entries often consisted of four words: "Unwell. Not doing much." Details buried the dead and penciled their names on pine boards. Hardly a boat passed without picking up soldiers "prostrated and reduced to the extremity of suffering and weakness by the poison inhaled from the miasmas of the low marshy grounds," an officer wrote. As summer approached and no rains came, the water level dropped, exposing the muck in which parasites thrived. The men worried it would sink so low no ship could rescue them. Of the 530 men who had arrived at Fort Burton, fewer than 200 were fit for duty six weeks later. Townsend went to New Orleans for elixirs to cure the illnesses or treat the symptoms. After his return some men with chills swallowed Hosteter's Bitters in large doses and "became staggering drunk," Townsend wrote. The president of the regiment's temperance society, he realized too late he had supplied them with whiskey.

As Townsend and others begged in vain to have the regiment transferred, the men concluded they had been left to die. They saw their mission as commercial, not military. Each day, two or three boats steamed past from plantations north of the fort to deliver cotton to New Orleans. "One boat that went down day before yesterday had about 100,000 dollars worth, quite a pile for one boat," Andrew Farnum wrote his father. As Townsend put it, "No one can deny that the lives of New Hampshire men were imperiled for a few bales of cotton and hogsheads of molasses."

Salvation came at last in the person of a lowly captain. Hearing of the regiment's plight, Alpheus Hyatt of the Forty-seventh Massachusetts somehow requisitioned steamers at Brashear City, seventy-five miles away, to relieve the garrison. One evening, the stern-wheel transports *Corine* and *Kepper* appeared at Fort Burton. That anyone was alive struck Hyatt as a miracle. He noted the contrast between the muscular crewmen who loaded the sick onto the ships and the emaciated soldiers who tried to help. Gazing down from the pilot house to the deck, he saw "solid piles of motionless, blanketed men stretched out straight on their backs, quiet as the dead they so closely resembled."

The rescue made some men giddy. The faces of the sick, wrote one soldier, "are animated with the glow of pleasure at having received marching orders, and many a poor invalid, heartsick at the slowness of convalescence in this depressing climate, evinces erectness of form and strength of step." Townsend shook himself to be sure he was not dreaming. Had the rescue ships not come, he wrote, the regiment's only hope would have been capture by rebels coming east to retake the Mississippi River.

Before leaving, men carried off the two cannons and destroyed the magazine and anything else at the fort that might aid the enemy. They torched the barracks that had so pleased them at first. They burned warehouses and "bade farewell to that dear old place, having already bidden farewell to the health and vigor of our regiment." The soldier who made this comment added that only at Fort Burton had the Sixteenth turned its back to the enemy. "If we fought its *Generals* much longer," he wrote, "none would be left to tell our fate of *yellow* destruction and *bilious* deeds."

The Sixteenth left a boatload of sick men in New Orleans, reducing its strength to fewer than 200 rifles. "Fred" wrote from Port Hudson in mid-June that 100 soldiers and 18 officers, including the new assistant surgeon, were in the hospital there. "Such is the condition of the regiment that we have been pronounced unfit for duty by the Medical Director, and left in the rear to guard ammunition," he wrote. Able soldiers turned out almost daily for the burial of another comrade with "the muffled drum, the mournful fife, the trailed banner . . . and the parting volley." During the final week at Port Hudson, the number of men fit for duty each morning averaged eighty.

On August 1, the regiment formed for the last time on southern soil. It was now the size of a single company. Captain George W. Bosworth of Lyndeborough looked down his company's streets and saw "one of the saddest sights I ever witnessed." Sick men lay everywhere. When it came time to board the *Sallie List*, Bosworth left a lieutenant in charge of his few able-bodied men and supervised the ambulances himself. One by one, the sick were borne a mile to the bluff above the steamer's mooring and laid on the ground with knapsacks for pillows. Stretcher-bearers carried them to the steamer. Captain Howard was assigned to load the knapsacks even though he had just three men who could lift them. After midnight, the post quartermaster checked the regiment's supplies for the journey. He sent more pine coffins but still feared the Sixteenth might run out before reaching Concord. Men who could barely raise their heads watched the coffins being loaded. Some died before the *Sallie List* docked at Natchez. At Vicksburg, General Grant's post surgeon ordered forty men to a hospital boat. Many cried when they heard they would be left behind, and with good reason. Few of the forty made it home alive. So it went all the way up the Mississippi River to Cairo, where the men left the steamer and boarded a train. Caring people met and fed them at every depot, but the regiment buried comrades in every state between Illinois and New Hampshire.

Tears of joy and tears of grief flowed at their homecoming. Women embraced sons and husbands. Fathers who did not at first recognize returning sons were relieved to find them alive. There were other scenes at the station. Women peered into the cars looking for a familiar face. "Where is George?" they asked. "Where is my Eddie?" Soldiers who had watched so many comrades die now saw their mothers and wives buckle in anguish at news of their deaths.

A formal escort gathered at Railroad Square to accompany soldiers who could march to the Phenix Hotel on Main Street. It included a drum corps, a band, and members of the Fifth New Hampshire, which had come home to recruit after Gettysburg. A few musicians from the Sixteenth formed a band under the direction of a Newport soldier, Marciene Whitcomb. A dinner prepared by Joseph G. Wyatt, the popular cook at the military training camp in Concord, awaited the regiment at the Phenix.

Afterward it was time for speeches, but the circumstances were awkward. The Sixteenth had served just nine months and made no gallant charges. Yet nearly 200 of its men had died, and more were dying. A hundred more officers and men were gone by Christmas, raising the death toll to nearly a third of the 914 who had answered their country's call in the fall of 1862. Governor Gilmore and the regimental commander, Colonel James Pike, spoke of these somber circumstances. "There is no regiment which has gone from our state that has suffered more from sickness, fatigue, or done more irksome duty than the Sixteenth," Gilmore told the men. "There is no New Hampshire regiment whose record is such that we need to blush to receive them, and I can congratulate you, officers and soldiers of the Sixteenth, on having done all that you were told to do." Colonel Pike thanked the governor and said: "I regret that we have not been in a position to win for ourselves, for you and our state that imperishable renown that it has been the lot of the Second, Fifth, Eighth, and other New Hampshire regiments to achieve. But we have the proud consciousness, sir, of having been where we were ordered to go and having done what we were ordered to do." Pike noted the price the regiment had paid. "Our thinned ranks and the enfeebled condition of many of our men attest that the cup of sorrow has not been allowed to pass us by. . . . Those who have fallen and lie beneath the sods of that unhealthy clime are martyrs in the glorious cause as truly as though they fell on the battlefield."

SHIP'S BOY

ALVAH HUNTER, A SLIGHT SIXTEEN-YEAR-OLD FROM GILFORD, was passing time aboard a floating barracks in Boston Harbor when he saw a strange black vessel chugging like a raft through the dappled water. His eyes widened. That was to be his ship, the *Nahant*, brand new and patterned after the celebrated Union ironclad, the *Monitor*. Alvah pointed out the *Nahant* to an old sailor nearby. The sailor answered with a stream of swears. "Them newfangled iron ships ain't fit for hogs to go to sea in, let alone honest sailors!" he said. "You'll all go to the bottom in her, youngster, there's where you'll all go!"

The sailor would prove nearly as prescient as he was profane, but his outburst did nothing to dim Alvah's enthusiasm. He was at war. Perhaps he had sensed this possibility as early as 1860, when he and his brother cut down a tree, fashioned it into a pole, and attached a Lincoln for President flag in the yard at home. Certainly he had longed for it since April 1861, when rebels fired on Fort Sumter.

The South and the sea were worlds away from Gilford, the town in central New Hampshire where Alvah was raised. His small size had led to childhood trials, including the winter day when schoolmates deposited him in a deep snow bank at recess, legs stiff and arms out. But he was tougher than he looked and mechanically inclined. He helped his father work the farm and run his small mill, where they split shingles and ground grains. He loved to fish and swim. One day he swam seven times: three in mill ponds on the way to Lake Winnipiseogee with friends, then in the vast lake and the three ponds again on the way home. He inherited his father's aversion to alcohol.

In the summer of 1862, still just fifteen, Alvah went "simply wild" with envy watching ex-schoolmates "but a little older than myself" drilling on Main Street as they prepared to form a company in the Twelfth New Hampshire Volunteers. He settled on a bold gambit. He went to the Twelfth's recruiting office in Laconia, mentioned he was acquainted with the fife, and found himself signed on immediately as a musician. The ploy carried him as far as Concord. It ended the day the men reported for physical exams. "My goose was cooked," Alvah wrote, "for the surgeon . . . had taught the school in Gilford village, and it was of no use to lie to him about my age. He knew me!"

Alvah clung to his hopes. He went to Boston, where two sets of aunts and uncles lived. One uncle was a sea captain. Alvah, who had no nautical experience, made liberal use of this uncle's name through days of sitting in the Navy recruiting office. The commodore's gruff declaration that he already had more ship's boys awaiting assignment than he could possibly place did not faze him. Finally a sympathetic onlooker suggested that Alvah apply directly to the first officer of the *Nahant*, under construction at Loring's shipyard in South Boston. It worked, and when Alvah returned to the recruiting office with a card bearing instructions to sign him on, even the commodore managed a half-smile. As 1862 drew to a close, Alvah reported for a year's duty aboard the *Nahant*.

He was one of four ship's boys and, in his words, the only Yankee. Two others were Irish, and the third was black. They were responsible for keeping the officers' quarters clean, serving them meals, and tending to their other needs. Alvah soon distinguished himself by the earnest performance of his duties—discovering, for example, that coffee could be boiled for the officers early, before the galley fires were lit, by placing the pot on a shovel full of coals in the engine room. Among his rewards were the run of the ship and the chance to commit its many peculiarities to memory.

Alvah found the *Nahant* lovable and fascinating, but it is easy to understand why seasoned sailors looked with doubt upon the monitors, as all ships of similar design came to be known. That it floated seemed a miracle. The *Nahant* was 200 feet long, but its deck rose just 18 inches above calm water and was covered in layers of half-inch iron plates bolted in place. The sides carried even more armor, as did the revolving turret amidships, which contained two huge cannons. Atop the turret was the pilot house, sheathed in iron and perforated with peepholes through which officers could see to steer. From the deck aft of the turret rose the smokestack. The hatches leaked. Alvah recorded all these details, and others: how special gearing lifted the immense turret a half inch before rotating it, how holes cut in the ship's iron ribs let any seawater flow aft to the pumps, how the oscillating arms on the *Nahant's* steam engine moved like the legs of a grasshopper.

So slow was the *Nahant*, and so difficult to steer, that she had to be towed south. The sound of "angry seas . . . hissing across the deck" gave rise to

THE *NAHANT*, ALVAH HUNTER'S MONITOR, DOCKED BESIDE
A TWO-MAST SAILING SHIP (HENRY P. MOORE PHOTO).

Alvah's first fears, and with hatches closed, he became seasick in the stale
air below. En route the crew learned that the original *Monitor* had sunk in a
storm off the Carolina coast, where the *Nahant* was bound. It took six days
for the *Nahant* to reach Hell Gate in New York, where she paused for a week
to take on stores. Another week's journey took her to Newport News, the
scene some months before of the first battle between ironclads, the *Monitor*
versus the *Merrimack*. The *Nahant* reached the naval base in Port Royal on
February 20, 1863—nearly two months after leaving Boston, and about as
quickly as Alvah might have walked there. The *Nahant* joined a large naval
force assigned to blockade Charleston Harbor and—if possible, given its
formidable fortifications—capture the city.

The sinking of the *Monitor* made clear, if it hadn't been already, that such
ships were vulnerable to the sea. But they were still thought invulnerable
to cannon fire on the morning of April 6, when the *Nahant*, seven other
monitors, and their flagship, an armored frigate called the *New Ironsides*,
steamed into the outer harbor of Charleston to attack Fort Sumter, a mile
and a half away. The men expected to fight immediately, but in the way

of all things military, they waited a day at anchor instead. The mail came, bringing Alvah two letters, which he read while sitting in the fresh air atop the *Nahant*'s gun turret. The boy next to him peeled off a loose stamp and fixed it to the turret, saying, "There. One big shot is going to strike just where that stamp is." For emphasis, Alvah used his penknife to scratch an arrow in the paint just above the stamp.

Aligned in single file and ordered to sail as close to the fort as possible, the attackers finally got underway on April 7. It took time to get them up to speed. "Those of us who were stationed on the berth deck, where we could hear little and see nothing, found the long wait very trying on our nerves," Alvah wrote. It was three hours before the crew heard the battle's first shots, and ten minutes more before the *Nahant*'s two guns fired in quick succession. The rebels shot back. "At first the hits were few and scattering," Alvah wrote, "but, as we drew nearer to Sumter, they were more frequent." It was like being inside a beaten drum. One of the *Nahant*'s guns fired seven times, the other eight. The rebels hit the *Nahant* 36 times. In total, they fired 2,206 shots at the Union fleet, delivering 439 hits, while the Yankees got off only 139 shots in return. The *Keokuk*, the monitor next in line to the *Nahant*, went down the next day.

Damage to the *Nahant* was less severe but sobering nonetheless. One shell hit at the base of the turret and jammed it. Another struck the turret's top, blasting the ship's boy's stamp into oblivion and leaving a deep dent at the arrow Alvah had scratched in the paint. A third hit the pilot house, causing a nut and bolt end to break loose inside and ricochet about, striking the quartermaster in the forehead, the pilot in the neck, and the captain in the foot. The pilot, Isaac Sofield, was temporarily paralyzed, and the quartermaster, Edward Cobb, was less fortunate still. "We on the berth deck knew nothing of this tragedy till the turret-chamber door opened and three men came through bearing the body of poor Cobb," Alvah wrote, "and my first sight of a wounded man was when I heard a gasping moan, turned around and looked directly down upon the gaping wound on the side of Cobb's head. Then, for a few seconds, I wished I was back in Boston." At about the same time, the impact of a rebel shot sent a seventy-eight-pound chunk of iron flying across the gun turret, knocking out the steering assembly. The *Nahant* drifted under the guns of Sumter for ten minutes before the steering was repaired and the attack called off. Sofield recovered, but Cobb died in his hammock on the deck. Dismay settled over the fleet. "We had failed," Alvah wrote, "and failed disastrously."

The attack eventually cost the admiral who ordered it his job, but many had overestimated the capabilities of the ironclad navy. So startled were Congress and naval officials that they ordered one monitor, the *Passaic*, back to Washington so they could inspect the damage. The *Nahant* was towed to Port Royal for repairs, and Alvah's spirits soon recovered. Fishing helped, as did blackberrying expeditions and permission granted the ship's boys to swim each day. Before departing for Washington, the *Passaic* made a gift of its dinghy, a boat small enough for two boys to row, and soon Alvah and a comrade were happily ferrying officers to other ships or ashore on errands.

One June morning, Alvah and a comrade, Barney Doyle, were invited aboard the dinghy by the ship's sailing master, William Carter, for a fishing trip. Alvah had just caught, killed, and tossed back the first fish of the day, a small shark, when he spied the top of a man's head in the tall plants along the shore. Carter teased him for his active imagination, but the officer was watching too when the head appeared again, to be joined by a second. The trio quickly rowed to a nearby gunboat, which dispatched ten armed sailors to investigate. They soon found two rebel deserters bearing news: a powerful ironclad ram named the *Atlanta*, built with donations from the residents of Savannah, was about to put to sea, threatening the Union fleet.

The *Nahant* was sent to the mouth of the Wilmington River, the *Atlanta's* likely route to the ocean. There it joined the monitor *Weehawken* and a wooden gunboat on blockade. The *Nahant's* guns were kept loaded, her boiler stoked, and her anchor ready to be uncoupled at a moment's notice. That moment came on June 17. Alvah rose early, as was his habit, and had just rolled up his hammock when he heard feet scrambling across the deck. "The quartermaster came running-tumbling down the ladder," Alvah wrote. "He seized the boatswain's mate by the arm and exclaimed, 'Call all hands, quick, sound to quarters. She's coming right down upon us!'" Alvah ran topside, wrapped an arm around the flagstaff to brace himself, and saw the *Atlanta* coming a mile away, a white wave at its bow. He watched until the *Atlanta's* first shot skipped across the water, drenching him with spray as it passed forty feet from the *Nahant*. Alvah went below to his duty station, where he heard five or six distant shots before the command came to fire the

Nahant's big guns. But nothing happened. Later he learned that in tracking the *Atlanta*, the *Nahant's* turret had turned so far that its guns had nearly blasted its own smokestack.

After half an hour of mystifying silence a call came for a boarding party. When the hatches opened, the boys scrambled on deck. The *Atlanta* lay a quarter mile away, the American flag on its mast and the *Weehawken* close by. "It was plain that she was our prize," Alvah wrote. One of the *Weehawken's* five shots had punctured the *Atlanta's* armor and the planking inside, the shower of oak splinters wounding sixteen rebels. Disappointment that the *Nahant* hadn't gotten off a shot was tempered by the graciousness of the *Weehawken's* captain, who allowed the *Nahant's* boarding party to accept the surrender. This time inexperience had cost the enemy's crew. The *Atlanta* could have steamed past the sluggish monitors but slowed to fight instead.

Back at Port Royal, senior commanders planned another offensive in Charleston Harbor. The target was Fort Wagner at the harbor's mouth. On July 18 came the terrible result: a night infantry attack, supported by naval bombardment, resulting in heavy loss for the Seventh New Hampshire and blood-soaked fame for the Fifty-fourth Massachusetts. Alvah watched the attack from the roof of the *Dandelion*, a tugboat carrying him back to the *Nahant* after a bout of sickness. He and the tugboat captain saw the flashes of muskets, "and some of the rattle of it came to us over the water." After watching a while with fading hopes, the two turned in for the night.

From this point the campaign took a wiser turn. Frequent bombardments kept the defenders of Fort Wagner pinned down and the defenders of Fort Sumter preoccupied. This allowed the infantry to work siege trenches closer to the fort until Wagner could no longer be held. The *Nahant* played its part in the grinding assault, alternating duty outside Charleston Harbor with breaks at Port Royal. On quiet summer nights Alvah often lay topside watching the burning fuses of Union shells against the dark sky. On September 6, the monitors and onshore siege guns all fired on Wagner, and the rebels abandoned it. Later the Yankees would turn its guns on Sumter and the remaining harbor defenses.

The passage of time brought stresses in life aboard the *Nahant*. One day the black ship's boy, George Patterson, accused Alvah of stealing an issue of *Harper's Weekly* filled with accounts and illustrations from Gettysburg. Alvah was proven innocent, but George jumped him anyway. An officer intervened, shouting, "Put that damned nigger in double irons in a coal bunker, and keep him there a week!" When George was freed, Alvah offered his hand, but it was not taken, and relations among the ship's boys were never again the same. Two of Alvah's favorite officers went home sick. Alvah found their replacements lacking, though the new officers saved the ship during a passage. Concerned by the amount of seawater the *Nahant* was taking on, they turned it back to Port Royal. There they saw that a load of supplies had lowered the bow, allowing more seawater in, and that wood chips and rags dropped by carpenters and mechanics had blocked the passages through which the water was supposed to flow aft to the pumps.

Still, as the end of Alvah's year-long hitch approached, the reduction of Sumter seemed near, and he wanted to see the campaign through. On December 6, as the *Nahant* lay at anchor in heavy seas, he wrote two letters home saying he liked the service and intended to re-enlist. He had just sealed and stamped them when he heard a commotion above. He climbed through the hatch and saw the *Weehawken*, anchored several hundred yards away, lean to the right and sink by the bow. Only a few feet of its smokestack remained above the waves. Alvah watched in horror as boats rushed to help sailors struggling to stay afloat. Twenty-four seaman and officers died, among them a ship's boy. An inquiry would determine the cause to be the same lack of trim that had nearly doomed the *Nahant*. After a long stare at the *Weehawken's* smokestack, Alvah went below and tore up his letters.

Two days later, as was his practice, he came on deck bearing the watch officer's first cup of coffee. Anchored nearby was a supply ship on its way north. Alvah saluted and reported that his term of duty aboard the *Nahant* had expired. He would always love his newfangled iron ship, but he was going home.

THE *WEEHAWKEN*, WHICH SANK BY THE BOW
AS ALVAH HUNTER LOOKED ON.

February 20, 1864

OLUSTEE

THE QUICKEST WAY TO BATTLE WAS A STRAIGHT ROAD, and on February 20, the Seventh New Hampshire found itself on one. Not that the men expected a battle. They had met no opposition, and the flat north Florida country was so poor it seemed unlikely the rebels would defend it. The invaders saw pine trees, palmettos, the railroad tracks that ran alongside the road, and little else. "Everything about the march for the first fifteen miles was as pleasant as could be desired," wrote Sergeant Robert O. Farrand of Fisherville.

The Seventh had regrouped since its disastrous assault on Fort Wagner the previous July. Colonel Joseph C. Abbott of Manchester trained the

JOSEPH C. ABBOTT

men promoted from the ranks to replace the eleven officers lost that day. Now wearing the epaulettes of a first lieutenant, Ferdinand Davis, the sergeant who had made a desperate escape across the sands of Morris Island, was one of these. Three hundred recruits filled vacancies, restoring the regiment to 650 men. Except for "the rougher element," the recruits were soon "ground by the iron heel of military discipline into soldiers," Davis wrote. "It is surprising how quickly a man, however much of a greenhorn when he joins a company of disciplined soldiers, will become adjusted to his surroundings."

The Seventh arrived at Fernandina, Florida, on the *Ben De Ford* in early February and shared a steamer with the Seventh Connecticut up the muddy St. Johns River. At Jacksonville these two regiments and the Eighth U.S.

Colored formed an infantry brigade in a force totaling 5,500 men under Brigadier General Truman Seymour, an eighteen-year army veteran from Vermont. Although Seymour answered to higher-ups in South Carolina, he had just been promoted to head the Department of Florida. His orders directed him to secure a depot for cotton and lumber, disrupt rebel supply lines, recruit black soldiers, and entice Florida back into the Union. How to do these things was left to him as long as he kept his main force near the coast and avoided a major battle. Many veterans in the ranks distrusted Seymour and blamed him for the Fort Wagner defeat. Their worries were well-founded. When President Lincoln sent John Hay, his secretary, to assess military prospects in Florida, Hay found Seymour "subject to violent alterations of timidity & rashness." This may explain why Seymour obeyed his orders one day and ignored them the next. After securing a coastal base, he led his force inland toward Lake City. Without reconnaissance he had no idea what he might meet along the way.

His men marched forty miles west to Sanderson, a train depot amid the scattered hovels of turpentine farmers. There Lieutenant Davis and the rest of the Seventh received bad news. Over Colonel Abbott's protests, half the men were ordered to turn in their Spencer carbines, seven-shot rifles which they believed to be the best available. They handed the carbines over to a mounted infantry regiment and took Springfields in return. "I counted more than twenty in our company that were entirely useless," a soldier wrote the *Mirror* in Manchester. "Many of them had no ramrods and others no locks." Some who received the Springfields had never fired one. With this slight in mind, the men marched on, cavalry before them, sixteen cannons rolling along the straight road, and the infantry on the flanks. Davis's company led the right wing.

Suddenly rifle fire erupted ahead. Skirmishers moved up to probe, and the Seventh was ordered forward at quick time with the Eighth U.S. Colored on its left. Although Florida had been meagerly defended to now, a rebel force of more than 5,000 men awaited Seymour's expedition. Brigadier General Joseph Finegan's Florida and Georgia soldiers deployed in a solid line between swampland and a pond near the Olustee depot. As the Yankees approached, these men advanced to a position where they had good cover and could plainly see their adversaries through the few pine trees on the flat terrain. "Nothing could have been better planned or more

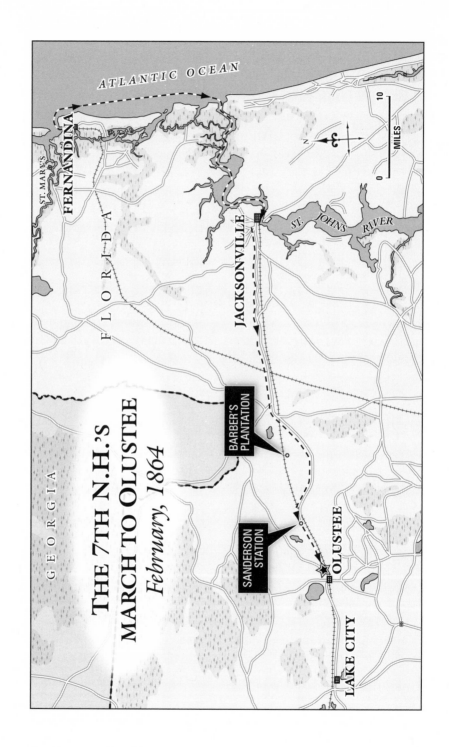

THE 7TH N.H.'S
MARCH TO OLUSTEE
February, 1864

ATLANTIC OCEAN

ST. MARK'S

FERNANDINA

FLORIDA

GEORGIA

JACKSONVILLE

ST. JOHNS RIVER

BARBER'S PLANTATION

SANDERSON STATION

OLUSTEE

LAKE CITY

MILES

civilly acquiesced in than was this whole scheme," a Union soldier wrote. "General Seymour accepted the issue just as it stood." A reporter likened the rebel force to a spider waiting for a fly.

The Seventh New Hampshire was soon caught in the web, its men marching along four abreast when the first balls thudded into them. Abbott ordered them to break into companies, a command they "promptly executed under a heavy fire." He next tried to form a battle line, the long ranks designed to maximize a regiment's firepower, but the din drowned out his voice. As Davis struggled to hold his men in line, two captains ran to Abbott for clearer orders but found him conferring with Colonel Joseph Hawley, the brigade commander. In the panic caused by the confusion of orders, many men fell back and hid behind trees. One of them, Corporal Joseph K. Harris of Enfield, later wrote that these men "commenced bushwhacking of their own responsibility." Davis's company now stood between the bushwhackers and the rebel line, both blazing away. He and his captain, James Chase of Hopkinton, decided "to retire the company while we still had it under control." All but about a hundred men of the Seventh broke toward the rear.

As the regiment collapsed and Hawley and Abbott tried to rally it, the rebels kept up their fire. Forty-four-year-old Private James Flynn, who had joined the Seventh as a substitute in Concord, was shot in the lower rib cage, the ball exiting between his shoulder blades near his spine. He wrote his wife and son five weeks later from Tallahassee, but they heard no more from him. Sergeant Thomas Simington, the color bearer, held his flag high until a ball in the thigh brought him down. Davis moved back into the fray with his company and took a bullet in the leg for his trouble. Chase, whom Davis described as "coolness itself in battle," was also hit. But most of the men who ran from the field did not come back. "I nearly killed myself trying to rally the 7th N.H.," Hawley wrote his wife Hattie. He glossed over the Seventh's failure in his official report but advised Hattie to "say nothing of their conduct."

For its skedaddle the Seventh would later blame the raw recruits in its ranks, the loss of the Spencer carbines, and the confusing orders. But the Eighth U.S. Colored, which went in on the Seventh's left, did better despite similar obstacles. These men had trained for only weeks, and many had yet to fire a weapon. A bullet in the heart killed their colonel early in the battle. Lieutenant Oliver Norton's soldiers ran toward the enemy lugging full knapsacks and empty rifles. Hit by a sheet of fire, "at first they were stunned, bewildered, and knew not what to do," Norton wrote. "They curled to the ground, and as men fell around them they seemed terribly scared." Yet they formed a battle line under "the most destructive fire I ever knew," he wrote. It did them no good. They could not load or shoot well enough to fight a concealed enemy. They bunched up, and into these bunches "the rebels poured the deadliest fire, almost every bullet hitting some one," Norton wrote. The rebels delighted in shooting them. "Do as they would, the nigger couldn't stand the fire, and small wonder, too, for it was terrific," wrote William Penniman, a Georgia private. "They would huddle ten to twenty behind each of the few scattering pine trees. Word was passed down the line to cross the firing." Once the New Hampshire men ran, the rebels opposite them joined the crossfire, "the result being that the negroes lay in piles around the bases of pine trees," Penniman wrote.

After four hours of fighting, Seymour knew he was beaten and ordered a retreat. "Our defeat was so severe and unexpected . . . that we were compelled to leave our killed and most of our wounded in rebel hands," wrote Sergeant Henry Little of Manchester. Hundreds of Seymour's men were captured. Behind his tree, Corporal Harris "found it impossible to get off and was obliged to surrender." A dozen rebels surrounded him, took his overcoat, watch, and money, and marched him away. Buckshot hit Sergeant Robert Farrand in the temple, and his younger brother Joseph was shot in the chest. Both were taken prisoner. Some wounded black soldiers faced a worse fate. T. W. G. Inglett, a Georgia soldier, left one of several accounts of rebel infantrymen executing these men. "Our boys just knocked out their brains with their guns after the Negros was wounded," Inglett wrote his wife. Others described shooting wounded black soldiers or clubbing them to death with logs.

Lieutenant Davis of the Seventh was one of the wounded who got away. As on Morris Island after the Fort Wagner attack, he made a harrowing escape, this time with a hole in his leg and much more ground to cover. Before setting out, Davis rested against a pine tree with balls hissing around him as George P. Dow, a sergeant from Atkinson, tied a handkerchief around his leg to stop the bleeding. Surgeons treated Davis at Sanderson, but the only thing useful in their care was the cup of whiskey they gave him to ease the pain. "I didn't stand on prohibition then but gulped her down," he wrote. In a futile probe for the ball a surgeon stuck his finger in the hole in Davis's leg, curled the joint, and rotated the finger like a well-digger's auger. Later, Davis had almost fallen asleep when he heard the surgeons packing to leave. He buckled on his sword, draped a blanket over his shoulders, and limped into the night with the "disorganized mass." He and Joseph C. Clifford, a wounded captain from Loudon, kept overtaking one another as each engaged in "a contest between grim determination and complete exhaustion." Every time Davis rested, "Clifford's form would loom up in the moon light, and we would hail each other as he passed." At three in the morning Davis reached the Seventh's campfires. His welcome there was "balm for the soul." He had walked sixteen miles since being shot.

The next morning dawned clear and cool, and Davis could walk no more. Mules had pulled a train bearing provisions to Barber's Plantation, and the train was to carry the wounded to Jacksonville. "Every car was loaded with the wounded, even to the roofs of the boxcars," Davis wrote. A man with a head wound jumped down and insisted Davis take his spot on a platform car. With his legs hanging over the side, Davis started by mule power for Jacksonville. A locomotive replaced the mules five miles from the city. The train stopped at a pier on the St. Johns River, where the *Cosmopolitan* waited to transport Davis and other wounded men to departmental headquarters in Beaufort, South Carolina.

Rumors of Seymour's disaster reached Beaufort as officers there prepared for a ball. Ambulances carried them to a festive hall and the band struck up one tune after another. Yet there remained "a slight palpable shadow over all of us from hearing vague stories of a lost battle in Florida, and from the thought that perhaps the very ambulances in which we rode to the ball were ours only until the wounded or the dead might tenant them," Colonel Thomas W. Higginson wrote in his diary. The generals left early, but the band played on. Then, in the middle of the Lancers Quadrille, General Rufus Saxton, military governor of the department, walked back in and the music stopped. Saxton had just visited the *Cosmopolitan* with its cargo of 240 wounded men from Olustee. The officers at the ball had not been fed, and some muttered about being hungry, but the dance was over. Higginson visited the *Cosmopolitan* and wrote: "Among the long lines of wounded, black and white intermingled, there was the wonderful quiet which usually prevails on such occasions." Only the groans of men being carried ashore broke the spell.

Doctor Esther Hill Hawks, who now served a black regiment at

THESE SIX MEN WERE AMONG THE SEVENTH NEW HAMPSHIRE'S
MORE THAN 200 CASUALTIES AT OLUSTEE (CLOCKWISE FROM
TOP LEFT): PRIVATE DANIEL JONES OF BOSCAWEN, KILLED IN
ACTION; LIEUTENANT CHARLES FARLEY OF HOLLIS, WOUNDED
AND CAPTURED, DIED AT LAKE CITY FEB. 24; PRIVATE THOMAS
HALEY OF FISHERVILLE, WOUNDED AND CAPTURED, DIED
MARCH 3; LIEUTENANT TRUE ARLEN OF CANTERBURY, DIED
OF WOUNDS, MARCH 25; PRIVATE JEFFERSON R. SEARLES
OF WEBSTER, CAPTURED, DIED AT ANDERSONVILLE JULY
5; PRIVATE DANIEL E. ABBOTT OF BOSCAWEN, WOUNDED
AND CAPTURED, DIED AT ANDERSONVILLE OCT. 31.

Fernandina, detested General Seymour. Three days before the battle, he
had attended the hanging of three black soldiers court-martialed for raping a white woman. "Served them right," Seymour crowed as the men
swung. "Now let any other man try it if he dares." Had the same punishment been meted out to white soldiers for raping black women, Hawks
wrote in her journal, Seymour "might have grown hoarse in repeating his

remarks." The night after the battle, Hawks left for Jacksonville, riding with the colonel at the head of the Third South Carolina. She found the four-hour march "quite jolly," all things considered. The men tramped behind her bellowing, "Hang Jeff Davis from a sour apple tree." Hawks and her husband Milton cared for hundreds of soldiers at a Jacksonville field hospital. Seymour's force had suffered more than 1,800 casualties—a third of his command and twice the rebel loss. Casualties in the Seventh New Hampshire numbered 208, in the Eighth U.S. Colored 310. Despite this carnage, Hawks saw hope where only an abolitionist could, rejoicing when white soldiers shared tobacco with black. "I concluded that the end of the war is near for the millennium had begun," she wrote.

On the battlefield, the rebels stripped Yankee corpses and buried them in shallow graves, where wild hogs soon rooted many of them out. Among the prisoners sent west were more than 100 men from the Seventh New Hampshire, including the badly wounded Farrand brothers. Some died along the way, but a few weeks after the battle, many reached a new prison camp on a Georgia plateau near the tiny village of Andersonville.

February 21, 1864

LOVE HURTS

ONE WINTER'S DAY IN 1864, M. Annie Thompson went to Andover, Corporal Frank Buzzell's hometown, to post the formal declaration of their intention to marry. A twenty-year-old teacher, Thompson lived with her parents in nearby Salisbury. The groom-to-be was off with his regiment and could not go with her. A twenty-six-year-old minister's son, he had been a farmer before volunteering with the Fourth New Hampshire in 1861. But Frank Buzzell had a secret. He had just re-enlisted for three years without telling Thompson. His decision had the potential to keep the couple apart until early 1867.

When Buzzell broke the news by mail, Thompson found it a "kind letter," but she had expected him home in months and the prospect of more years of danger for the man she loved brought her low. What hurt most was that he had acted on his own. She made this point between the lines of her response to him on the pleasant Sunday afternoon of February 21, the day after she received the news. She was so upset she could not go to church that day, and it took her six pages to pour out her emotions. "Oh Frank," she wrote, "you do not know how my heart aches—how each beat is laden with deep *deep sorrow*." She hated the idea that "another three years must wear away" before they could be together. And yet she saw her pain as a sign of the depth of her love for him. "I never felt the need of your sympathy and love as I do to-day—never knew before yesterday and to-day how much I love you," she wrote. She sometimes dreamt of him the night before a letter arrived, as she had before his latest letter. He had talked about re-enlisting, but she had hoped he would come home to her instead. "*God* knows I would have you do what you think to be right and I would *try* to help you tho it cost a *mighty struggle* with my own feelings." She took him at his word that his decision was best for both of them. "*I will not murmur*," she wrote. And then she murmured: "*Angels cheer your way*—though *you will never know* how *hard* it has been for me to do so."

She told him she would be with him wherever the war took him. "Whenever you are *lonely*, *sad* or *weary*, then remember that Annie though far, far from you still loves you and sympathizes with you in all your trials and hardships." Her hurt made her long for him as never before. "I love you as ever and wish more than ever to see you and receive your loving embraces," she wrote. She hoped he would get the commission he wanted, especially if being an officer made soldiering safer. She prayed for a furlough so they could be together, even if only briefly. She respected him for becoming a soldier. "I am glad that as things occurred to bring about this cruel war, you were one of those who possessed sufficient patriotism to enroll your name among the many that were bound to serve their country and strive to defend and protect its rights. . . . Yes, I love and pity the poor, suffering soldier." She did not mean any soldier, of course. "Some day, I hope not far distant—may see us happy together—but alas only for a few short days. . . . How I would love to put my arms round your neck and say 'good bye' with a good kiss and receive one too. Just imagine me doing so, and believe me to be—*yours* as ever."

Frank Buzzell knew a good thing when he saw it. He came home on furlough even sooner than Annie had asked him to. On March 20, less than a month after her letter, the couple rode to Fisherville, where the governor's son, the Baptist minister Joseph H. Gilmore, performed their wedding ceremony.

Four months later, in the trenches at Petersburg, a rebel marksman shot Buzzell halfway between the right elbow and the wrist, shattering his ulna. A surgeon removed four inches of bone. Buzzell's recovery was long and difficult. Gangrene nearly cost him his little finger, and in time both that finger and his ring finger became deformed. The other fingers stiffened and curled so that his right hand was useless. His arm atrophied.

In the unpredictable way of war, Buzzell's re-enlistment did not lengthen his service. True, his treatment lasted until February of 1865, when he was discharged at Depot Hospital in Concord, but it would have been long in any case. For re-enlisting, he received a bonus, a promotion to sergeant, and the furlough during which M. Annie Thompson became Annie Buzzell.

Frank brought home her beseeching letter, and they kept it. Each added a note to the end. Frank wrote his while still a soldier: "God bless you Annie B. I have kissed your name for I wished to kiss you and could not." In a corner of the same page, she wrote: "This is the last letter that M. Annie Thompson wrote to F.A.B. and signed her name." She meant her maiden name, and to emphasize the point, she underlined "Thompson."

April 21, 1864

MAY GOD HAVE MERCY

BETWEEN THE SHOOTING OF THE SHAKER LEADER and the trial of the veteran who killed him, enough time passed for the victim's admirers to publish *A Biography of the Life and Tragical Death of Elder Caleb M. Dyer.* That Dyer was worthy of such tribute was beyond question, within the Enfield Shaker village where he lived and for miles around it. "As a businessman, he was fair, plain, honest and upright," his biographer wrote, "but square and decided in all his dealings; and would sooner suffer wrong, than knowingly do wrong. He was active and energetic, and a thing once undertaken was rarely abandoned." Dyer was sixty-two when he died, and, as his friend Aaron Cragin put it, he had been the mainspring of Enfield Shaker life for nearly a quarter century. His accomplishments were many: the stone dwelling house, six stories tall, finished about 1840; a sawmill in 1844, another in 1847; a bridge across Mascoma Lake and a machine shop in 1849; a village office in 1850; a great barn in 1854; side buildings in 1855; a dam, a bedstead factory, and a grist mill, all finished by 1858. There was more, including thousands of dollars of business transacted in the flannel trade on the Shakers' behalf in New York, as well as jobs for many in Enfield who did not follow Shaker ways. "In addition to the sense of grief and loss so keenly felt," Cragin said in his eulogy, "the manner of his death is calculated to impress us all with horror."

Like Dyer's achievements, the "manner of his death" was not open to question. Nor could the contrast between his life and his killer's have been much greater.

Thomas Wier was a strange figure in and around Enfield before August 1861, when he enlisted in the Fifth New Hampshire at the age of forty-five. He was the father of five daughters, a shoemaker by trade, a pauper by circumstance, a man of excitable temperament. In 1843, he had left his home to wander with William Miller, who promised salvation to those who would wait with him for the end of the world. Wier believed he had lived as a perfect, sinless Christian for seven years.

His motives for enlisting at an advanced age are unclear—beyond a boast that he intended to return with Jefferson Davis's head or without his own—but poverty seems a more likely factor than patriotic bloodlust. His wife Mahala was ill, and Wier asked Dyer and the Shakers to take in the daughters still at home, Ellen and Sarah, ages eight and ten. The Shakers, who were celibate, depended on such commitments for new members. But Dyer was reluctant. He knew Wier, who had worked for the Shakers, and feared he would change his mind. Dyer would have worried even more had he known Mahala was unaware of her husband's request. In the end Dyer agreed to take the children because doing otherwise would seem unneighborly, given the family's plight. On August 29, in the presence of Dyer and a witness, Wier signed a contract committing Ellen and Sarah to the order's care, making Dyer the guardian of his children until they came of age.

Wier was mustered into the Fifth as a corporal on October 12, 1861. A few days later two of his three grown daughters died. Mahala recovered from her sickness, but Wier fell ill during the Fifth's first months in the field. By spring he had been discharged and sent home with chronic diarrhea. To Wier's professed astonishment, Dyer would not release the children upon his return. Wier pleaded, threatened mobs and murder, and asked lawyers to intercede on his behalf. But the contract was binding. In the fall of 1862, Mahala tried to take Sarah and Ellen by force, an abduction thwarted in part when the children resisted. Wier, who had been allowed unsupervised visits with his girls, found this privilege revoked.

On Saturday, July 18, 1863, just after five in the evening, Wier appeared at the village. After praising several Shakers for the beauty of their garden, he approached Dyer outside a hen house and asked to see his daughters. Citing the lateness of the hour, Dyer refused. "You can have your choice," Wier said. He drew a Colt revolver and fired at Dyer as the Shaker turned away, the bullet striking Dyer above the left hip and penetrating his abdomen to the navel. Wier pulled the trigger again, but the gun jammed. "I am shot, but not killed," Dyer told the Shakers who came to his aid. Wier left the village in the company of half a dozen silent Shakers. They walked two miles to the center of town, where Wier surrendered to Sheriff Wyman Pattee.

Despite Dyer's optimism and the care of several doctors, he died three days later. His funeral drew hundreds of mourners to the Shaker village. "I would that this page of our community's history might be obliterated, blotted out," said one eulogist, Charles Jackman. "The thought almost nerves one to madness."

The day after Wier's arrest, Pattee escorted him home for a shave and a change of clothes and allowed him alcohol, which Wier said he needed for medicinal purposes. His guards gave him three or four drinks a day, of whiskey and a pint of gin—perhaps more than Pattee intended but less than Wier wanted. Indicted in the fall, he pleaded not guilty by reason of insanity, and his trial was set for the following April in Haverhill, the seat of Grafton County. One measure of public interest was the presence of a reporter from the Manchester *Daily Mirror & American* to record the trial in detail.

The prosecution's case was straightforward. First, through the testimony of three Shakers who witnessed the crime, Attorney General William Clarke established that Wier had shot Dyer. "After Wier fired the pistol he went upon what I should call a trot, three or four rods, and then broke into a walk," testified Trueman Johnson, who followed him to town. "We said nothing to him but kept along by the side of him." Shakers and villagers who had heard Wier threaten Dyer and speak of the consequences of killing him also came forward. "He talked a great deal about the Shakers and the children," testified James Huse, who made bedsteads in North Enfield. Wier told Huse that after killing Dyer "he should die in peace, and it would be the happiest time in his life." William Smith, a surveyor, said Wier's threats began in the fall of 1862. "Those threats, my impression is, were to mob the Shakers if they would not give his children up. The next threats, in the winter following, were to take the law to them." By summer, Smith testified, Wier said those who had promised to help him had all backed out. He threatened to handle the matter alone even though this "would cause him to pull hemp."

Smith and two other witnesses had approached Dyer on Wier's behalf—in Smith's case, with an offer that Wier would compensate the Shakers for his children's board if they would release them. Dyer told Smith the Shakers wanted no money and the children could go if they chose. Smith met alone with Ellen and Sarah. "I was considerably acquainted with the children," Smith testified, "and tried in all my power to persuade them to go to their father's home, but could not persuade them to go."

Cragin, Dyer's friend and eulogist, was the second of two lawyers Wier asked for help. He testified that Wier believed Dyer had deceived him and the contract had been doctored. Cragin took his concerns to Dyer. "I was very strongly impressed that some trouble might grow out of it," he testified. He asked Dyer "if he didn't think he better give them up. I told him he must be aware that it was a case that would appeal strongly to the sympathy of the people outside of their society." Dyer knew this, Cragin said, and again offered to let the children go if they wished. On the Monday before the shooting, Cragin conveyed Dyer's offer to Wier. "Mr. Wier said, then all hope is gone," Cragin testified. Wier believed the Shakers had turned the children against their parents. "He said that he should have to take the matter into his own hands, that he should settle it that week," Cragin testified. "He was very much excited."

The defense focused on Wier's behavior after his return from the army and the delusions he suffered. One witness said Wier was serious about bringing Jefferson Davis's head home. Another said he denied signing a contract with the Shakers. Hubbard Harris testified that he had been hoeing with Wier on the east side of Shaker Pond in June 1863 when two boats passed bearing Shakers on an outing. Wier insisted his children were aboard and accused the Shakers of lying when they denied it in response to his calls. Others testified that Wier, long peculiar, had grown more so since returning from the war. If the wind was right, a minister said, he could be heard singing from half a mile away. "At different times in the store, I have seen him sitting apparently in meditation," testified Harry Leeds, "and all of a sudden he would rise up and without any provocation, would clap his hand over his mouth, commence swaying backward and forward, and burst out in a boisterous unearthly laugh, would suddenly stop laughing, set up straight, and become and remain quiet." Wier would often "draw a hand-sled down street and back, without anything upon it," Leeds said. Even in warm weather he wore his haversack, canteen, and overcoat and carried a blanket. Lewis Biathrow once saw Wier in a field, hoe in hand, doing army drills. "He then holloaed 'March,' then stepped a few steps," Biathrow testified. "He was using his hoe-handle as a gun. He would say, 'Shoulder arms,' 'Present arms,' as he maneuvered. . . . He was at work all alone."

Defense lawyers did not ask for special consideration for Wier as a veteran or make an issue of the Shakers' pacifism. Nor did they raise past controversies over the Shaker practice of breaking up families—though they might have, in a case involving Dyer himself. His mother Mary was a prominent Shaker critic, having accompanied her husband and five children into membership in the Enfield village in 1813 and later reconsidered. She waged a decades-long campaign in pamphlets, before the courts, on the streets, and in the Legislature to extract her children from the village, all to no avail.

When defense lawyers asked if witnesses considered Wier insane, prosecutors successfully objected. Only professionals could make such a judgment, the judge ruled. All three prosecution experts observed the trial and reached the same conclusion. Prosecutors asked John Tyler, who had served five years as superintendent of the New Hampshire Asylum for the Insane, if Wier was sane. "I see no reason to doubt it," Tyler said, adding that he had seen no sign of mental illness in Wier's expression or manner. Defense lawyers pressed Tyler. In binding his children to the Shakers, and then insisting he had not, wasn't Wier demonstrating insane delusions? "I should think not," Tyler said. "It would indicate a mistake or a delusion, not clearly and of itself an insane delusion."

To settle the issue of what Wier had signed, prosecutors introduced the contract into evidence, along with testimony from Shaker Mary Fall, who had witnessed its signing. Dyer said he would take the children only if Wier signed the agreement, she testified. "Wier said he thought there would be no need of it, he might not ever return from the army, and that if he did, he should not want his children," Fall said. Dyer read the document aloud and handed it to Wier, who looked it over. "Thomas then took the pen and signed and passed it back to Dyer," Fall testified, "and we signed as witnesses."

Prosecutors closed their case by calling Shaker William Perkins back to the stand. As the first witness, he had described the shooting. Now he repeated Wier's words during his walk with the Shakers from the scene of the crime into Enfield: Deal honestly with others and tell no lies. "He said he expected to be hung," Perkins said, "and deemed it a privilege, rather than to be abused so."

Wier's fate went to the jury at four o'clock on April 20. Jurors delivered their verdict the next morning: guilty of murder in the first degree. Wier had sat quietly throughout his trial, wearing black pants and his blue army overcoat, collar turned up, buttoned to his chin. Now the clerk asked if he had anything to say. The *Mirror* reporter saw Wier fight back tears before saying in a quiet voice: "I don't know. It is a little matter to be judged of men. I appeal to that higher Court where we must all soon appear. I don't know as I have anything else."

In passing sentence, Judge Everett Sargent said the law gave him no discretion in cases of murder in the first degree. He expressed no regret over this. He did not mention Dyer's exceptional life or Wier's army service. "While we cannot nor would not censure you for loving your children, which is the duty of all parents, yet you should reflect that they were placed with the Shakers by your voluntary act," Sargent said. Any disagreement with Dyer "could not justify your act in taking his life in the midst of his usefulness." In accordance with state law, Sargent sentenced Wier to be held until April 28, 1865, when he was to be hanged between nine and noon.

With the Army of the Potomac preparing for a spring offensive under its newly promoted commander, Ulysses S. Grant, hopes for Union victory were high, and the only remaining question seemed to be whether Wier would survive the war in which he had served. "May the God of Infinite Grace have mercy upon your soul," the judge said, and Wier was taken from the courtroom.

CORPORAL DAVID A. STEVENS OF BOW AND PRIVATES JOHN F.
HAM OF BOW, PARCHUST D. QUIMBY OF CONCORD, ALONZO P.
HALL OF PITTSFIELD, AND CHARLES HART OF ANTRIM, ALL
MEMBERS OF THE FIRST NEW HAMPSHIRE HEAVY ARTILLERY,
STRIKE A POSE ON THEIR RETURN FROM PICKET DUTY IN 1864.

Part III

TO THE
BLOODY END

"This inhuman war will not cease until
the arrogant South is brought under the
rod and made to *feel* that the North is
a *power*, to be *respected* and *feared*."

—Colonel Samuel Duncan, March 23, 1865

May 12, 1864

SPOTTSYLVANIA

AS THE NINTH NEW HAMPSHIRE VOLUNTEERS marched through Washington on a fine spring day, Corporal Elmer Bragg looked up to the balcony of Willard's Hotel and saw Abraham Lincoln. "I was surprised to see how careworn the President was looking for he seemed to be *really ill*, and who can wonder that this is the case in times like the *present*?" Bragg wrote his father. Beside Lincoln stood Ambrose Burnside, Bragg's whiskery corps commander, who had brought his troops east to join Grant's gathering army. Spectators crowded the sidewalks, and Burnside's corps took an hour and fifty-seven minutes to pass in review. "New England troops—God bless them!" Bragg heard someone say. "We all felt as proud as though we were fancy troops who had never seen hard service," he wrote. Where the parade might lead was "all a mystery," but his faith and idealism made the destination unimportant. "As we move on to meet the enemies of Freedom we go with a sacred trust on our hands," he wrote, "and if we are *true men* and Brave soldiers we can *meet duty* wherever it calls and far above the smoke and carnage of the Battle field a righteous peace will ere long shine down on a *free* and *happy* people."

ELMER BRAGG

Larkin D. Mason, a Tamworth probate judge appointed by Governor Joseph Gilmore to assist New Hampshire troops, watched the parade from the window of his room in Willard's. He could see Lincoln and Burnside on their perch. Looking to the street, he picked out three New Hampshire regiments, including Elmer Bragg's. With two Maine regiments and a Vermont regiment in the mix, they were part of a New England brigade commanded by Colonel Simon G. Griffin of Concord. Mason had heard enough around the capital to know he would soon have work to do. "Everything indicates a terrible battle on the Potomac within two weeks," he wrote the governor.

The Ninth New Hampshire was not the confused mob that had been thrown into the battles of South Mountain and Antietam before many of the men even knew how to load their rifles. They were veterans now, having fought in those battles, put Vicksburg to siege, and sacked Jackson, Mississippi. They carried light loads and could march long distances. On the negative side, bullets and disease had shortened their column. Company E, which Bragg and his friends had joined at Lebanon as a tightknit band of scholars from Kimball Union Academy, now numbered forty-four

SIMON G. GRIFFIN WITH HIS STAFF DURING
GRANT'S SPRING OFFENSIVE IN 1864.

rifles—less than half its roster when it left Concord in August of 1862. Its leader was Lieutenant Oscar D. Robinson, who had been valedictorian of Kimball Union's class of '62.

Marching out of Washington after the presidential review, the Ninth crossed Long Bridge, the same span over which it had passed before heading north to counter Lee's 1862 invasion of Maryland. Pursuing Lee again, Burnside's corps headed toward the old battlegrounds of Virginia and paused at Manassas. "Wrecks of Ambulances, dismounted pieces of Artillery *too large* for a curiosity gatherer to carry off, broken muskets, rusty bayonets, fragments of exploded shells & solid shot still lie and will lie in mixed confusion telling passers by of *the awful destruction* of war, and yet how *feebly*!" Bragg wrote his father. "For the dying groans and death struggles of the thousands who were called to die on the field are hushed and all are enclosed neath the green sod."

Larkin Mason, the governor's emissary, had been right about the imminence of battle, and for Bragg's regiment his estimate of two weeks was correct to the day. By then the big guns had been booming for a week as Grant's army fought near the old Chancellorsville battlefield. On May 11, his generals advised him to disengage, but Grant instead wrote to Lincoln: "I propose to fight it out on this line, if it takes all summer." At that moment the New Hampshiremen were loading up fresh beef in the rear and expecting another nervous day in the trenches at Spottsylvania.

Before dawn the next morning they lay in a ditch in a drenching rain on the far right of Burnside's line. Their task was to connect with the left of the Second Corps, which had already advanced into battle. Many weapons were wet, the underbrush in the pine woods before the men was thick, and it was dark. They charged into a fog as the enemy fired blindly at the noise they made. They missed the Second Corps's left, and Major George H. Chandler went looking for it, taking a bullet through the thigh for his troubles. Men stopped to shoot only to have their wet charges misfire. They dried their rifles and reloaded. They moved so near the enemy that the flash of a charge sometimes lit up a startled face. Many were hit several times at point-blank range. The regiment retreated after ten minutes, but some companies could not escape. Bunched up with their flanks exposed, they fought on with swift and predictable results. The Ninth left dozens of dead and wounded men behind, including Sergeant George Tracy of Robinson's company. A ball shattered Tracy's tibia just above the ankle. Unable to flee,

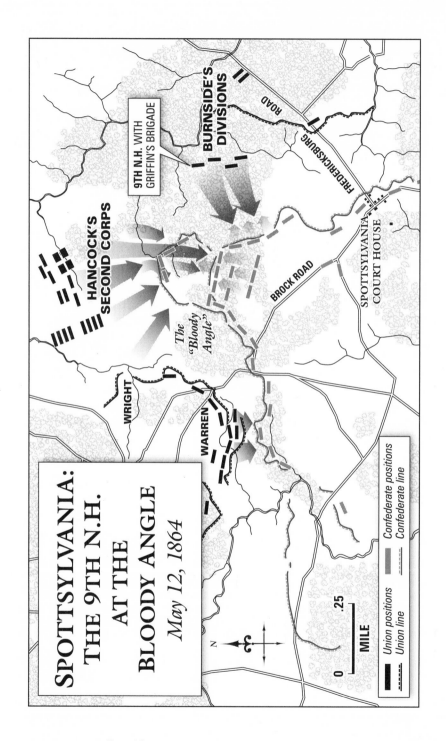

SPOTTSYLVANIA:
THE 9TH N.H.
AT THE
BLOODY ANGLE
May 12, 1864

BURNSIDE'S DIVISIONS

9TH N.H. WITH GRIFFIN'S BRIGADE

HANCOCK'S SECOND CORPS

FREDERICKSBURG ROAD

SPOTTSYLVANIA COURT HOUSE

BROCK ROAD

The "Bloody Angle"

WRIGHT

WARREN

Union positions
Union line
Confederate positions
Confederate line

N

MILE

0   .25

he crawled about picking up knapsacks to pile around him. The rebels who overran him paused to steal his ammunition but also gave him more knapsacks for his makeshift breastwork. "I had quite a little fort," he wrote in his diary. "It was not an agreeable position; but God mercifully preserved me."

Counting heads after the retreat, Lieutenant Robinson saw no sign of Corporal Bragg. Of his 44 men, 20 were gone. The regiment, which had begun the day with 500 men, had lost 42 dead, 94 wounded, and 70 missing. Robinson could only hope Bragg was among the missing. A comrade reported having seen him fall during the retreat. The rebels pulled back after the fight, and Robinson crept along between the picket lines in his futile search for Bragg. Men from the company did find Sergeant Tracy forty hours after the battle and brought him in in a blanket. His foot was amputated, and he died. Over two days 37 men of the regiment were buried in mass graves. Bragg was not among them. "We feel sure he was not killed for all the bodies have been recovered from that portion of the field," Robinson wrote Bragg's father. Sergeant Franklin Burnham of Plainfield, who had last seen Elmer "banging away at the Johnnies on our front," assured the Braggs he had looked into the face of every corpse found where the company fought. The family finally received two letters from Elmer, the second one from Richmond, sharing the barest information: He was wounded and doing as well as could be expected.

Elmer Bragg kept a diary and eventually told his father what had happened. A rebel ball hit him near the left temple, shattering a bone and knocking him out. When he awoke, his face was bloody and his regiment gone. "Just then one of the Rebels put his bayonet into my stomach near my heart and as I was insensible he robbed me," Bragg wrote. He lost his watch, rubber blanket, knife, and stockings. After the rebels led the wounded to the rear, he counted 150 prisoners in his group. "'Tis sad to see how some of my comrades are suffering in the hands of the enemy," he wrote. He cooked for them and saw surgeons arrive to amputate. His wounds were dressed on the fifth day. He and the others reached a prison hospital in Richmond on May 21.

He tried to stay brave even as men died around him. "God help me to be ever contented with my lot," he wrote in his diary. Patients gauged how the war was going by the influx of rebel wounded. In early June, around the time of the battle at Cold Harbor, they correctly guessed Grant was near Richmond. Bragg wanted money, knowing he would crave books once he felt better. The ball hurt his head so much he finally allowed a rebel surgeon to remove it. By August the handwriting in his diary became unsteady. Three months from the day he was shot, he was among 400 prisoners paroled and sent to the naval hospital in Annapolis. He wrote his sister that he had become sicker in captivity and suffered from crazy spells. He obsessed about repaying his father for the watch the rebels had snipped from his pocket. "Father will *never loose a cent* if I can ever get *enough*," he wrote. On August 18, he scratched in his diary: "Troubled a great deal with my head aching. But how much better I am cared for now. Thank dear Father in Heaven." When William Bragg arrived the next morning to see his son, he hardly recognized him.

Two nurses wrote to William Bragg the day after he left. John Hanby got right to the point: Elmer had gone into convulsions in the night and died in the morning. Maria M. C. Hall conveyed the news more gently, beginning: "But yesterday you were with us & enjoyed the pleasure of seeing your son alive again from Richmond & its prison. But our Father's word tells us that in the midst of life we are in death—and my heart fails me as I write that the case of your own child is a striking illustration of the truth of these solemn words." Hall wished William had stayed longer. Elmer had told her how happy the visit made him. Near the end, she wrote, he had "severe spasms," lost his voice, and gasped for breath. He choked to death at half past ten. "His death came upon me like a thunderbolt," Hall wrote. She sent the Braggs a lock of Elmer's hair. When William retrieved the body, he brought home and kept the rebel ball that had killed his son.

Bragg was dead by the time news of his transfer to Annapolis reached his comrades in the trenches before Petersburg. Thinking him still alive, they wrote to cheer his return to Union soil and to describe the trials the Ninth New Hampshire had endured since Spottsylvania. In a letter detailing the regiment's losses at the Crater near Petersburg on July 30, Newell T. Dutton of Claremont, another young scholar from Company E, wrote: "How often as seated in our circle sipping the 'Life of the soldier' we've wished we could carry to you a cup of the strength giving beverage (coffee)." Lieutenant Robinson wrote Bragg that he looked forward to "the pleasure of conversing with you *face to face*," signing himself "truly your comrade & brother soldier."

In the time it took Bragg to die, the war again transformed the Ninth

SGT. MAJ. NEWELL T. DUTTON (LEFT) WITH THE REST
OF THE NINTH NEW HAMPSHIRE'S NONCOMMISSIONED
STAFF: HOWARD M. HANSON OF SOMERSWORTH,
THE COMMISSARY SERGEANT; SYLVESTER J. HILL OF
MANCHESTER, THE HOSPITAL STEWARD; AND CHARLES
L. RUGG OF KEENE, THE QUARTERMASTER SERGEANT

New Hampshire. At first, despite constant fighting and lack of sleep, Robinson's men remained "cheerful & confident & I have yet to know the first instance where one man has refused to try to perform his duty." As for himself, he wrote, "My greatest surprise & wonder is that I am alive." Grant's relentless campaign required draftees and substitutes to replace the men lost at Spottsylvania, Cold Harbor, and the Crater. Robinson described the regiment's decline in a letter to Bragg's father. The officer corps now comprised a captain and three lieutenants, and half the soldiers had never faced fire. The army had provided new rifles to be tested—Lindsey's patent double shooters. Robinson found them "miserable things & especially objectionable for new men." Battlefield defeats had hurt morale. "Our Regt. suffered severely in the last engagement & it is not strange that the men have some dread for the next," Robinson wrote. To the regiment's sparse old guard, the pride of marching past the president in the spring and the wild-eyed excitement of double-timing up South Mountain two years earlier seemed like distant dreams.

May 19, 1864

FRIENDS TO THE END

AS THE TWO MEN SETTLED INTO CONNECTING ROOMS at the Pemigewasset House in Plymouth, New Hampshire, Franklin Pierce left the door open between his room and Nathaniel Hawthorne's and set his lamp so he could see Hawthorne from his bed. The former president and the author of *The Scarlet Letter* were fifty-nine years old, and time was closing in on them.

They had been dear friends since their student days at Bowdoin College, a span of four decades. If anything, the war had strengthened this bond. At a time when many people in his own state reviled Pierce, his friendship with Hawthorne counted more than ever. Hawthorne brought out Pierce's humanity, a trait often hidden in a politician who scorned all who strayed from his rigid ideology. Hawthorne did not stray. He had written Pierce's campaign biography in 1852 and, like Pierce, believed that abolitionists threatened the Constitution's necessary compromises. Though wrong, slavery would wither on its own "when all its uses have been fulfilled," he had written. As president, Pierce had commissioned a portrait of Hawthorne and hung it in his office.

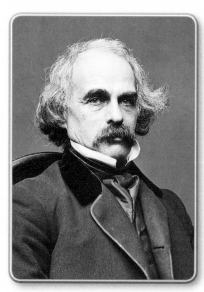

NATHANIEL HAWTHORNE

Unlike his friend, Hawthorne had taken time to visit President Lincoln at the White House. His account of their 1862 encounter was balanced. James T. Fields, editor of the *Atlantic Monthly*, printed only its laudatory side. Hawthorne cast Lincoln as "a man of keen faculties, and, what is still more to the purpose, of powerful character. . . . The President is teachable by events, and has now spent a year in a very arduous course of education; he has a flexible mind, capable of much expansion, and convertible towards far loftier studies and activities than those of his early life; and if he came to Washington a back-woods humorist, he has already transformed himself into as good a statesman." Fields cut the passage about Lincoln's folksy side: "It is the strangest and yet the fittest thing in the jumble of human vicissitudes, that he, out of so many millions, unlooked for, unselected by any intelligible process that could be based upon his genuine qualities, unknown to those who chose him, and unsuspected of what endowments may adapt him for his tremendous responsibility, should have found the way open for him to fling his lank personality into the chair of state,—where, I presume, it was his first impulse to throw his legs on the council-table, and tell the Cabinet Ministers a story."

Days before Pierce's Fourth of July speech in Concord in 1863, Hawthorne insisted on dedicating *Our Old Home* to him over Fields's protests. The book contained sketches of English life that Hawthorne would not have observed had Pierce, as president, not appointed him consul to Liverpool. "If he is so exceedingly unpopular that his name is enough to sink the volume, there is so much the more need that an old friend should stand by him," Hawthorne wrote. He did revise the dedication, hoping to appease the Pierce haters. As published, it read: "To Franklin Pierce, as a slight memorial of a college friendship, prolonged through manhood, and retaining all its vitality in our autumnal years, this volume is inscribed by Nathaniel Hawthorne." But Hawthorne could not resist writing in his foreword that Pierce had once "filled what was then the most august position in the world." The implication that Lincoln had diminished the office angered many readers, including Benjamin Brown French, a onetime crony whom Pierce had banished from the Democratic Party. French, who now worked for Lincoln, wrote that Hawthorne's "insertion of 'what was then'—is mean and contemptible."

That December, Hawthorne attended the funeral of Jane Pierce, the ex-president's wife. Framed in an ornate coffin, her face looked to Hawthorne like a carved image. "There was a remote expression about it as if the whole had nothing to do with things present," he said. As the two men lingered by the grave in Concord's Old North Cemetery on a frigid day, Pierce pulled Hawthorne's collar up to keep off the wind.

Pierce knew his friend's health was failing, but Hawthorne's wife Sophia believed in the healing power of travel and liked Pierce's proposal that the two men tour the North Country together the following spring.

"I think the serene jog-trot in a private carriage into country places, by trout-streams and to old farm-houses, away from care and news, will be very restorative," she wrote Fields. "They will fish, and muse, and rest, and saunter upon horses' feet, and be in the air all the time in fine weather." Pierce had been "a most tender, constant nurse" to Jane Pierce, Sophia wrote, and now that she was dead, "His love for Mr. Hawthorne is the strongest passion of his soul." To Pierce, she wrote: "I know his youth will return to him in the country wandering with you."

Hawthorne had just taken a trip with William Davis Ticknor, his publisher and Fields's partner. After Ticknor died suddenly in a Philadelphia hotel, Hawthorne came home "sadly exhausted, with his face ploughed up with deep furrows of pain and distress," Sophia wrote Pierce. "I never saw him look so ill." It troubled her husband that Ticknor had been unable to say goodbye to his family. "Oh it was so dreary to die in a Hotel!" she wrote. Now she would entrust him only to "such gentle and tender hands as yours. . . . I know you will guard him from *people*." After Ticknor's death Hawthorne "was nearly killed with persons who went to see him."

Her husband's next journey days away, Sophia wrote Fields that he was "not fit to be left by himself, as his steps are so uncertain, and his eyes are very uncertain, too." Because he refused to see a doctor, she asked Fields to arrange for Doctor Oliver Wendell Holmes to run into him in Boston before he left for New Hampshire. Holmes caught up with Hawthorne trudging up the street in front of his hotel, the Bromfield House. "He seemed to have shrunken in all his dimensions," Holmes wrote. Hawthorne spoke of a persistent "boring pain" in his stomach. Weak and docile, he told Holmes his writing days were over. Although he had always spoken deliberately, Holmes now found that "talking with him was almost like love-making, and his shy, beautiful soul had

OLIVER WENDELL HOLMES

to be wooed from its bashful prudency like an unschooled maiden." When Holmes saw him again the day he and Pierce left, Hawthorne could barely walk or whisper.

Pierce met Hawthorne at the Bromfield House, and they took a train to Concord, New Hampshire. They started north in Pierce's carriage on May 15, hoping to travel "far beyond the White Mountains to the wild scenery of Dixville Notch." Pierce quickly saw that his friend was "more comfortable in the carriage with gentle motion than anywhere else." They stopped at Centre Harbor, where Hawthorne slept fitfully and ate a light breakfast. At noon they strolled onto the hotel piazza to look out upon Red Hill, Lake Winnipiseogee, and Mount Belknap. "He was weak, but not suffering from pain, and evidently enjoyed the hour," Pierce wrote. During the fifteen-mile carriage ride to Plymouth, Hawthorne asked if Pierce had read William Makepeace Thackeray's obituary. A stroke had killed the English writer in his sleep the previous December. Hawthorne said that when his time came, it would be a blessing to go without a struggle.

The Pemigewasset House, their destination, was a large white hotel built by the railroad as a rest stop for travelers bound for the White Mountains. A fire had damaged it in 1862, but it had been repaired. Pierce and Hawthorne arrived as the sun sank behind the hills. Hiram Bell, the proprietor, met them at the door, where he and Pierce spoke of the hotel as just the place for Hawthorne to rest and recuperate. But Pierce had already decided to travel no farther and to advise Sophia and the Hawthornes' daughter Una to rush to Plymouth. Hawthorne had to be carried up to his room.

As night fell, he drank tea, ate toast, and dozed on the couch. He went to bed after an hour, and Pierce placed his lamp where he could see his friend six feet away. Pierce fell asleep at ten o'clock but awoke before midnight. His friend "was lying in a perfectly natural position, like a child, with his right hand under his cheek," his face toward Pierce. When Pierce awoke again three hours later, Hawthorne had not moved. Pierce tiptoed into the room. Hawthorne's features looked normal, but Pierce "could not perceive that he breathed." He felt his left temple, wrist, and side for a pulse, "but the great, generous, brave heart beat no more."

Pierce sent for a physician and woke two acquaintances who happened to be staying in a nearby room. He wired Sophia Hawthorne and started a letter to her before the body had even been moved. "He lies upon his side, his position so perfectly natural and easy, his eyes closed, that it is difficult to realize, while looking upon his noble face, that this is death," Pierce wrote. "He must have passed from natural slumber to that from which there is no waking without the slightest movement." As he gathered Hawthorne's belongings to send them home, he found a picture of himself in his friend's valise.

Pierce joined Sophia and the family for the funeral in Concord, Massachusetts. Had the widow been composed enough to plan it, he would have been a pallbearer. "But it mattered not where you stood or walked because you were in his and our hearts," she wrote him. Although the day was bright, with apple blossoms drifting on the breeze at Sleepy Hollow Cemetery, the funeral surely reminded Pierce of the December day his friend had stood at his side over Jane Pierce's grave. The men who bore Hawthorne's casket included Fields, Holmes, Henry Wadsworth Longfellow, Ralph Waldo Emerson, Bronson Alcott, and Louis Agassiz. Pierce was a pariah to most of them. Emerson wrote in his journal that day that he had hoped Hawthorne would outlive his "perverse politics & unfortunate relationship for that paltry Franklin Pierce." Fields was kinder, seeing in Pierce a friend for whom Hawthorne "would willingly, at any time, have given up his own life."

Despite Pierce's political triumphs from the 1830s through his presidency, he was a man of many sorrows. His three children had all died young, including eleven-year-old Benny, who was killed in a train accident just before Pierce's inauguration. Jane Pierce had struggled with depression and other illnesses for years before her death. Hawthorne had been a sympathetic ear and loyal friend through all this tragedy and through the abuse that was a politician's lot. "I need not tell you how lonely I am, and how full of sorrow," Pierce wrote a mutual friend. A man of unbending opinions, he had been no less committed to the friend who had stood by him.

May 30, 1864

A HARD CHOICE

WAR HAD BEEN GEORGE WASHINGTON GORDON'S LIFE and liveli-
hood since his enlistment ten days after the surrender of Fort Sumter. With
military schooling in his past, he was named sergeant major of the Second
New Hampshire Volunteers and soon promoted to lieutenant. He left his
wife Angeline and their two children, six-year-old Etta and three-year-old
George, in Suncook, a mill and farming town north of Manchester. He
wrote home faithfully and longed to be with his wife and kiss their children
good night. His regiment's strength withered in a succession of battles:
Bull Run, Williamsburg, Fair Oaks, the Seven Days, second Bull Run,
Gettysburg. Gordon survived them all. He kept one eye on the future, wir-
ing home money through Adams Express Company and advising Angeline
on finances, from the purchase of property to the price she should get for
a sleigh they no longer needed. As his three-year enlistment neared its end,
he faced a big decision: Should he go home to his family or re-enlist and
see the war through?

GEORGE WASHINGTON
GORDON

The carnage on the battlefields of
the Virginia Peninsula in 1862 sick-
ened Gordon. "It almost deprives a
man of all humanity to follow the
fortunes of war," he wrote. On the
battlefield at Williamsburg in May
he was shocked that "so many so
young and fair lay cold and senseless upon the cold earth awaiting
some friendly hand to bury [them]."
For days the hot, humid air carried
the smell of death. The corpses
attracted gawkers, and "men went
around and covered the faces of
the dead from the gaze of curiosity."
At Fair Oaks in June, the Second
camped where thousands had died.

"Most of them are buried on the field and so many it is impossible to bury them decent," Gordon wrote. "In some places anamiles have dug bodies quite out of the ground."

Gordon was wounded at second Bull Run that August and lost his possessions when the Second's camp was burned to deprive the rebels of food and supplies. From the hospital he wrote that even though war had created "a land of mourning," it must be fought "with all vigor although evry home in the nation shall be made desolate, for it is desolation unless we do conquer . . . for it would be slavery and nothing more." In the Peach Orchard at Gettysburg on July 2, 1863, he was hit in the neck, arm, and side. He described these wounds as "not dangerous although quite painful." He considered the battle less decisive than the papers reported, telling Angeline: "There is more fighting to be done and hard fighting." Gettysburg bled his regiment again. When Gordon, a captain now, returned to camp, Company I—his command—consisted of eleven men.

For rest and reinforcement, the Second was sent to Point Lookout, a crowded camp for rebel prisoners on the Maryland shore. Surrounded by a fourteen-foot wooden fence, it covered forty acres. The prisoners slept in tents, rations were paltry, and more than a quarter of them died of illness, but duty was safe and pleasant for Union officers. Angeline visited and met the wives of Captain James H. Platt of Manchester, Chaplain John Wesley Adams of Salem, and Edward Bailey, the regiment's twenty-one-year-old colonel. Her touch lingered in Gordon's mind after she left. "Oh! that I was with you tonight—all would be bliss," he wrote. "It does seem sometimes as if I would surrender my standing, honor and everything else for the sake of being with my beloved wife and family, but I have gone forth to do my country service in battle and I did not act until I had well considered the deprivations connected with such service." He would do his duty no matter what, and yet "If you could be with me, all could be sunshine." He hoped the feeling was mutual. "Now I do not believe I am licentious minded . . . except with you, and that is not criminal," he wrote. "If I was at home, you would not object to *sleeping* with me, would you? Or would you rather sleep awake? I guess you would."

For all his conjugal tenderness, some soldiers who served under Gordon found him petty and arbitrary. Before Private Martin Haynes married, he resented Gordon's rule favoring married men for furloughs. When he asked Gordon if being engaged counted, "he looked as if he thought I was trifling."

The company's few remaining Abbott Guards, Manchester militiamen who had enlisted together in 1861, got up a deliberate snub of Gordon, and Haynes relished it. They raised $150 to buy a sword for Colonel Bailey, their original captain, not Gordon. "The breach between Captain Gordon and the old men is now very wide and the feeling very bitter," Haynes wrote his wife, the former Cornelia Lane. "In this way the old men can show, in a way not open to criticism, how much more they think of their first captain than of their last." When it appeared Haynes might be transferred back to Gordon's command, he considered applying for a commission with a black regiment. Strangely, Haynes even believed Gordon favored paid substitutes and bounty men over the first volunteers. "Since these mercenaries came along with hundred-dollar bills sticking out of their pockets," he wrote, Gordon had used a special company fund accumulated from soldier donations to buy food for "our cussed Subs."

Though not by choice, Gordon was, in fact, devoted to making soldiers of these men. He caught his first glimpse of the future when the Fifth New Hampshire Volunteers joined the Second at Point Lookout. The quality of the Fifth's new recruits shocked him. Gone were the heady days when friends enlisted together from their towns and academies to save the Union. The draft ruled now. "The 5th N.H. arrived here last night and went into camp up above the rebels camp with their conscripts and such a set, d——d them," Gordon wrote Angeline. "Oh! if I had a company of those fellows I would want to kill some of the devils. I suspect that we will be filled up with such skulch on this new call. If we are, God help them." Three weeks later, twenty replacements joined his company. "Such devils," he wrote Angeline. "We have lost the name of N.H. now certain for not one of them were born in N.H." The new men, mostly paid substitutes, were Irish, Scottish, German, Swedish, Dutch, French, Swiss, "and everything imaginable. Well I shall make them soldiers or give them a ticket for somewhere but not heaven, I know."

This was no idle threat, and Gordon's assignment to court-martial duty in the spring of 1864 put him in a position to carry it out. The main obstacle to training his recruits was their inclination to desert in hopes of joining the enemy or slipping back north to collect another bounty. Estimates of the number of deserters from the Second varied, but Chaplain Adams put it at seventy. Most were caught. "Their utter ignorance of the geography of the country has in many instances led to their undoing," wrote Haynes, who saw in the situation the unraveling of a once-proud regiment. "When the bulk of the old men are discharged, and the subs have all run away, and most of the officers have been mustered out, where will the glorious old Second Regiment New Hampshire Volunteers be?" he asked. One night four deserters stole a boat and with boards for oars rowed down the York River and up Chesapeake Bay. A ship captain arrested them, and their desertion cases soon came before Gordon's court-martial board.

Private John Eagen was condemned to be shot April 13, and the regiment was called out to witness his execution. As Eagen neared the firing squad, word reached the officers in charge that Major General Benjamin Butler had called it off. "The miserable fellow threw off his cap and danced for joy," wrote Haynes. Gordon fumed. "We marched back to camp blue as whetstones and not a little mad," he wrote Angeline, "for such measures are necessary to keep men with the commands to which they belong. It is rather hard but fair." Two days later, the Second was ordered back to the steep bluff above the York River to witness the death of Eagen and Henry Holt, a second deserter convicted by Gordon's court. The gunfire did not kill Holt instantly. Lying on his coffin, he raised a hand several times before his body fell still and the coroner stepped in. Two more men condemned by Gordon's court, a Norwegian and an Irishman, were shot two weeks later. "We are getting a pretty hard name for a court," he wrote Angeline. "We have got four of them shot and more are deserving of being shot if I am judge." Whatever his opinion of Gordon, Private Haynes was of like mind, writing: "These measures were harsh, but they had a most salutary effect and the desertions were immediately checked."

Gordon and Haynes had something else in common. Both had decided to go home when their three-year enlistment was up in early June. In sharing the news with Cornelia, Haynes quoted a comrade: "When I get my discharge in my hand, I shall feel as if I had shaken off a man who for three years has had his hand at my throat, trying to strangle me." Gordon was proud of his battle record but had done his part. "I have gone so far and got honorable scores enough and now I can go home and live contented in relating the adventures of camp life while in the army," he wrote.

On May 30, as his regiment prepared to move, he closed a note to Angeline with his usual affectionate words. His children were nine and six years old by now, but in his eyes they remained much younger. "Love to you and the babies and kiss them for me," he wrote. He had nine days left.

June 2, 1864

A CHAPLAIN'S PROVINCE

JOHN WESLEY ADAMS, JUST TURNED THIRTY-TWO, wore a broad-brimmed hat and rode a roan mare named Flora. Dark hair curled out behind his hat brim, and a bushy beard hid his chin. As the Second New Hampshire's third chaplain, he had quickly learned that in a hard-fighting regiment, the chaplain's province was violent death. He dreaded the coming battle just the same. He had been under fire before, but at Cold Harbor the armies were gathering in multitudes. As much as any private, Adams doubted his courage and wondered if he would die. To minister to others, he would first have to tend to himself.

JOHN WESLEY ADAMS

Adams's first brush with death in wartime had occurred in April, when he was sent to talk with two of the men condemned by Captain Gordon's court-martial board. This made the two officers partners in dispensing justice even though Gordon had let Adams know he disliked chaplains. Earlier he had written his wife that chaplains "steal articles sent to sick soldiers by the various organizations at home to save the expense of feeding themselves, and they can get things that way that cannot be bought here."

One of the condemned men was James Scott, a Norwegian immigrant who had Anglicized his name or had it Anglicized for him. "I became greatly interested in him, and took his case upon my heart," Adams recalled. He found a Norwegian-English Bible and pointed to comforting passages, telling the prisoner: "Scott, that is plain—that reaches your case. Can't you believe that?" Scott shook his head. Finally Adams read the "royal epitome of the Gospel," adding phrases to suit the moment: " 'God so loved the world'—even James Scott the deserter—'that He gave his only begotten Son that whosoever believeth in Him'—not excepting the vilest of the vile—'should not perish but have ever-lasting life.' " At this, Scott shook Adams's hand and knelt beside him.

An hour before the execution, Adams returned to Scott's cell. They were praying when the jail doors opened. It was time. A band playing the death march led the procession, followed by two coffins, the two deserters, and Adams, with guards in the rear. They entered a square with one side open and crowds of men filling the other three. Adams, Scott, and Owen McDonough, the other deserter, stood in the open end, the coffins behind them. Adams prayed again after the death order was read. "Forget about what is about you now, and only look to Jesus, and all will be well," he told Scott. The convicts were blindfolded, and a dozen riflemen entered the square. At the drop of a white handkerchief, they fired. The deserters "threw up their arms, fell backward lifeless upon their coffins, and the stern penalty of military law was paid," Adams wrote.

For the sake of his regiment's reputation, he wished the state could meet its draft quotas with a better grade of recruit. "If this regiment does not retain its character for efficiency in the future," he wrote the *Independent Democrat* in Concord, "the people at home may blame themselves, and not us." To another paper he was even more candid: "Our good name is dear to us, and we will not cheerfully surrender it. But let New Hampshire beware how she insults those who have served most faithfully in her veteran ranks by filling them up, when depleted, with professional deserters and men who have to be 'discharged on account of mental imbecility.' " On a personal level Adams took "sad pleasure" in helping Scott, but the strain cost him "days of nervous prostration, quite unfitting me for service," he wrote later. He had no time to cope with these emotions. The regiment was moving on, its destination a mystery. "However much the rebels may know of the plans of our leaders," wrote Adams, "we confess our own ignorance of them."

The regiment's next stop was below Richmond on Drewry's Bluff, where Fort Darling's cannons had repulsed Union attacks in 1862 and still controlled traffic on the James River ninety feet below. On a Sunday morning Adams ran into Captain Platt, whose future wife had once boarded with Adams's relatives in Massachusetts. She and Adams's wife had been friends at Point Lookout. Adams considered Platt uneducated and blunt but decisive. As they lay behind trees in sight of the fort, he tossed Platt a *Lawrence American*, and Platt made a request familiar to chaplains: Should anything happen to him, would Adams please care for him and inform his wife of his fate? Adams promised he would. During an attack the next morning a rebel ball hit Platt in the head, or, as Adams put it, "The fatal messenger found its way to his brain so intelligently and faithfully serving our cause." Someone shouted, "Platt is killed!" and Adams ran to him. He helped load the body into an ambulance and rode with it to the rear. He

JAMES H. PLATT

asked a soldier to make a coffin, wrote Platt's wife, and arranged for a furloughed soldier to take the body to Baltimore. A few days later, Platt was buried in the Valley Cemetery in Manchester.

The Union assault on Drewry's Bluff having failed, the Second steamed down the James River aboard the *General Lyons*. It was a tense journey. The three-year term of the original volunteers was due to expire on June 8, and any men who did not re-enlist could go home then. It was just their luck to be moving toward battle. Asked to preach aboard the steamer, Adams chose a passage from the fifth chapter of Isaiah in which God created smoke by day and fire by night but also "a tabernacle for a shadow in the day time from the heat, and for a place of refuge, and for a covert from storm and from rain." The *General Lyons* rounded the Virginia Peninsula and headed up the York River to the mouth of the Pamunkey. Adams's description of the river was a metaphor for the war. "Nature perpetrated the crookedest transaction I ever knew her to when she traced the channel of the Pamunkey River," he wrote. "How we ever reached our destination, when so much of the time we were going the other way, is a mystery." The *General Lyons* got stuck in the mud and the men set out on foot. Felled trees and other obstacles blocked the road, slowing the advance and giving Adams too much time to think.

It was here he faced his demons. He had comforted a condemned man and witnessed executions. His friend Platt had chatted with him one morning and been killed the next. He had survived enemy fire. But the rebels waited at Cold Harbor in force. Adams knew "a carnival of death" was coming and doubted his strength in the face of it.

The sound of the guns on June 2 calmed his mind. "As the distinct clatter of dozens of muskets swelled into the continuous roar of many thousands, I thought of the wounded I might rescue, and the dying whom I might minister," he wrote. The comforting fictions of the infantryman, combined with faith, steeled the chaplain for battle. "I am as safe here as anywhere," he told himself. "The post of duty is the safest place. . . . If Heaven wills that I should fall, that is best. I am absolutely in God's hands."

At Cold Harbor Major General William F. Smith ordered three brigades to make a frontal attack. Gilman Marston, the Second New Hampshire's first commander, was a brigadier general now. His brigade formed the left. On the right, the Twelfth New Hampshire was the lead regiment of another brigade. As the line charged across 400 yards, the enemy shot the Twelfth to pieces. The Second went in next, attacking rebels who were dug in chest-deep, their horseshoe-shaped line allowing them to fire on both flanks. Some Union soldiers dug for their lives with tin plates, knives, and bayonets. Any small dent they could scratch in the earth gave them some cover.

As the charge began, Chaplain Adams stood beneath a pine tree with Charles Carleton Coffin, the Boscawen man now famous as the *Boston Journal's* war correspondent. As he answered Carleton's questions, a shell struck the tree. Falling limbs shook the ground, and Carleton left to find a safer vantage point. Adams's duty on this day was medical and spiritual. He guided the wounded to ambulances and assisted the field surgeon. He gave water to the thirsty and

HARRIET P. DAME

helped move the dead from the field. He teamed with Harriet P. Dame, the Concord woman who had been the regiment's angel for years, in caring for the most grievously wounded. "Miss Dame is almost ubiquitous . . . a ceaseless, tireless worker," wrote R. S. Stubbs, a U.S. Christian Commission delegate. Sergeants Nathaniel Freeman of Hinsdale and Allen Hayward of Swanzey each had a mangled arm, Freeman the left, Hayward the right. Adams hurried them to the field hospital. When a soldier he described as "a German infidel" screamed for water, Adams offered his canteen. The man kissed his hand. Because an ambulance ride might be torture to William H. Smith, a captain from Exeter who was shot in both legs, Adams called for a stretcher. Later he saw that Smith made it to the hospital at White House Landing, where Dame cared for him until his death.

Like many other original members of the Second, Captain Gordon planned to go home in less than a week. He had been working on the discharge papers of Private Haynes and other men in his company. While Gordon led these men, along with his recruits and re-enlisted veterans, a bullet ripped through the top of his head. Although the captain disdained chaplains, Adams felt only sorrow as he helped him into an ambulance.

After the guns fell silent, Adams worked amid the chaos of the field hospital, where hundreds of men lay in tangles on the ground. Men begged him for water, for shade, for help in getting a surgeon to take them next. He comforted men with gaping wounds, shattered limbs, broken backs. "The dying were there," he wrote, "and the spiritual agencies were blended with the material." He saw Captain Gordon's corpse. He heard Freeman and Hayward joking about their missing arms, one swapping the other a left glove for a right. He saw the tent of Major James M. Merrow of Rollinsford, the regimental surgeon, and beside it a ditch filled with feet, hands, legs, and arms "that had in childhood been fondled by loving mothers but

ALLEN B. HAYWARD WITH HIS EMPTY SLEEVE

June 2, 1864 ▪ *A chaplain's province*

now had done their last work." Down a slope in a larger ditch lay scores of bodies wrapped in blankets, more dead of Cold Harbor. "In this way," Adams wrote, "the soil of Virginia is becoming truly sacred."

To the wounded and dying, he saw himself as a surrogate mother, sister, or wife. "I had no memories more sacred and satisfying than these," he wrote long afterward. Someday in heaven he hoped to hear a familiar voice hailing him, "Chaplain!"

July 30, 1864

A RACE WITH TIME

COLONEL EDWARD E. CROSS, A MAN WITH A ROMANTIC BENT and a way with words, had included the nineteen-year-old Lieutenant Frank Butler in his inner circle. Six-foot-six, thin, and awkward, Butler had a good education and "irreproachable morals and habits"—traits that irritated

FRANCIS W. BUTLER

certain superior officers. But Cross liked him, and it was Cross's way to groom men as leaders in his own Fifth New Hampshire Volunteers and to support their ambitions outside the regiment. Butler took advantage of this, graduating from signal school and rising to chief of ambulances for the Eighteenth Corps and aide-de-camp to the corps commander, Major General William F. Smith.

In addition to youthful energy, a quick mind, and devotion to duty, Butler possessed another quality Cross appreciated: he liked to write.

In a poem from the front he described the realities of war. Its next-to-last stanza read:

> Thousands who began this journey
> Full of hope bright buoyant strong
> Ere their sun had reached its zenith
> They had joined the greater throng.

The more battles a soldier survived, the more likely he was to fear that he, too, would join the greater throng. Some kept this fear to themselves. Others brushed it aside with bravado, noting in letters home that while comrades had fallen at their sides, God or luck or fate protected them. As Butler came through battle after battle, as the war killed off men he knew, including Cross himself, he began to wonder if he would survive. In his diary and letters, October 12, 1864, the last day of his three-year enlistment, took on new importance. By early summer of that year he considered himself a short-timer, but he hedged his bets. As though trying to prepare his family for the worst, he kept saying in his letters that he might not make it.

Behind these fears lay the scenes Butler saw or heard about. After the battle of Fredericksburg, in which he served as a signalman, Butler peered through a glass at rebel soldiers stripping the Union dead and emptying their pockets. They left the corpses naked in the streets. Butler rode to Gettysburg with Cross and witnessed his painful death. Nearly a year later, at Eighteenth Corps headquarters, he saw cannon and sharpshooter fire snatch lives in an instant. The general staff was out in the open, exposed to hollow pipes packed with explosives and iron balls—"bees," Butler called them. He opened a pipe that failed to explode and counted seventy-eight balls. "The man who can kill the most men is the greatest hero," he wrote. After his corps lost more than 6,000 men at Cold Harbor, he visited the Fifth, his old regiment, and learned that many of its officers had been slaughtered. Among them was Lieutenant Mason W. Humphrey, who had recently written Butler to complain about a safe assignment and express a "longing to go to the field, where every true soldier should be." Now Humphrey, "my friend, as they all were, was decapitated—or rather his head was split by a shell & his brains brushed out as clean as a cloth could have wiped them," Butler wrote.

Early in the war the Union cause and the will to win sustained Butler amid the carnage. The sour taste of defeat at Chancellorsville only strengthened his resolve. During the battle, in which he served as a courier for Major General Henry W. Slocum, commander of the Twelfth Corps, Butler had defied death and won the admiration of soldiers and generals alike. Slocum sent Butler to order Brigadier General John W. Geary to move the Second Division. Butler rode to Geary through a crossfire. "Bullets were scarce, but the shot & shell were thick," he wrote home. The Fifth New Hampshire was positioned near Geary, and as Butler passed, "the boys saw me and cheered." He found Geary's division bracing for an infantry attack. "Don't swear now, my men," Geary shouted as Butler rode up. "Don't swear." When Butler delivered his order, Geary replied: "Tell General Slocum I'm doing the best I can and not to send me any more orders. I'm in a tight place." Butler admired Geary, who had been governor of Kansas before the war. The respect was apparently mutual. They met again the next day, "and we went off together talking over matters. Oh! I love him. Brave! No braver man lives. He is one of my kind—& I tell you he likes me for I was as cool as could be & helped him get out his Div. as if I had been one of his own Genls. and he gives me credit for it."

As bad as his family might feel about the army's defeat at Chancellorsville, he wrote, "to us who are *actors* the sting pierces beyond yr imagination." He was tired of losing. "I'd just as lief be dead as to live & have it said *we* were conquered," he wrote. Perhaps it was a similar declaration that prompted a warning from a fellow officer: "Be careful, Butler, you may be in hell tomorrow before 10 o'clock." An officer who had seen Butler ride the gauntlet to reach Geary piped up: "Butler is bulletproof. If he is to be killed in this war, he would have been killed at Chancellorsville."

As the summer of 1863 waned and the second anniversary of his enlistment approached, Butler began to think about getting out. He was conflicted. He could have resigned, but the thought of leaving before his three-year term was up seemed not to have occurred to him. And even as the memory of a New Hampshire autumn turned his heart toward home, he realized he loved the soldier's life. He wrote his family that he would be home "just in time to do the harvesting—apples, corn & potatoes &c.—for '64 unless I get harvested before." As much as he looked forward to working again on the family farm in Bennington, he wasn't sure he could give up soldiering. "I think after a few wks of Citizen life I shall enlist again if the war lasts & you are willing." His parents had only reluctantly approved of his going to war as a nineteen-year-old, but even as a man, he was prepared to listen to their opinion.

By June 1864, after the brutal Union defeat at Cold Harbor, Butler was counting down the days. He calculated that only fifteen Sabbaths remained until his discharge. He still mentioned the possibility of re-enlisting but did not take his survival for granted. How could he? At Cold Harbor his horse was shot, a shell hit his coat, and a bullet scarred his hand. He blamed poor generalship for the bloodbath there and found no consolation in defeat this time. "Oh God! 'Tis enough," he wrote. "I'm sick of the music, glory and war & when Oct. comes I'm off living like dogs & fighting without a Genl. . . . I'm disgusted. My friends are kild all around—I don't care for anything." He knew the summer months held "dangers in store for soldiers & none can count on safety."

His job as chief of ambulances for the Eighteenth Corps gave him some comfort. His friend George Gove, a lieutenant in the Fifth, considered it "one of the best positions in the army." But in mid-June, as the corps crossed the Appomattox River to join the siege of Petersburg, the medical director replaced Butler over a policy dispute. Ordered back to the Fifth, he resigned himself to "going to my Rgt to be slain in the fray."

This was not to be. General Smith heard Butler was available and made him an aide-de-camp. This meant serving at Smith's headquarters, which seemed safe enough behind three dug-in lines and a reserve of black infantrymen. "Altho ours is a post of danger, I prefer this to marching with my Rgt.," Butler wrote. Soldiers in the trenches dared not raise their heads during the day, and rations and troops were moved at night. Orders, however, had to be carried wherever and whenever necessary. On June 21, Butler was sent out twice in daylight "and got several shots but was as fortunate as ever."

Nine days later at the future site of Fort Stedman, he surveyed the lines, sensed danger, and turned to warn General Smith. Just then a minie ball struck Butler in the knee, and he collapsed. The wound seemed minor. "I rejoice to-night in being able to say that the surgeon gives great hopes of his being not long disabled," Smith wrote Butler's father. By chance, Captain Thomas Livermore arrived just after Butler was hit. Both men had been Colonel Cross's protégés, and Butler was Livermore's "most esteemed friend in the army." He had helped Livermore land a job on Smith's staff. Livermore rode to the hospital and found his friend "not at all dispirited and apparently not badly wounded." Butler wanted to convalesce at home and told Livermore he expected to be back in thirty days. Livermore lent him fifty dollars for the journey.

Butler's servant, a sixteen-year-old black youth named Luther, went north with him. What little is known of Luther must be deduced from a letter his mother, Margaret Craig, wrote to him from Virginia two years later when he was still living with the Butlers. He came from a large family, which the war had scattered. His mother served a white family on Cedar Grove Plantation, probably first as a slave

MAJ. GEN. WILLIAM F. SMITH

and then as a free woman. When Luther's letter arrived, she had not heard from him in years. Several of his cousins who had left during the war were dead, and she presumed he was, too. Her joy upon receiving a letter from him leapt from the pages of her response. Along with news about their far-flung relatives and her hope that he might save his wages and come to Virginia for a visit, Margaret Craig could not resist a dose of motherly advice: "You must do your best at learning & not let them out-do you."

Butler arrived in Bennington five days after he was shot. His mother Mary, a devout woman who served as secretary of the Soldiers' Aid Society, prayed for him and joined her daughters in nursing him. Optimism turned to worry when gangrene set in. His doctors recommended amputation. Butler rallied briefly after the operation, but on July 30, a month after he was shot, he died. The family buried him the next day, a Sunday.

Friends and neighbors rallied around the family. Like most who wrote letters of condolence, George W. Burns felt a kinship in grief with the family. "Having myself more than once passed through the deep waters of affliction, having lain my loved ones in the grave, I can judge something of the deep sorrow that fills your heart," he wrote. Laura Robinson, a teaching assistant at Kimball Union Academy, where Butler had studied, wrote to one of his sisters: "I know there are times when the kindest words, the softest tones seem like pointed arrows piercing deeper the aching, bleeding heart. But sympathy is always sweet." Robinson had reread Frank's letters. He seldom expressed religious feelings in his correspondence, but it seemed he had to her. "If we never meet again upon Earth, may we meet in Heaven," he had written.

At least two of Butler's soldier friends contacted the family. Months after his death, Captain Orlando W. Dimick of the Eleventh New Hampshire escaped from a rebel prison and returned to Lyme on furlough. He had attended Kimball Union with Butler. Their mutual friend, Edwin B. Hale, had stayed home to enter Dartmouth College, choosing the path Butler left to join the army. When Hale told Dimick about Butler's death, their talk turned to "the departed one of our *once happy three*." Dimick asked Butler's father for a photograph of Butler and one further favor: "I would like much to know of his wounds and death . . . if it is not trespassing upon your feelings."

Captain Livermore wrote the family after Butler's mother requested that her son's belongings be sent home and his debts settled. She also described Frank's dying days. Livermore responded that the courage the Butlers had seen in their son on his deathbed stood "in beautiful similitude to his vigorous and noble-hearted service while his sword was unsheathed for his country." Butler had been Livermore's "brother in affection and my companion in battle and in campaign," but now he, too, had died a soldier's death.

September 9, 1864

THE DURGINS' WAR

IN THE SPRING OF 1861, Jeremiah and Caroline Durgin lived with their daughter Sarah and youngest son Scott in Fisherville. Their two older boys, Abner and Hiram, worked for uncles near Boston. In days gone by, Jeremiah had handled horses and tended inns at way stations for stagecoach lines. Now a civic-minded Republican, he had come to town to run the

THE DURGIN CHILDREN, ABNER, HIRAM,
SARAH, AND SCOTT, CIRCA 1855.

Washington House, a hotel and tavern near the train depot. Caroline kept house and garden and saw to the schooling and Christian upbringing of the children.

When war came, Jeremiah helped organized the home guard, a militia company comprising the older men of Fisherville, and became its captain. Abner and Hiram rushed home to answer the first call for troops. Abner, who was twenty-one, had inherited his father's interest in horses, and Hi was a strapping nineteen-year-old known around town as a skillful baseball player. After they joined the Second New Hampshire Volunteers, Abner went to Bull Run as a teamster, Hiram as a corporal in the lines. The carnage that day caused some men to flinch, but not Hiram. "I was not the least moved in time of battle," he wrote. He calmly tied his blanket strap around the nearly severed leg of a man near him. In praise of his brother's coolness under fire, Abner wrote: "Hi is 'in town.'" Abner proved himself during the chaotic retreat. As other teamsters abandoned wagons and equipment, he drove his team all night to Washington, losing only one horseshoe along the way. He later sent home a rebel cavalry officer's saddle, pistol, and valise. Inside the valise were half a cake of French shaving soap and a daguerreotype of a "fair and comely" woman of twenty or twenty-five. The booty was displayed at Ward & Humphrey's hardware store on Main Street in Concord.

Caroline Durgin missed her sons and wrote them cheerful letters sharing her hopes and fears and news of family and village. The chapel where they worshiped needed a new roof, she wrote, or it was time to paint boxes for her dahlias. One morning during the war's first winter she looked out the window on the vastness of the snow and wrote: "I would like to just step in and see you this morning, but knowing I cannot have that privilege, I deem it a consolation that I can write a few lines to you." Her pleasant tone did not always hide a mother's worries. Rumors of a massacre during the Bull Run retreat reached Fisherville before any official report. Thinking she had lost two sons, Caroline couldn't sleep. To her relief, the regiment's major wired the capital the next day that the Concord and Fisherville boys were safe.

When her husband decided to volunteer, Caroline knew she couldn't stop him. "Your mother is wilting I should go out to war," Jeremiah wrote his sons, but finally she told him to enlist and be done with it. Commissioned a captain at the age of forty-nine, he went to E. W. Woodward, a tailor in the Phenix Hotel on Concord's Main Street, and bought a uniform for eighteen dollars and shoulder straps for three. He donned the uniform and stood at attention with his hands cupped for a photograph by Herman J. Currier, his daughter Sarah's boyfriend. The new uniform fit loosely but could not conceal the paunch of middle age. Jeremiah began enlisting men for a company of the Seventh New Hampshire Volunteers. One cold morning about seventy of them marched to the mast yard, a piney plain along the Contoocook River that in colonial days had supplied masts for the royal navy. Caroline stayed home but noticed how the sun and wind had browned the men's faces by the time they returned. Her only complaint was that Jeremiah's regiment would train in Manchester, not Concord.

The day before he left, Jeremiah took the third Durgin

JEREMIAH DURGIN

September 9, 1864 = *The Durgins' war*

boy, thirteen-year-old Scott, to visit the training camp of the Fifth New Hampshire in Concord. "Can it be possible you will need many more of our men out there?" Caroline wrote Abner and Hiram. "I suppose a great many of you will like [it] so well out there that you would not be contented here at home." Scott begged to go south with his father, but Caroline said no. Though she missed Jeremiah, the family swelled with pride when the Fisherville Cornet Band closed a concert with "Captain Durgin's Quickstep."

Jeremiah's first assignment was to help make Saint Augustine safe for Union occupation. He served as provost marshal, rousting disloyal residents from their homes and sending them to rebel territory. He liked the job at first, but after putting eighty-six people aboard a steamer one day and facing an order to send off a hundred more the next, he reconsidered. "It is hard to drive ould & young from their homes not to return again, but such is the fate of war," he observed. Some deportees cried, telling him they would rather be shot than leave home and family. "Sad, sad, but it is my misfortune to have it," he wrote Caroline. When his regiment was ordered to Charleston, he felt confident the Seventh would help capture this bastion of the Confederacy. "We will whip them or die in doing it," he wrote. Should it be the latter, he told Caroline not to cry, for they would soon meet again in eternity. As he led a patrol, a cannonball went through a house where he was cooking dinner. He told a comrade "he preferred to season his own soup."

Abner and Hiram Durgin returned to Bull Run in August of 1862. This time, the Second New Hampshire charged with fixed bayonets and broke through two lines before being stopped. But the advance went too far. "We soon found ourselves exposed to a terrible fire on three sides," wrote Lieutenant Edmund Dascomb of Manchester: "It was a tempest of lead that flesh and blood could not withstand." Thirty-eight men were killed, and Sergeant Hiram Durgin was among them. "Experience teaches a very dear school sometimes and I think we are receiving a very dear one indeed, although we shall come out right side up yet," Abner wrote his mother.

As much as Caroline wanted to keep Scott home, time worked against her. He visited training camps whenever he could. Once he set out to see an uncle but changed his mind and spent the day at the camp of the Third New Hampshire. Invited to share beef and bread with the soldiers, he told his mother the meal was "better than he gets at home." Abner's attempts to cool Scott's ardor sometimes backfired. He urged Scott to be diligent in learning to read, write, and care for horses, but he could not hide his bellicose views. When rumors of war with Great Britain circulated in the Union camps, Abner wrote Scott: "There isn't a soldier In our Regt. but would sooner die the death of a rooster than be subject to British rule." Caroline's only hope of keeping Scott home was his youth, but the short war so many had predicted became a long one. Just turned sixteen in 1864, Scott joined the Eighteenth New Hampshire as a corporal.

ABNER DURGIN

With all the Durgin men gone to war, it was Abner who spelled out the cause for which the family had sacrificed its domestic tranquility. Family letters had avoided the subject until he wrote his mother on September 9. He was by then a strikingly handsome twenty-four-year-old man. He had re-enlisted, won a lieutenant's commission, and become regimental quartermaster. One day, when he was sent to Norfolk on business, a prediction his father had made before the war came back to him. Jeremiah had said that no matter how unpopular abolitionists seemed, their philosophy would prevail within ten years. Abner disagreed at the time but now believed his father had been right.

What he saw in Norfolk caused him to reflect on the family's wartime sacrifices. Major General William T. Sherman had just captured Atlanta and burned much of it. Through long occupation by Union troops, Norfolk had been punished, too. "The city shows the effects of war more than most southern ones and the citizens look as though they had received their portion for the part they took in bringing on this war," Abner wrote. "Though it seems hard at sight, it is no more than right for they did do their share in causing us to suffer so much." He thanked God for the Union victory that recent events portended, observing that at last "it looks as if it is possible for us to soon see sunlight ahead and march onward and upward and homeward very soon." Rather than "judge that our long suffering shall be for nothing but disgrace," he believed the public would sustain the government, as it must. "The enemy is a wily one and stalks abroad very powerfully but barks, growls and boasts more than it must be allowed to accomplish," he wrote.

For him and his family, Hiram's death put a sharp edge on the coming election. Like many soldiers, Abner blamed McClellan, the Democratic presidential nominee, for failing to reinforce Major General John Pope's army at Second Bull Run. Had Pope been so strengthened, perhaps Hiram Durgin would not have died. "I am satisfied McClellan is a traitor and many of our fallen dead have been *sacrificed* to accomplish Porters and McClellans foul and rebel designs," Abner wrote. The Union men killed at Bull Run "were murdered by intrigue and by Fitz John Porter and McClellan. . . . Will a patriotic and able General withhold reinforcements from another general who is known to be actively engaged with a superior force?" No. "If the Spirits of the Departed would speak to us, would they say elect an imbecile traitor like him?" No. Abner hoped his sister and brother-in-law would "work diligently for Abe Lincoln and a country undivided."

This is how the seasoned soldier Abner Durgin distilled the Union cause: a united country without slavery. Whether Caroline Durgin, reading his letter, thought about the war in such terms she did not say. More likely she remained absorbed in the personal dangers her men still faced, as well she should have.

The three Durgin men made it home after the rebel surrender, but their war never ended. Outward signs of age had begun to bother Jeremiah during the summer of 1864, when he asked Caroline to send him a bottle of Batchelder's Hair Dye, whose New York manufacturer promised instant results and "No ridiculous tints." Jeremiah survived the Seventh New Hampshire's long turn in the South, but camp life ruined his health. He was just fifty-four when he died in 1867. Family and neighbors said

CAROLINE DURGIN

Scott Durgin was never the same after the war. He shot himself in the head in 1870 at the age of twenty-two. Abner's regiment stayed in the South after Appomattox, and he contracted malaria in September 1865. Still gravely ill three months later, he received a monthly war pension of seventeen dollars beginning the day after he left the army. He could not hold a job and often forgot who and where he was. Friends and co-workers testified that he suffered from an "aberration of mind." Doctors diagnosed him with "malarial poisoning resulting in insanity." At the age of thirty-six, after more than a decade of suffering, Abner was committed to the insane asylum at Concord. Doctors there reported to the pension office that his condition was deteriorating, his chance of recovery "essentially nothing."

At least the last of Caroline Durgin's sons was alive and close to home. And Abner's doctors listed two positive factors in their assessment. He appeared to be physically healthy and seemed to have neither a thought nor a care.

December 23, 1864

ANDERSONVILLE

THE LAST THING SERGEANT ROBERT O. FARRAND ever saw was two colonels talking things over during the battle of Olustee. As he watched them, buckshot hit his left temple just behind the eye. When he awoke, his regiment was gone, but he heard gunfire. For safety's sake, the rebels were firing loaded weapons scavenged from the battlefield. Farrand felt a ball hit his knapsack and another glance off his heel and hit his thigh. He could do nothing to protect himself. The buckshot had penetrated his head and severed both optic nerves, and he was blind. When the shooting stopped and he heard a man walk past him, he rose to his knees and waved toward the sound. He was cold, and he asked the man to take him to a fire or a doctor. The man guided him, telling him along the way that the Yankees had been driven off with heavy losses. As Farrand warmed himself by the fire, he fainted from loss of blood.

What had happened on the battlefield was bad enough, but it was just the beginning of Sergeant Farrand's nightmare. There was no hospital near, the meanest among his captors saw him as easy prey, and in just over a month he would find himself at Andersonville, a Confederate prison camp whose inmates likened it to hell on earth.

Farrand was a new American. A slight man of 5-foot-4 and 136 pounds, he had been born in England in 1840 and come to the United States in 1855 on the *Parliament*, a sailing packet ship. He moved to Fisherville two years later and apprenticed with the village's only tinsmith. He helped tin the bell deck and the tip of the spire on the new Baptist church. When Jeremiah Durgin began recruiting a company for the Seventh New Hampshire, Farrand and his brother Joseph volunteered. On July 18, 1863, the regiment marched into the slaughter at Fort Wagner, where Robert was shot in the wrist.

Seven months later, when he regained consciousness beside the fire at Olustee with a more serious wound, he was not alone. A gang of rebel soldiers saw him stir and told him to take off his pants. They had already stolen his shoes and everything of value except a gold pen they had somehow overlooked in his vest pocket. He refused to give up his pants, saying he could not see to find another pair. The men threatened to cut his throat and pull the pants off his corpse. He told them the pants were old and heard them move closer, presumably to inspect them. They left him alone. He waved toward the sounds of passing horse teams until a wagon stopped and brought him to the train station. Someone lifted him out, and he fainted again.

When he awoke three days later in Lake City, his nose told him he was lying in a stable. Comrades from the Seventh were there, too. He wanted to wash himself and clean his wound, and he recalled that Elizabeth Gould, a woman he had met in St. Augustine, was from Lake City. A black man guided him toward her house, but on the way they met another prisoner from the Seventh, Charles Danforth of Hopkinton, who had been shot in the lung. He took Farrand to a different house. The woman there gave Farrand hot water, towels, soap, and a sponge, and washed the blood from his face. Beneath a thick scab she found his wound. He put his finger in the hole and felt no pain. The woman brought him biscuits, johnny cake, butter, and tea and escorted him upstairs to sleep on the floor in a heated room filled with wounded prisoners.

The men were taken to Tallahassee and held in a church that had once

served the local black population. Farrand found a buyer for his only posses-
sion—the gold pen—and spent some of the thirty-five Confederate dollars
he received for food. His brother
Joseph also made it to Tallahassee,
but the two never found each other.
Joseph died of his chest wound on
March 8. Robert did his best to keep
his own wound clean. Before apply-
ing a new dressing, he pushed on his
left eyeball to force blood and other
matter out of the hole in his temple. One day as he performed this
task, the eyeball burst. Liquid and
chunks of eyeball drained from the
socket for three days. The buckshot
was still behind the right eye socket
and would remain there.

JOSEPH FARRAND

The guards told the prisoners
in the church they were about to be
moved to a new hospital with good
beds in Georgia. They went by steamer to a train depot above Fort Gaines
Landing on the Chattahoochee River. There, twenty-two wounded men
were locked for the night in a boxcar with a muddy floor. As the train pulled
away the next day, townspeople gathered along the tracks to get a look at
the Yankee prisoners. The men reached Andersonville station on March 22.

Slaves had built what there was of Camp Sumter at Andersonville. They
dug trenches, cut pines, and set thick logs five feet in the ground to create
a fence twenty feet high. The posts were joined snugly enough to prevent
prisoners from seeing through. The enclosure was rectangular, penning in
about sixteen acres. A smaller fence twenty feet inside was called the "dead
line." Guards were instructed to shoot any man who ventured beyond it.
The stockade held six thousand prisoners when Farrand arrived, a number that would grow more than five-fold by summer, leading to a ten-acre
expansion.

When Farrand and the men in his boxcar were assigned to companies,
they replaced men who had died. He was glad his company included sixteen men from the Seventh New Hampshire. The prisoners had to fend for

UNION PRISONERS AT ANDERSONVILLE
(A CONFEDERATE PHOTOGRAPH).

themselves, but he knew his comrades would help a blind sergeant when they could. Food was every prisoner's first concern. Horse-drawn wagons delivered it each day, and the men watched as the supply was divided again and again until each received his share. A full day's ration came to half a normal meal—about a pint of corn and cob ground together plus a one-inch-square chunk of bacon. Captain Henry Wirz, a new commandant, cut the ration by a third, but he had little choice. Higher-ups ignored his efforts to improve conditions at the camp. The bacon was usually "alive with maggots," Farrand later remembered. The men cooked it on tin plates, sending the maggots scurrying, and fried the cornmeal after mixing it with water and patting it into cakes. Farrand relied on others to cook for him.

Neither the planned barracks nor any semblance of a septic system materialized at Andersonville. The only water came from a brook through the stockade. The brook first passed through rebel camps, where cooks dumped in grease and dirty water. "When we drank from it our mouths would feel and taste as if we had been eating fat meat," Farrand recalled. In time prisoners dug wells. Friends built Farrand the standard camp quarters: a two-man shelter of pine boughs with pine needles for a carpet. A prisoner from the Sixth Illinois Cavalry lived with him and cared for him. The prisoners had no way to wash, and lice infested their clothing. Farrand felt fortunate to have fragments of a blouse and pants. He had no shirt, socks, or hat and had not replaced his stolen shoes.

Somehow Farrand avoided the worst diseases at the camp. Pneumonia and intestinal infections had already begun killing prisoners when he arrived, and the death toll swelled as the population grew and the days warmed. Two smallpox deaths frightened the camp administration into a vaccination campaign, but dirty vaccination tools often caused gangrene, leading to amputation and death. Farrand skipped the vaccination. More than 7,800 men died from disease that summer. As their corpses were found, they were carried to the gate and laid side by side. Each morning those who had died during the night were hauled out to join them, and a death cart arrived to transport them for burial. Of the men captured at Olustee from Farrand's regiment, forty-two died at Andersonville, ten of them from scurvy.

Symptoms of this disease, which is caused by a vitamin deficiency, began to show in Farrand's gums in late summer. His legs swelled until he could not walk. When the daily death toll rose to ninety men, the rebels finally began sending away prisoners for exchange or relocation. Men too ill to move were left behind. Blind, sick, and unable to march, Farrand perceived this as a death sentence but resolved to get out if he could. The prospect of going home gave him courage. The night before his detachment was to leave, a friend brought him a bucket of cold water. He bathed his knees and massaged his leg muscles until he could hobble. The next morning he repeated the treatment, fell in, and left Andersonville linked at the elbow with a fellow prisoner.

The column halted near the Andersonville depot, and Farrand sat to rest. His legs bent oddly, his feet touching his hips. When the column was ordered forward, he could not move. Comrades pulled him along by the arms, his feet beating against three sets of railroad tracks. He left the depot as he had arrived, in a boxcar. When the train reached Charleston, two men carried him to the river to bathe for the first time in more than six months. A rebel soldier who saw them on the way asked what was wrong with Farrand. He gave the men a towel and soap and later brought Farrand a shirt, cotton pants, and ten dollars. Along with others who could not walk, Farrand was loaded into a wagon to be driven across the city. A voice he recognized approached the wagon and called, "These are for the blind man." The rebel soldier who had helped him earlier tossed three loaves of bread into the wagon. Farrand ate one and gave two to the other prisoners.

As he waited to be exchanged, Farrand got diarrhea and went to the hospital. Chronic diarrhea had been a death sentence for many men at Andersonville, but here good care and food revived Farrand. On November 28, ambulances came to take him and other hard cases to town, where they were loaded into boxcars again for the journey to Savannah ninety miles away. Rebel soldiers telegraphed ahead from every depot for the latest intelligence. Although Sherman and his army were on the way, the rebels still held Savannah when the train arrived nineteen hours after it had started. The prisoners were escorted from the city to a Union steamer. "It would be hard to find a happier set of men than we were when we found ourselves once more under the protection of the stars and stripes," Farrand later said. They ate hardtack and fat pork after boarding—"the sweetest and best meal I think I ever enjoyed in my life."

ROBERT FARRAND
AFTER THE WAR

Having been paid and issued new clothing, Farrand arrived in Fisherville at four o'clock the afternoon of December 23. Of the twenty-two men who had ridden in his boxcar to Andersonville, only he and Private Charles Danforth, who had led him to caring hands at Lake City, had survived. Although Farrand had been gone from the prison for nearly three months, lice sores still covered the length of his spine. The pain did not stay his tears of joy. He was home for Christmas, and it was a miracle.

Christmas 1864

WAITING FOR CUPID

THE LETTER SURPRISED JULIA JONES. She had not seen Samuel Duncan for two months and had perhaps forgotten his promise to send her his picture. But here it was, a portrait of the young Dartmouth College tutor ready to join the other faces in her album. His note betrayed a facetious formality. "I fear," Duncan wrote, "lest it may be presumptuous of me to offer this card for an album that contains so many of the handsome and distinguished of the National Capital; and lest, too, our acquaintance was so limited that I may have passed entirely from your recollection: but the promise! Fidelity in the execution of promises must override the dictates of prudence and judgment."

Jones saw the note as an epistolary challenge. "Quite a commotion was created among the notables of my photographic album the other day by the announcement from me, in glad surprise, that Tutor Duncan of Dart. Col. was about to become one of their number," she wrote. "John P. Hale glanced smilingly & would have extended a hand, I'm sure, had he not been deprived of that same by the artistic cloud. Old father Pierpont looked, for all the world, just as if he were going to wink & say, 'I've heard of him'—while the distinguished Sumner, who is said to be totally indifferent to everything but abolition & his own promotion, gave you something like a very cordial bow. . . . I need not alarm you with the rage of a young officer, who tries to look daggers, swords and revolvers; nor flatter you with the blushes of several pretty young ladies, who declare that yr entrée was '*so* unexpected.'" Jones poked at his airs, writing that she had meant to thank him sooner, but "since yr return to Hanover, you had mounted & were wandering about on those famous, old stilts, known as dignities, & this consideration—together with the mathematically correct note—was quite enough to alarm me into protracted silence."

From Duncan came this rejoinder: "Didn't you romance a trifle about the commotion in your album caused by the arrival of the Tutor? He never made so much disturbance before, and never expects to again to his dying day."

So began a flirtatious correspondence between a popular young woman from a small New Hampshire town and a scholar who would soon join the Union army as a major. Considering the uncertainties of war and the many suitors of Julia Jones, the chances this exchange would lead to romance seemed slight.

Jones had grown up in East Washington, where her father Solomon was a prosperous shopkeeper and civic leader. He sent Julia, a good musician with a quick mind, to the New London Literary and Scientific Institution. She became a teacher and later a school principal in Concord. Twenty years old when the war began, she was charming enough to capture the attention of Colonel Edward E. Cross, Captain Frank Butler, and other officers. The Joneses sometimes stayed in Washington, D.C., where the family had connections with leading Republicans. Jones's older brother Amos served with General John C. Frémont, the 1856 presidential nominee, until Frémont resigned his commission in mid-1862. Julia Jones was in the capital when Duncan sent her his picture.

Their early letters tracked war news and found common ground in the Union cause. He was the optimist, she the skeptic. In June 1862, Duncan rejoiced that McClellan's army seemed on the verge of capturing Richmond. "It does seem as if the beginning of the end were already at hand—as if the ruinous structure of southern independence must soon crumble, and our brave soldiers be released from their dreadful toils and sufferings to return once more to their cherishing houses," he wrote. Jones was circumspect. "My policy is to claim superiority for him until he proves himself *inferior*," she wrote of McClellan. When he dawdled after the battle of Antietam, her patience ran out. She wrote Duncan on washing day, an occasion she loathed, and for a moment imagined herself at the head of the army. "If any twenty-four hours of the week's calendar are to be looked upon apprehensively, it's the twenty-four hours immediately succeeding the peaceful Sabbath!" she wrote. "That bristling, bustling, boiling, scrubbing Monday! In the words of the Episcopalian litany, 'Good Lord deliver us' from any more *to-days*." She considered the rebel sacking of Chambersburg, Pennsylvania, a disgrace. "I don't *like* being indebted to the Rebs for all the lively incidents of the War," she wrote. "I wonder how an American Joan of Arc would prosper?"

Duncan joined the Fourteenth New Hampshire in the fall of 1862, and the regiment settled into camp in Maryland. "Our warfare so far has been mainly directed upon the barnyard fowls, the beehives, & roasters of the good sesech population of Poolesville; and we have shown ourselves valiant champions, too." After his letters stopped for two months, he wrote claiming he had answered her last letter. The pretense bothered her more than the delay. She scolded him, writing that he reminded her of the Prodigal Son forcing her to play "the tender-hearted old Father, so pleased to see the truant back that the deserved reproof is quite forgotten." She added that while "willing to believe almost *anything* to oblige you, Maj. D . . . do not expect me to rely on *everything* if you are addicted to making such apologies as may be found in your last letter—when you pretend to have answered *my* last letter or at least to *think* so—all moonshine!" After Duncan's next long silence, he tried flattery where a clumsy excuse had failed him before. He just hadn't found time to compose a proper letter, he wrote. "Does my friend of friends, my pet child, saint—imagine that I would or could so long neglect her—with plenty of time at my command? O never—so intense my love. I would write & write & write an uninterrupted strain of devotion—till our glorious meeting swallow up that delight in still more entrancing ones. It's merely impossible for me to write you an ordinarily sensible letter. You are not on my calendar of material effects—you belong with light, fleeting clouds—& to me the palpable part of the poetry of sunset & of the chaste holiness of moonlight. So my pen recoils at the grave language of earth & will indite only the more graceful & beautiful words when speaking of you."

He also teased her with news of a momentous decision. "Now for a secret—Can you keep it—or like a real woman, will you let it out? I'll trust you and try you." He had volunteered to lead a black regiment. "I don't know your ideas of negro regts, but I think I can serve my country better there than where I now am." He was thinking "of having one company of octoroons (feminine)—how would you like the command of the company?" If he feared her reaction to his news, he needn't have. "'Tis true I should not like to have a regiment of octoroons, but I think it just as noble to command colored troops as white—more so—even—because say what people may about equality of the blacks and whites—a white officer does make some sacrifice of his own feelings—to command blacks or to have *any* intercourse with them otherwise. So, Sam'l Duncan, soldier, when you assume the responsibilities of your new position, you will do so with the hearty 'Godspeed' of Julia Jones, civilian." Duncan responded: "As you suggest, I would choose whites for my associates (octoroons of the feminine gender no exception;) but I am equally agreed that it is as much to a man's credit and honor to lead a black regt, so [long as] he does it successfully, as a white one."

Traveling in Ohio in the fall of 1863, Jones met the family of Brigadier General Eliakim P. Scammon, whose daughter Maggie became the object of a running joke between her and Duncan. Tongue in cheek, Jones sang Maggie's praises and Duncan longed to meet her. Scammon was "the most beautiful character I have ever met," Jones wrote. "I *do* wish you might see her! She's my exact opposite in everything. Such a lovely, pure nature—& she's so smart—& intellectual withal." Duncan expressed "a longing desire to see that same lovely, amiable & attractive Miss Maggie S——, whose beauty and many motives you praise so highly." Might she not send him her picture? "Perhaps she is romantic enough to be willing to exchange 'faces' with me—if not, you might represent to her that it would be an act of patriotism, regarding me as one of the 'defenders,' needing such acts of encouragement from the fair ones left behind."

After months of such flirtation it was Jones who blinked. Why she abandoned their bantering tone to profess her love is unclear. Their letters contain no evidence they had seen each other since their brief meeting in the spring of 1862. But suddenly, here was Jones writing him that "but one girl in the universe knows how to love properly & that girl *I*—& that no one in the wide world was ever so completely environed, encompassed & enshrouded in another's love as you in hers—that is—*mine* . . . The idea of yr being able by any effort of yr mind—however strenuous, to forget me, is very painful, & I can't harbor it at all." She might call him by the name of another in a mischievous slip of the pen, she wrote, but his letters "thoroughly convince me of yr sincerity—& I am so jubilant." If she was wrong about this, she wrote, "Don't for a moment hesitate to ask me for a release, if you wish it—& if you don't receive a *full, unhesitating* one—Julia Jones is *not* herself, I assure you." She praised his military calling and understood his quest for glory, but above all she wanted him to stay safe. "Oh I *do* admire a *brave man*, Col. Duncan," she wrote, "& I believe *you* are one."

When she sent him a photograph, he responded with a soliloquy whose tone must have both pleased and vexed her. "I should be loath to deny that the *miniature* you sent me doesn't stir *the waters a little deeper*," he wrote. And what had he done with this gift? "First I took off the gilt frame work, to see if [I] could get at anything that would speak—it seemed as if the living original could not be far off. That wouldn't work. Next a powerful magnifier brought out the picture life size with great beauty and clearness. Then I held it up beside my own sunburnt, ugly phiz, & looked into a mirror, to see how the two would appear together:—and then—well! I fell to musing, and what my tho'ts were, you conjecture if you can."

Seven months later, after he was shot in the foot at New Market Heights, Duncan came home. The wound provided a chance at last, after more than two years, for Duncan and Jones to see each other. Over the Christmas holiday they sleighed, touched, embraced, kissed, and talked and talked. Spoken words and quiet moments nurtured the feelings that written words had sown. Each vowed to kiss no other. She asked him to stay longer, but he reminded her of "the stern imperative demands of the hour." On their last night together Julia sang to him. Their professions of love were a Christmas gift that each soon cherished in memory, but for Duncan the gift also raised the stakes of the military life. Suddenly he had something precious, and the risk of losing it began to prey on him.

As Samuel wrote Julia in January, her song echoed in his ear, bringing joy salted with the sorrow of parted lovers. "I cannot quite dispossess myself of the notion that there may have been a prophecy to me in that sweetly sad song you sang to me the last evening of my stay in Concord," he wrote. On his way back to the hospital he attended a skating party in a Philadelphia park and felt the rub between war and peace. "None but those who have stood upon the bloody field where the human harvest was bending before the sickle of the reaper Death as he reaped with resistless might, can understand my feelings as I gazed upon this carnival of pleasure. Can it be that there is war in the land? I mused." As for his own future he saw his December parting with Jones "with the full & present conviction that it might be a last farewell. God grant it otherwise; but if it be his will that more should fall in our holy cause, who shall hold his life above the sacrifice? . . . What greater fullness of life can there be than that of an earnest patriot fallen amid the clash of arms? Not by years or wealth, but by noble action, should life be measured."

The time for teasing each other about rival love interests was over. Duncan and Jones had arrived at the intimacy in which lovers share their deepest feelings. The war held his life and their fate in limbo, and Duncan wanted to be sure Jones knew it.

January 2, 1865

ESCAPE

IN THE CHILL OF NOVEMBER AN ESCAPED YANKEE PRISONER lay sleeping in a ditch by the road a few miles from Columbia, South Carolina. Beneath his overcoat Orlando W. Dimick wore all the clothes he had. Although his shoes were falling apart, he was determined to walk through the Carolinas and cross the Smoky Mountains to Union lines in eastern Tennessee. When he awoke, Dimick considered his options. He needed food, but the harvest had passed. He needed help, but who could he turn to? Maybe the slaves, he decided. He stopped at the first plantation he came to, crept up to a fence, and spied a black man working in the field. The man's name was July.

Dimick, who lived in Lyme, had joined the Eleventh New Hampshire in August 1862. The regiment fought with Ambrose Burnside's Ninth Corps at Vicksburg and in several battles in the East. Dimick was a twenty-four-year-old lieutenant when his regiment crossed the James River shortly after the battle of Cold Harbor. Just south of Petersburg on the night of June 16, 1864, the men were ordered into line. When they charged with fixed bayonets, Dimick led two companies past a house and tried to reunite them beyond it. "I approached

ORLANDO W. DIMICK

toward the left what through the darkness seemed a squad of my men," he later wrote, "but I had made a serious mistake."

Rebels surrounded him and took him prisoner. The only other man captured from his companies was Corporal Webster Huse of Enfield. The two were taken to Petersburg, where a mounted officer demanded Dimick's sword and pistol. His captors confiscated "anything resembling a weapon," put him in a room with twenty-one Second Corps officers, and allowed him to write a note home. They loaded the officers and 500 enlisted men into boxcars. Dimick traded a guard his watch, a "pocket instant," for a loaf of bread; other officers sold silver watches for $125 or $225 in Confederate currency. Breakfast at Greensboro, North Carolina, cost $10, and small corncakes could be had for $2. Traveling only by day, the train reached Andersonville Station in Georgia on the sixth day. The enlisted men were marched to the prison camp, where Corporal Huse later died, but the officers stayed at the station.

In the morning they rode the train to Camp Oglethorpe in Macon. There, on a three-acre former fairground, Dimick joined 1,400 other officers. A high board fence topped by a guards' walkway enclosed the camp. Cannons pointed in from each side. No prisoner was allowed beyond the "dead line," a picket fence inside the main one. Finding all the structures that housed prisoners filled, Dimick and two Pennsylvania officers burrowed beneath a frame building for shelter. They dug a small area deep enough to stand and created a two-foot opening to sleep in. There they lived for six weeks.

By then Dimick had accepted that he was a prisoner of war. "A more depressing feeling I have never experienced," he later wrote. "Probably many who could otherwise have endured their physical hardships sank under the terrible weight of this depression." Occasionally war news arrived with new prisoners. The officers played cricket, baseball, dominoes, checkers, and chess and carved napkin rings and chess pieces with their pocketknives. They worshiped in the building above Dimick's warren. And they dug constantly, but futilely, trying to tunnel out of the camp.

Sherman's invasion of Georgia, which was at last destroying the South's ability and will to fight, forced the evacuation of Camp Oglethorpe in late July. Dimick was moved to Savannah, where the officers ate better, lived in tents, and slept in bunks. They even set up a language class. But still they dug. They had nearly finished a tunnel when a cow wandered into the opening outside the wall. The guards saw the cow disappear and watched the prisoners more closely after that. One night, as Dimick stood in the mouth of a new tunnel with a load of dirt that had just been removed, a guard lifted the tent flap and saw him. Both men took off running, the guard for help, Dimick for his tent, where he lay down and feigned sleep.

Sherman's army came on, and the prisoners moved again, first to

Charleston, then Columbia. They were held in the Charleston jail as a deterrent to Union gunners on the islands and on the ships, but scarcely a day passed without "the welcome messengers from Union guns," Dimick wrote. In October, when the prisoners reached Columbia, they sang patriotic songs to a crowd assembled "to see the Yankees." They walked two miles to Camp Sorghum, named for the lightly salted meal they were fed. Here they lived in an open field near the Congaree River, 1,500 officers with no shelter. A few tried to run, an idea that lost its allure after guards shot and killed a Pennsylvania cavalry officer. Dimick received his only letter as a prisoner on October 31. He turned it over and drew a crude map of an escape route to Knoxville, Tennessee, on the back. He found real maps in camp and used them to improve his own. He placed his letter over them, stuck pins where the cities and towns were, and traced the railroads, rivers, and major roads. Knoxville was more than 250 miles away through enemy territory.

In November, a new camp commander allowed prisoners to leave camp to collect wood. Escapes started immediately. Dimick and Lieutenant William C. Holman of the Ninth Vermont Volunteers stuffed food in their pockets and set out for what the prisoners called "God's country." They hid in the woods till dark, fell in with other escapees, and moved by night. Dimick estimated they made six miles the first night, twelve the next. The third night they hit trouble. Holman got sick and turned himself in. Dimick and the four others strayed too close to a well-lit house. Dogs barked and a man yelled, "Halt!" He turned out to be a rebel sergeant home on leave. They were captured again.

The next morning the sergeant loaded his captives into a wagon hitched to a mule team. As soon as they realized only three men were guarding them, they all jumped out. Dimick ran until he was alone in the woods, rolled up in his overcoat, and dozed in a ditch. His shoes were falling apart and he had no food, but he still had his map and a compass. He awoke and went looking for a slave who might help him. At the first plantation he came to, he crawled to the fence and called to a man on the other side. This was July. He brought Dimick boiled sweet potatoes, pork, and "dodgers"— corncakes. "It was my first 'square meal' in five months and . . . I did it full justice," Dimick wrote. July fed him again that night and offered to look after him until a cobbler he knew could mend the shredded shoes. After that, he would send Dimick on his way with as much food as he could carry.

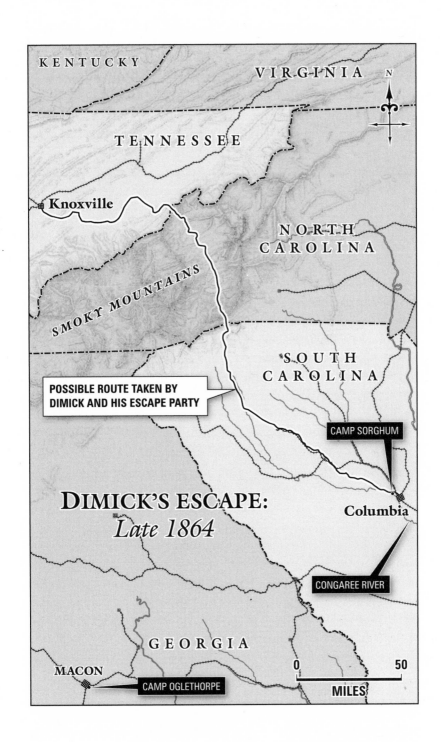

KENTUCKY

VIRGINIA

N

TENNESSEE

Knoxville

NORTH
CAROLINA

SMOKY MOUNTAINS

POSSIBLE ROUTE TAKEN BY
DIMICK AND HIS ESCAPE PARTY

SOUTH
CAROLINA

CAMP SORGHUM

DIMICK'S ESCAPE:
Late 1864

Columbia

CONGAREE RIVER

GEORGIA

MACON

CAMP OGLETHORPE

0   50

MILES

The plan changed abruptly when five more escapees from Camp Sorghum arrived. Dimick bade July goodbye. The escape party decided to follow the railroad tracks. The men started at around nine each night and walked six hours before lying "spoon fashion" under a single blanket to take "the fugitives' rest." Dimick's shoes fell apart, but he patched them and trudged on. The escapees relied entirely on black people for sustenance. In essence they discovered an Underground Railroad with the roles reversed. Late each afternoon they sought food, and in every instance the black people they called upon helped them. "Taking us oftentimes into their cabins, they would give us the best at their command, whether of their own or 'Marsa's,'" Dimick recalled. The men ate corn, sweet potatoes, and even an occasional goose.

The Underground Railroad changed when they reached western North Carolina. Slaves were scarce, and the Yankees' only hope was to find white people with Union sympathies. Dimick ventured forth while the others hid. When he approached a farmer shucking corn in his barn, he told the man the truth: he was an escaped prisoner who needed help. "I never have shot at a Yankee yet and I never will," Henry B. Grant told Dimick. In the first of several such encounters for the escapees, Grant and his wife fed them. After the war, Dimick would write: "No higher type of loyalty existed than was found in western North Carolina and East Tennessee, where the devotion to the flag meant ostracism and persecution of self and kindred, and oftentimes the loss of property and destruction of home, and sometimes the death of dear ones." Grant's nephew, a sixteen-year-old rebel soldier whose unit was guarding the road to the Smoky Mountains and east Tennessee, guided the Yankees right past his camp. Another North Carolinian gave them food and showed them the way through the mountains.

They reached Knoxville in early December, and on January 2, 1865, Dimick came home to Lyme. It had been nearly six months since his capture and two since he walked out of Camp Sorghum in Columbia. The man he most wanted to tell about his escape was his old school chum Frank Butler, but Butler was dead. After two months recuperating in Lyme Dimick rejoined the Eleventh New Hampshire in Virginia.

February 22, 1865

'THE REBELLION MELTS AWAY BEFORE IT'

BEFORE THE WAR SAMUEL A. DUNCAN had been a man of words, a Dartmouth College scholar. Now he was a man of action, a brevetted general leading a brigade of black soldiers through the South in Sherman's avenging army. But Duncan retained the habits of a lettered man, and he was surprised when it occurred to him he had not read a newspaper in seventeen days. "In fact I am getting indifferent to the newspapers," he wrote to his beloved Julia Jones. "When men are making news and history, the mere reading of them becomes tame indeed."

The chance to make history had inspired Duncan since the summer of 1863, when he took command of the black brigade. Recalling the dull duty and bickering of his old regiment, the Fourteenth New Hampshire, he wrote his brother: "I shall always rejoice that I freed myself from all connection with the rotten concern." James W. Patterson, a Dartmouth math professor and now Duncan's con-

SAMUEL A. DUNCAN

gressman, supported his decision. "This war must settle the humanity & the consequent rights of the black images of God," Patterson wrote Duncan. "If military law recognizes the rights of men in black & white alike, why should not civil law when the war ceases?" The new job would take Duncan "where powder & lead are thrown about with perfect looseness," but it also afforded a chance for glory. "Col. Shaw has won a place in history which he might have failed to reach if he had lived to four score years in quiet times," Patterson wrote.

Duncan saw hope in the slightest gains among his men. "The colored soldiers develop remarkable qualities for marching, and I think will be equally brave in battle," he wrote. On an early expedition his men chased off rebel pickets and fired a volley at what looked like a straggler. It turned out to be an empty coat, but Duncan was pleased to find nine bullet holes in it. His one reservation about leading black soldiers was that it would not "win me much credit in Richmond, when they get me there a prisoner."

On May 4, 1864, the Army of the James, in which his brigade served, steamed up the river toward the rebel capital. As the black division took the lead in Major General Benjamin Butler's army, Duncan gazed back upon "a truly magnificent sight. Monitors, gunboats, ironclads, & transports of every conceivable plan and capacity, black with the soldiers of the Union, came pressing on." The *Greyhound*, Butler's command ship, came alongside the boat carrying Duncan and his men. "As she was rushing past, Gen'l Butler stood upon her deck, his hat in his hand, & the fresh wind streaming his thin long hair behind him. Approaching our boat, his right arm was moving energetically like a piston; and amid the din of voices and the whirring of the boats, we could not fail to hear him shout, 'Push on! push on! push on! More steam! more steam! Hurry up!'" The brigade's mission was to capture City Point, a strategic outpost with direct routes to Petersburg and Richmond. Even ten months after the Fifty-fourth Massachusetts regiment's charge on Fort Wagner, many soldiers in the flotilla on the James doubted the black troops, and Duncan wanted a chance to prove them wrong. He didn't get it this time. His two regiments, the Fourth and Sixth United States Colored Troops, landed without serious opposition. "We captured 35 prisoners and one rebel flag," he wrote.

The brigade's trial by fire came five months later as the men led what was meant to be a coordinated assault on New Market Heights, a rebel stronghold north of the James. In the foggy darkness, they charged through young pines and over 800 yards of open plain. Shouts of "Niggers, boys! Niggers!" inspirited the defenders on the heights before them. The attackers crossed a swamp, a river, and a field covered with manmade obstacles. Hundreds of them fell. A black sergeant in Duncan's Fourth regiment, the first in, called the attack "sheer madness." Duncan was hit four times, "only one shot proving serious," he wrote. "The others gave my coat & hat rather a seedy appearance. I shall keep the old hat as a trophy." His brigade was mauled, but in the newspapers, as in his mind, the bloodshed served a purpose. "Who dare say, after this, that negroes will not fight?" wrote Henry J. Winser of the *New York Times*. Thomas Morris Chester, a black correspondent, informed readers of the *Philadelphia Press* that the soldiers had won "undying laurels for their steady and unflinching courage." Using the same adjective, Duncan said his men had faced "the red tempest of death with unflinching heroism."

Wounded in the foot, Duncan spent four months recuperating before returning to join Sherman's campaign to subdue the South. He arrived on February 22, Washington's birthday, as his brigade was about to parade through Wilmington, North Carolina. The city had been a rebel port on the Cape Fear River just inland from Fort Fisher. Union troops had taken the fort a month earlier, ending a lively trade between southern cotton and tobacco wholesalers and British blockade-runners bearing food, clothes, and arms. The day Duncan arrived was lovely, and the rebels abandoned the city without a fight. His soldiers took pride in liberating the local black population. "They stepped like lords & conquerors," Duncan wrote his fiancée. "The frantic demonstrations of the negro population will never die out of my memory. Their cheers & heartfelt 'God bless ye's' & cries of 'De chains is broke; De chains is broke,' mingled sublimely with the lusty shouts of our brave soldiery that welled up as they caught sight of 'Old Glory' floating again over the dwellings of the loyal citizens." Duncan spoke with newly free black people and concluded that "the rebels can derive but little, if any advantage from the arming of their slaves. The slaves comprehend the great question at issue. They knew full well what our army signified to them as we passed into the city." His men met weak resistance beyond the city. "For a half hour I rode amid the dropping patter of the leaden rain, for a minute and a half amid the thickest of the bursting shower, and yet came out without the smell of fire upon my garments," Duncan wrote.

He set up quarters in the mansion at the end of a cedar-lined lane on a cotton plantation. "The blighting influences of slavery are all around me," he wrote. "The institution of slavery is simply damnable. No wonder that the seven vials of wrath are being poured out upon our country because of its tolerance of such an abominable system." He liked being part of Sherman's "all-conquering army that is now sweeping like an avalanche over the domains of the rebellion." He believed South Carolina had gotten what it deserved. "The vengeance which our warworn veterans have been nursing against that nesting place of traitors vented itself to the full," he wrote. "Our columns have blackened a path a hundred miles in width—cattle are driven off, the supplies consumed or destroyed, & the mansions burned. It seems a terrible retribution to befall a people, but in its connections I believe it a mercy. This inhuman war will not cease until the arrogant South is brought under the rod and made to *feel* that the North is a *power*, to be *respected* and *feared*." Anyone who failed to see this was wrong in his view. "Is *rebel property* more sacred than the *lives* of our *loyal soldiers?*" he wrote. "Yet so the braggart miscreants of the South & the too tender hearted people at home would seem to assert when they raise their hands in holy horror because a rebel's house or cotton has been given to the flames."

Duncan scoffed at the old claim that Sherman was a "lunatic." As he watched soldiers crossing a pontoon bridge toward Goldsborough, he wrote that Sherman's army "possesses the best morale that an army ever had. It is invincible. It views the enemy with utmost supreme contempt. It moves forward whithersoever it chooses, & the rebellion melts away before it. Sherman is worshipped by all. I shall ever esteem it a piece of good fortune that I am serving under him. No other place in the army would suit me so well."

April 4, 1865

RICHMOND AT LAST

CHARLES CARLETON COFFIN, the reporter who had brought the war home to New Englanders for four years, wasn't about to miss one of its triumphant acts. He jumped on his horse and galloped toward Richmond. The horse stumbled just outside the city and threw him into a ditch. At forty-two years old, he checked carefully to be sure no bones were broken before remounting and riding on. Richmond had fallen. The Confederacy had torched its capital. President Lincoln was coming to tour the city. *Boston Journal* readers needed a witness, and who better than Carleton?

Fires still raged as he entered Richmond late in the day. Acting on orders, fleeing rebels had ignited warehouses filled with tobacco and cotton. The first Union troops to arrive fought the fires alongside civilians who lacked the means to leave. The task was overwhelming. Carleton turned away from Main Street, where fires were still bringing down walls. He took a side street, passed the rebel capitol, and found the Spottswood Hotel. He had been awake since three in the morning, when the explosion set by the rebels to destroy their navy's magazine near Richmond shook the earth at Petersburg and City Point, both more than twenty miles away. Flames had consumed buildings on three sides of the

CHARLES C. COFFIN

hotel. Carleton, the lone guest, had his choice of rooms. On the register he counted twenty rebel officers who had checked out that day. He took a first-floor room so he could jump to the street in case of fire. He gazed out at the damage—streets impassable, chimneys and walls teetering, Capitol Square littered with things saved from the fire. He saw women and children crying and men staring silently at the destruction.

Early the next morning, April 4, as Carleton walked the city streets, the pavement burned his feet. "Granite columns, iron pillars, marble facings, broken into thousands of pieces, with cartloads of bricks, blocked the streets," he wrote. He began listing destroyed buildings: the Bank of Richmond, the American and Columbian hotels, the offices of the *Enquirer* and the *Dispatch*, the post office department, the war department, the arsenal, foundries, the Presbyterian Church. There were perhaps a thousand in all. Union soldiers, black and white, had done their utmost to save what they could. They had climbed to the roofs of the capitol and the governor's mansion to douse cinders before they became flames. A citizen of Richmond told Carleton that without the soldiers, the whole city would be gone. "So the despised Yankees, the greasy mechanics and mudsills, became the saviours of their fond old city, which the leaders of the rebellion, who claim to be cavaliers, set on fire in their impotent rage," Carleton wrote.

Looters were everywhere. Fleeing rebel soldiers had started the rampage, but Carleton blamed their leaders. The soldiers "suffered privation and hardship," he wrote, while politicians in Richmond "have reveled in luxury, have had places of power, have plundered and robbed the nation, and with provident forethought have hundreds of thousands of dollars in London and Paris." Carleton saw a black man with three Dutch ovens on his head. Women carried away molasses, flour, salt, and bacon. "They had all but starved, but now they could eat till satisfied," he wrote. In Capitol Square the troops of Brigadier General Charles Devens's division, the first to occupy the city, shared their rations with women and children left homeless by the fire. The refugees had carried beds, kettles, pianos, crockery—anything they could—to the square. Carleton entered the capitol, where Devens and other officers had set up their command. Rebel legislators had left their papers at their rickety desks. The carpet was threadbare, the paint peeling. The windows were broken out.

As Carleton stood on the bank of the James River just after noon to get another perspective on Richmond's desolation, he saw twelve sailors rowing upstream. In the boat were President Lincoln and a military party headed by Admiral David Porter. Black spectators recognized Lincoln from his top hat and began to shout. On the dock, forty or fifty black workmen dropped their tools and ran to greet the president. Carleton told a woman, "There is the man who made you free." She replied, "Dat President Linkum?" Assured it was, she jumped up and down and cried, "Glory! Glory! Glory!" Carleton joined the presidential party for the three-quarter-mile walk to Jefferson Davis's mansion. "What a spectacle it was," he told his readers. "Such a hurly-burly—such wild, indescribable, ecstatic joy I never witnessed." A black man guided the procession. Behind him marched six sailors wearing round blue caps, short jackets, and baggy pants and armed with carbines. Next came the president, Porter, the other officers, and Carleton, followed by the other six sailors. This twenty-man parade passed through a swelling, teeming mass of humanity, black and white, hollering, dancing, singing, and waving caps and bonnets. Union soldiers joined the celebration. "All could see him—he was so tall—so conspicuous," Carleton wrote. A black woman standing in her doorway shouted, "Thank you, dear Jesus, for this." Her companion clapped and cried, "Bless de Lord!" A third woman lifted her bonnet and screamed, "God bless you, massa Linkum."

Just the day before, these women and others who hindered the progress of the presidential party had been slaves. "Now they were free, and beholding him who had given them their liberty," Carleton wrote. Lincoln silently acknowledged their greetings. "He was a man of the people among the people. It was the great deliverer, meeting the delivered." By the time Lincoln reached Davis's mansion, the crowd had grown immense. It jammed the front lawn, black faces outnumbering white by two to one. Major General Godfrey Weitzel greeted Lincoln at the front door. Wave after wave of cheers rose up until the door closed and the two men disappeared.

Carleton, one of the most trusted and seasoned correspondents of the war, doubted his ability to report what he had seen. His account began with this sentence: "Language fails me in any attempt to describe correctly the appearance of the city as I passed through the streets this morning at an early hour." As he reached the end of his story, nothing had changed his mind about his ability to tell it. Yet, in one long, loping sentence, he tried again to capture the moment:

"No written page or illumined canvas can give the reality of the event— the enthusiastic bearing of the people—the blacks and poor whites who have suffered untold horrors during the war, their demonstration of pleasure, the shouting, dancing, the thanksgiving to God, the mention of the name of Jesus—as if President Lincoln were next to the son of God in their affections—the jubilant cries, countenances beaming with unspeakable joy, the tossing of caps, the swinging of arms of a motley crowd—some in rags, some bare-foot, some wearing pants of Union blue, and coats of Confederate gray, ragamuffins in dress through the hardships of war, yet of stately bearing—men in heart and soul—free men henceforth and forever, their bonds cut asunder in an hour—men from whose limbs the chains fell yesterday morning, men who through many weary years have prayed for deliverance—who, when their children were taken from them and sent to the swamps of South Carolina and the cane breaks of Louisiana, cried to God and cried in vain, who told their sorrows to Jesus and asked for help, but who had no helper—men who have been whipped, scourged, robbed, imprisoned, for no crime."

All this, Carleton wrote, "must be kept in remembrance if we would have the picture complete."

April 15, 1865

PEACE, WITH A CATCH

ON THE WAY TO HIS FIRST BATTLE IN 1862, Oscar D. Robinson had established his priorities. Unable to keep up because he was carrying too much, he threw away his blanket and food but kept his pen and ink. Now

he was Captain Robinson, a veteran of Antietam, Vicksburg, the Wilderness, Spottsylvania, and the wearying siege of Petersburg. He and his pen had survived to tell his tale of the end of the war.

The beginning of the end was the fall of Petersburg. Robinson's regiment, the Ninth New Hampshire, formed in the trenches with its division at 3:30 a.m. on April 2. On command the men "leaped over our works and rushed for those of the enemy," he wrote. They captured the rebel pickets and charged fortified trenches that had held them back for months. Shells shook the earth. The Ninth overran the next

OSCAR D. ROBINSON

rebel trenches, and the next. "Thus the fighting went on during that long Sabbath day, our men taking fort after fort and battery after battery till darkness closed the scene," Robinson wrote. The next morning, plumes of smoke rose before them, a sign of the enemy's flight. They attacked at five o'clock, but as they neared the next line of fortifications, no one fired back. "Soon with loud cheers we pushed wildly forward over forts filled with abandoned artillery and thro' abandoned camps where the tents were still standing." They paused on Cemetery Hill to look out over Petersburg. "It was a glorious moment and one worth years of suffering to behold," Robinson wrote. "Behind us were the strong and hitherto impregnable works of the enemy which we had long confronted, while beyond were our own fortifications and camp and burying grounds of the various Divisions where lay so many of our noble comrades who had fallen while bravely fighting for what we that moment beheld." The grass was green and fruit trees blossomed in the city ahead. The rising sun lit up the spires and brightened Old Glory as it waved from the courthouse cupola. The victors raised cheer after cheer, their voices echoing through the hills. Robinson hoped the retreating rebels heard this "death knell of their hopes."

Robert E. Lee's army surrendered five days later, and Robinson's regiment was detailed to guard 8,000 rebel prisoners, including 600 officers, on the walk back to Petersburg. As seven captured generals rode in ambulances, Robinson's men herded the rest like cattle. The parade of loose ranks stretched nearly a mile. Guards with loaded rifles and fixed bayonets walked beside the prisoners, moving by day and sleeping at night. Much as Robinson disliked the job, it allowed him to size up the erstwhile enemy. "A few of the rebel officers were *plucky*, defiant and bitter, but the majority of them and nearly all the men were perfectly subdued and only wished for the chance to 'take the oath' and return home," he wrote his mother. Many said they wanted Jefferson Davis hanged. Some refused to believe Lee had surrendered, but most knew their cause was finished. "It would be as utterly impossible to organize them again to fight the North as it would as to resurrect the armies of Napoleon 1st," he wrote. He was pleased to see retribution "being visited on the Southern people for their crimes of oppression and treason!" Rebel leaders were in despair, their backers sinking into poverty. "Society is completely uprooted, households are in mourning for loved ones who have died in an unholy, a criminal *cause*, and those who have been lords and masters are bewailing the loss of power which they so basely abused."

What happened next changed Robinson's mind about the price the rebels should pay. On April 15, he heard that President Lincoln had been assassinated. Rain and cold that night dimmed the glow of victory. "The wind howls and moans over the forests," he wrote in his diary. "The camp fires gleam fitfully in the darkness; great, jagged dark clouds hang low around the horizon, deepening the sable fall of night. But a *deeper, darker, sadder* gloom than that of the natural elements hangs over our nation." His first thought, shared by many, was that rebel leaders had ordered Lincoln killed. "If things have come to such a state as this I think it is time to commence a war of *extermination*," he wrote his sister. "Such sentiments I know are dreadful to indulge but I believe it would be better to annihilate the whole rebel population than to suffer such a state of affairs to exist in this Government."

Although Lincoln's murder was a hard blow after years of hard blows, Robinson remained grateful that he and his brother had survived the war. "Thro' God's mercy I have been spared to behold the joyful day," he wrote his sister. "We as a family have great reason to be thankful that the close of the war leaves us *un*clad in the garments of mourning . . . while there is sorrow and weeping in so many households." But now the assassination had given victory a bitter edge. Would peace never come?

April 21, 1865

FLASHBACK

THE BOAT TRIP WAS NOT EVERYTHING Benjamin Brown French and his wife Mary Ellen hoped it would be. They traveled to Richmond and toured the city's streets, he on horseback, she by carriage, and visited the prison camp at Point Lookout, Maryland, where 18,000 rebels awaited their freedom. But when a senator in the traveling party fell ill, congressional leaders canceled plans to go to Charleston to witness the raising of Old Glory at Fort Sumter four years to the day after its surrender. So, on April 14, the steamer headed back to the capital. The Frenches arrived at their house on Capitol Hill just after dark and climbed into bed at ten o'clock.

French, who came from a prominent Chester family and started his career as a lawyer and editor in Newport, had been a fixture in Washington since 1833. A man of sixty-five with mutton chops and a high forehead, he earned his life of privilege by getting things done and serving men in power with discretion. Mary Ellen, thirty years his junior, had cared for his first wife, Elizabeth, in the final months of her breast cancer. Benjamin came to see Mary Ellen as an indispensable "gleam of the brightest sunshine." In 1862, sixteen months after Elizabeth's death, they married. Benjamin was commissioner of public buildings in Washington, a job he first held

under his onetime friend, Franklin
Pierce. The buildings in his charge
included the White House and the
Capitol. He reported to President
Lincoln, but the burden of his office
was Mary Lincoln, a First Lady jeal-
ous of her prerogatives and inclined
to overspend.

The morning after the Frenches'
return from the boat trip, Benjamin
awoke at first light. He dozed for a
few minutes, but when he noticed
the streetlights still burning, he
wondered why. He went downstairs
to investigate and found a sentry
marching in front of the house. A
soldier happened by and asked
French, "Are not the doings of last
night dreadful?" French had no idea

BENJAMIN BROWN FRENCH

what he meant. The soldier told him the president had been shot at Ford's
Theatre and Secretary of State William Seward's throat had been cut in his
home. French ran upstairs to tell Mary Ellen the news. He walked to the
Capitol and ordered the building closed and then to Tenth Street, where
Lincoln lay on a couch in a private home. Cabinet members, congressmen,
generals, and doctors crowded the room, but French made his way to the
president's side. Lincoln's breathing was labored. "I was told, what I could
myself see, that there was no hope for him," French wrote. No one spoke.
It seemed to French "almost sacrilege to interrupt the solemn stillness about
that dying couch." Amid the bowed heads and somber faces he saw General
Henry Halleck, the army chief of staff, moving quietly about "fixing his
large and most expressive eyes on everything that seemed to require attention." French walked to the parlor, where women surrounded the First Lady.
The president's elder son, Captain Robert Lincoln, who had just returned
from witnessing Lee's surrender, sobbed as French shook his hand. Mary
Lincoln had been French's nemesis, and she considered him an enemy, but
now he took her hand and shared her agony over the attack on her husband.

Thus began a week of toil for the commissioner of buildings. French joined in seeing to the details of the president's funeral. He coped with the widow's choking grief. He took charge of the president's body until it was put on the train to Springfield, Illinois. And one more thing: John William Westfall, who had policed the crowd for French during the inauguration six weeks before, reminded him that the two of them had encountered a man that day who seemed bent on doing Lincoln harm—a man they both now believed was John Wilkes Booth.

French described this incident to his son Frank days after the assassination. Reflecting on it, he believed he and Westfall had been "somewhat instrumental" in stopping Booth from killing Lincoln on March 4. As Lincoln passed through the Capitol rotunda on his way to the east portico to speak, French saw a man jump into the procession right behind the president. He told Westfall to order the man out. When Westfall grabbed the man's arm, he "began to wrangle & show fight." French confronted him. The man grew "very fierce & angry" and said he had a right to be there. French began to think he was mistaken and perhaps the man was a new member of Congress whom he did not recognize. "Let him go," he told Westfall. By then the president had passed through the rotunda. After Lincoln was shot, Westfall reminded French of the incident and showed him a photograph of Booth. French recognized it at once as the man who had broken into the procession. "He gave me such a fiendish stare as I was pushing him back, that I took particular notice of him & fixed his face in my mind, and I think I cannot be mistaken," French wrote. He knew the notion that he had helped forestall the assassination was "mere surmise," but he believed it was true.

When Lincoln died at 7:22 a.m. on Saturday, April 15, in the house on Tenth Street, French was already making himself useful. He had left in the president's carriage to pick up the wives of Gideon Welles, the navy secretary, and Phineas Gurley, the Lincolns' Presbyterian minister. Afterward, he stopped at the White House to order it closed to the public and ate a quick breakfast at home. Lincoln's body had just been carried into the White House when French returned there shortly after nine o'clock. He watched as soldiers lifted it from its temporary coffin and brought it upstairs for an autopsy. Finding Mary Lincoln too overwrought to discuss the funeral, French went to the Capitol to instruct workers on how to drape the building in mourning.

Once the body was examined and embalmed, it lay in the East Room of the White House, which would be reopened to the public for the viewing on Tuesday. The funeral was scheduled for Wednesday. Perhaps no one in a position of authority had more experience of East Room funerals than French did. He had been to five of them, from President William Henry Harrison's in 1841 through Willie Lincoln's after the boy's death of typhoid fever in 1862. It had been French's duty to make sure no one intruded on the Lincolns during their final visit to Willie's casket before his funeral. Now it was the president himself who lay on a bier in the East Room beneath an eleven-foot canopy. To French's eye Lincoln looked better in death as time passed. "But for the bloodshot appearance of the cheek directly under the right eye, the face would look perfectly natural," he wrote. French visited Seward, who told him the story of Lewis Powell's knife attack. He went to the Treasury Department to talk through the funeral with George Harrington, the assistant secretary in charge of the arrangements. On Tuesday twenty-five thousand people stepped through the darkened East Room to view the president. The air inside bore the pungent smell of the fresh flowers arranged around the casket. The mirrors were covered, their frames draped in black.

Pallbearers were chosen from the Veterans Reserve Corps, a unit for wounded and weakened men who re-enlisted for light duty. These veterans were assigned many tasks associated with the assassination. Private Newton Colby of Henniker had joined the corps after receiving his discharge due to chronic illness. In Washington he played the B-flat cornet in a band and served as a guard at the Old Capitol Prison. He was sent to patrol Ford's Theatre after the assassination. The initial fear was that accomplices might be hiding there, but in coming days his job was to protect the theater from curiosity-seekers. It turned out Colby and his bunkmate, Charlie Hart from Claremont, were also curious. They slipped into the president's box to look around and could not resist harvesting souvenirs. "We took our jackknives out and cut off strips from the red plush chair in which the president had been sitting," Colby wrote. "On these strips were long splashes of blood." They saw tickets lying on the floor. One of them, marked "Reserved," had a drop of blood on it. Colby sent his share of the booty home to his mother.

After 600 people crowded into the White House for the funeral on Wednesday, sergeants from the Veterans Reserve Corps carried Lincoln's casket to the hearse. French and a group of black soldiers fell in behind it and led a long parade of soldiers and freed slaves to the Capitol. French's

twenty-year-old son Ben Jr. had designed a catafalque for the rotunda. It was a simple thing, made of rough pine boards nailed together and surmounted by a domed canopy. The French men supervised its construction, and Mary Ellen French sewed its black mourning drapes. To muffled drums, Lincoln's pallbearers marched slowly into the Capitol and placed his casket on the catafalque. They opened the lid to allow mourners to see Lincoln's face. The nurse Sarah Low of Dover had gone to the White House viewing but left discouraged by the six-hour wait. The day after the funeral she and a friend tried again at the Capitol, "as we thought we might regret it if we did not." A heavy rain fell as the long double line inched forward. "In the dim light as we entered we saw on one side a line of officers sitting in full and brilliant uniform," she wrote. The coffin stood in the center, an officer at each end. The line split at the foot of the coffin with single files passing on each side. "The flowers on the coffin that had been beautiful the day before were faded," Low wrote. "It seemed forlorn that they had not been replaced by fresh ones." She found Lincoln's face thin, shrunken, and dark.

A week after he was shot, another procession carried his body to the Baltimore & Ohio depot for its long journey home. French walked in this cortege, too, behind General Grant and ahead of the new president. The sergeants loaded the casket into the funeral car, where Willie Lincoln's coffin already rested. It had been stored for three years in a vault in a Georgetown cemetery. Father and son would return to Illinois together.

It was April 21, and as the train left the station, French's tenure as chief caretaker of Lincoln's body reached its end. He had watched over the president in death as he had in life, but while he felt for Mary Lincoln, her behavior only deepened his frustration with her. The day before she finally left for Springfield with her two sons, French wrote his sister-in-law: "I think the tragic death of her husband has made her crazier than she used to be—but the most unaccountable thing she ever did was to purchase about a thousand dollars worth of mourning goods the month before Mr. Lincoln died. What do you suppose possessed her to do it? I will sometime tell you what I have gone through since Mr. L.'s death. I cannot write it." By then, he had moved past his own grief, believing that Lincoln's death and Andrew Johnson's elevation to the presidency were part of a divine plan. "The Nation has come out of the furnace of the Rebellion, and treason, and War and murder, and assassination unscathed, and with renewed youth & vigor, and will show all creation, and 'the rest of mankind,' that it can stand anything, and *lick* the universe."

May 23-24, 1865

THE GRAND REVIEW

CAPTAIN ELBRIDGE J. COPP WANTED AS MUCH AS ANY SOLDIER to parade down Pennsylvania Avenue in the triumphant march of the Union armies, but he could not ride a horse. His wound hurt too much. As consolation, Major General Christopher Columbus Auger gave Copp a ticket for the grandstand near the White House. From there, Copp recorded what he saw of both the passing armies and the grandees arrayed before him in President Johnson's reviewing stand.

Copp was a soldier for nearly the entire war. He had just turned seventeen in 1861 when he joined James F. Randlett's Nashua company of the

Third New Hampshire Volunteers. His father allowed it on the promise that he serve as a clerk, not a rifleman. To Copp's delight and his father's chagrin, he soon found himself in the ranks, and by the age of eighteen he was a lieutenant. Later, as the Third's adjutant, he was advancing at Drewry's Bluff with his sword held high when a bullet nicked the hilt and tore his riding glove. He was examining his minor flesh wound when a rifle ball slammed into his shoulder and knocked him to the ground. He staggered to the rear, where his black servant Tom led him away

ELBRIDGE J. COPP

on horseback. Three months later, in August 1864, Copp was back with his regiment at Deep Bottom. He slept the night before the battle under the same blankets as the Third's commander, Lieutenant Colonel Josiah Plimpton of Milford, who spoke of his fear of dying. Copp was hit standing behind the regimental colors. It felt as though nothing was left of him but his head. Twice he lost consciousness and awoke with the battle still raging. General Joseph Hawley ordered a member of his staff to help Copp to the rear. There he learned that Plimpton had been shot through the heart. The bullet that hit Copp shattered two ribs, went through his liver, and exited near his spine. It also punctured his canteen, depriving him of water when the thirst of the wounded overcame him. At Chesapeake Hospital at Fort Monroe a surgeon, without anesthetic, sank a steel probe six inches into his wound to remove bone fragments. The pain nearly killed him. For his recovery he credited God and his nurses, especially Harriet Preston, who took special care of him after both wounds.

Although Copp's war was over, he longed to be a part of the grand review honoring the victorious army. His older brother Charles, a Nashua bookseller who had employed him before the war, was a captain in the Ninth New Hampshire. Elbridge reached Washington on May 20 and hired a hack to carry him to the Ninth's camp near Alexandria, where he found the men cleaning, brushing, and polishing for the parade. His brother had a surprise for him. Elbridge's horse Don had been sold to an officer of the Ninth after Deep Bottom. Charles had arranged with the new owner to allow Elbridge to ride Don on an excursion to Mount Vernon. When he mounted the horse, "all that there is in life of the spirit of energy came back to me," Copp wrote. He loved his day in the saddle so much that he overdid it. When Major George H. Chandler offered to let Copp ride in the parade with the Ninth's staff, he had to say no.

On the morning of May 23, the first day of the grand review, Copp went early to the headquarters of General Auger, commander of the Department of Washington, to pick up his ticket. Looking up to a window there, he saw Secretary of State Seward staring out. Wrapped in a blanket, Seward was recovering from the knife attack on the night Lincoln was assassinated. His window looked out on Pennsylvania Avenue, but Copp's seat proved to be even better. Not only would he be able to watch the passing armies but he could also see directly into the presidential reviewing stand in front of the White House. Generals Ulysses S. Grant and William T. Sherman sat beside President Johnson. Cabinet secretaries, Supreme Court justices, senators, congressmen, foreign diplomats, and military officers filled the

THE PRESIDENTIAL REVIEWING STAND STOOD ACROSS
FROM COPP'S SEAT IN THE GRANDSTAND.

other seats. Grant's oldest son Fred stood at his side, and his two younger boys sat on his knees.

A signal gun sounded at nine o'clock, and General George Gordon Meade led the Army of the Potomac around Capitol Hill and down Pennsylvania Avenue past the White House. Copp listened to military airs and watched regimental flags with a veteran's reverence. Though tattered by storms and bullets, the flags remained "precious in the eyes of every soldier who had so bravely fought under their folds." He saw Meade leave the column and climb into the reviewing stand. General Philip Sheridan's cavalry came next, but without Sheridan, who was in Texas putting down last-ditch guerrilla fighting. Major General George Armstrong Custer, one of Sheridan's division commanders, lost control of his mount, and horse and rider sped along the flank of the parade. His hat gone with the wind, his curly locks and foppish tie flying behind him, Custer passed right in front of Copp. When he returned, the runaway horse at last under control, the crowd roared.

Copp's pride swelled when he saw his brother Charles march past, but he lamented that Ambrose Burnside was not at the head of the Ninth Corps, which had made its mark under him. Also absent were the generals whose names were synonymous with the Second and the Third Corps, Winfield Scott Hancock and Dan Sickles, both wounded at Gettysburg. Like Copp, Hancock could not ride and Sickles was a spectator that day. And yet Copp did not think the glory of the war rested chiefly in generals. Rather it belonged to the great waves of riflemen in the ranks, "the incarnation of strength, their faces brown as the Indians from years of exposure to the sun and storm."

Copp's brother met him the next morning in the lobby of the National Hotel, where Elbridge had spent the night. They walked through the crowded boulevard to the same grandstand Elbridge had occupied the first day. General Sherman soon rode into view. He dismounted in front of the Copp brothers and walked up the steps of the reviewing stand. His path to the president's side took him past Secretary of War Stanton. A few weeks earlier, Stanton had humiliated him, rejecting his surrender terms to General Joseph Johnston and suggesting in the press that Sherman was a mentally unstable traitor. Copp saw Stanton stand and offer his hand to Sherman. Reddening, Sherman brushed past without a glance. He shook hands with General Grant, the president, and others, leaving Stanton "like a whipped child to take his seat," Copp wrote.

After the spit-and-polish splendor of the Army of the Potomac, Sherman's army of 65,000 men was a sight to behold. Washington crowds had seen soldiers from the Eastern army throughout the war but had only heard about Sherman's men, and curiosity ran high. Sherman's idea, Copp observed, was "not to put on a holiday appearance, but to give the President and the people a sight of his army as it really was." To the tune of "Marching through Georgia," the soldiers swept along with a swagger—a "swinging independent s tep," Copp called it. Sherman's bummers, the foragers who had kept his army fed on its marches through the South, paraded down Pennsylvania Avenue with their captured mules and horses. Pots and pans clanged from the sides of some animals while chickens and geese weighed down others. Slaves who had freed themselves to follow Sherman's armies joined the parade. In front of some units, Negro women led mules carrying black children on their backs. All this gave the Western army "a most grotesque appearance," Copp wrote. A herd of cattle took up the rear.

When the last cow had passed, the Copp brothers lingered to watch the dignitaries leave the reviewing stand. As Sherman descended the steps, a crowd surged up to shake his hand and give him flowers. He smiled and accepted the adulation at first, but soon he could hold no more bouquets. The crowd grew to a crush, and his handshakes became rough, his "affability apparently departing," Copp wrote. Sherman pushed through the throng, ignoring outstretched hands and finally shouting, "Damn you, get out of the way!" The crowd parted. Sherman mounted his horse and fled.

The Copp brothers said their goodbyes back at the hotel, and Elbridge took the train home to New Hampshire the next day. The grand review had been a fitting final act to the trials of his young manhood. "I felt that the curtain of the great drama had been run down," he wrote, "the last scene of the tragedy of all tragedies closed."

June 8, 1865

HOMECOMING

SEVENTEEN DAYS AFTER MARRYING MARIA FRENCH in New London, Ransom Sargent took up his fife and mustered into the Eleventh New Hampshire Volunteers. For nearly three years, he wrote his bride faithfully from the battlefields of the South. He longed to "hear the sound of your sweet voice," he told Maria, "or look into those dear love lit eyes," but furloughs were hard for a musician to come by, and he never got one. The best he could do was dream of his wife and wake up sad that she was not really by his side. "Oh! I could read your thoughts sometimes, dear Maria, and what joy it gave me for I knew that tender look of passion was bestowed only on me," he wrote in the spring of 1865. "You are my only hope of happiness in the future. All my plans and bright anticipations could never be realized if you did not share my joys." On June 7, when the regiment came home, he ached to see Maria. But he arrived in Concord at the dawn of a new day, as the public began to recover from the shock of Lincoln's death and politicians turned to old rituals to guide a nation at peace. As much as he wanted to hop a train to New London, thirty miles away, Sargent had a part to play in these rituals and his final pay to collect. So, one last time, still "half crazy" from lack of sleep on the way home, he wrote Maria a letter. "I thought it best to get free from this hateful business entirely before coming home," it said. "I shall soon be where we can talk instead of writing, and that will be a great privilege."

The "hateful business"—the war—had been an ordeal even for a fifer. A farmer in a town of 950 people, Sargent had joined the Eleventh with thirty-eight other members of McCutchins Guards, a local militia. Because he was a musician, he had seen more than he had done. During Grant's 1864 campaign, musicians sometimes carried the wounded to safety, but their regular duties were to fortify a position for surgeons to operate and to collect rifles and bury the dead after a fight. At the Wilderness a tall rebel infantryman stepped from behind a tree and shot at Sargent, the ball zinging over his head. He dropped his stretcher and ran, learning that a soldier on the run was a tempting target. He became so used to maimed comrades that when a man in his company lost a leg to the surgeon, he coolly observed that the man would recover "and being a shoemaker, it won't be so bad as the loss of an arm." Near Petersburg he paused in a pine grove where almost every tree "was cut off by a shell or scarred by bullets." He counted a dozen dead rebels in view, most of them mutilated. Three had the tops of their heads blown off. From one man's pockets Sargent pulled a picture of his girlfriend, "a pretty but rather masculine young girl," and a letter in which she asked her beloved to shoot a Yankee for her. "I couldn't help thinking how sadly she had gotten disappointed," Sargent wrote Maria.

Now that the war was over, it was time to bury such memories and look to politicians to seize the fruits of victory, tell the future, and pay the bills. The process had begun the day the Eleventh reached Concord when the new leaders of the state's citizen legislature accepted their positions. The new governor's turn would come on the morrow—the annual Election Day, the occasion for a parade, a fair, and the governor's inaugural address. Willing or not, Sargent and his regiment were to march in the parade.

Lawmakers had elected two Republicans that morning—Ezekiel A. Straw, the big boss at the Amoskeag mills in Manchester, to preside over the Senate, and Austin F. Pike, a Franklin lawyer and businessman, as speaker of the House. Straw hailed the soldiers' return. "Let us hope that the victory they have won is worth its cost to our country," he said. The task at hand, in his view, was to pay the state's war debt of more than $4 million, repair the damage the war had caused, and "aid the other loyal States in exterminating that pest which brought the war upon us." Twenty-two of the thirty-six states had ratified the Thirteenth Amendment, outlawing slavery, and the Legislature would soon take it up. House Speaker Pike's theme was the coming of peace. "Darkness has indeed surrounded us for the past four years, but the bright sunlight has at length come, with genial warmth in its rays," he said. In the blood of martyred soldiers Pike saw "the seed of a purer Republic."

Late that afternoon Sargent and his 315 comrades stood bleary-eyed in the State House yard for their official homecoming. Pastor Nathaniel Bouton, a founder of the state abolition society three decades earlier, gave the invocation, and Joseph Gilmore, the outgoing governor, welcomed the men home. At the head of the Eleventh stood Colonel Walter Harriman, whose candidacy as a War Democrat had helped Gilmore squeak into office in 1863. Gilmore had so savored his easy re-election in 1864 that he sent Lincoln a celebratory gift: a jug of Shaker maple syrup "to mitigate the bitterness and smooth the roughness of your official life." Harriman thanked Gilmore for his welcome and mocked the recently arrested Jefferson Davis. "The din of arms has ceased, the Rebellion is dead, the South is conquered," he said. "We have got treason under our heel, and the chief conspirator has been captured in woman's uniform." *The Statesman* observed of the day's events: "Although Main Street is frequently the course over which processions pass, none are of so gratifying character as those composed of weary men coming home from war."

As Sargent's note to Maria the next morning made clear, he had no patience with such formalities or with the coming festivities. "They kept us parading up and down the street until dark, as tired as the men were," he wrote. "There is to be some great performance today if it don't rain, but there is some prospect of it." When the clouds broke and the sun came out, he and his regiment marched from their camp across the Merrimack River to the south end of Main Street to join the Election Day parade. Concord's rum shops were closed, but vendors of food, drink, and cheap ware and booths running games of chance and displaying war mementos were already busy. Normally, after winding through the streets the parade would have delivered the new governor to the State House, but not this year. The State House was being renovated, its new dome rising where a smaller cupola had stood since 1819. With the House and Senate chambers unfinished, the Legislature was meeting at the city hall and courthouse a block away. The governor-elect, Frederick Smyth of Manchester, would give his inaugural speech there.

Morning trains from Smyth's home city brought in veterans from the Amoskeag mills and the Manchester Veterans Association. The Governor's Horse Guard, a ceremonial troop under Colonel Henry O. Kent, collected Gilmore, Senate President Straw, and Speaker Pike and headed for the parade's starting point. The guards dressed in vests, trousers, and tall plumed hats, all green and trimmed in fur and gold lace. The officers wore blue and red, and the chief bugler shimmered in scarlet from head to toe. It is easy to imagine what the war-weary veterans thought of these dandies who pranced about with sabers drawn. Smyth arrived by train at around eleven and took his place beside Gilmore. Six black horses pulled their open barouche behind a cornet band and the horse guard. Somewhere in the procession marched Ransom Sargent. "The Eleventh New Hampshire attracted much attention from the great numbers who witnessed its passage through our principal streets," the *Independent Democrat* reported.

This auspicious escort ushered Smyth to the doors of city hall, where a crowd waited inside. Smyth, the thickly bearded son of a Candia storekeeper, was a prosperous banker and railroad man who owned a city block in Manchester with a hotel and theater. Lincoln had spoken at Smyth's Hall just as he was becoming a serious presidential contender in 1860. In fact, Smyth had ridden the train with Lincoln that day and introduced him in Manchester as "the next president of the United States." The words

GOVERNOR FREDERICK SMYTH

were unexpected but not unwelcome. Time had proved Smyth right, of course, but Lincoln's election had widened the sectional rift and hastened the rebellion. Now it was Smyth's challenge to look both backward and forward, to honor the sacrifice the war had required while articulating what the Union victory meant for his state's future.

If Smyth's bold introduction of Lincoln as the next president in 1860 had cast him as a man of rare foresight, this reputation suffered a blow when he lauded Andrew Johnson at the start of his inaugural address. "We cannot fail to see . . . that the same beneficent Power which gave us Abraham Lincoln has raised up out of the crucible of fiery trial a successor fitted for the period and its requirements," he said. The heart of his message came moments later. "The soldier has done his work, the statesman has now to do his," he said. The statesmen, he believed, owed a debt to the soldiers who had come home and the families of those who had not. Smyth said the state had sent 33,427 soldiers and sailors to war, lost 5,518 dead, and welcomed home 11,030 disabled veterans. "Has our land been purified and redeemed?" he asked. "It is by their blood." He urged business owners to favor veterans in hiring. If veterans and their families had to resort to welfare, he said, they should be spared the public shame and legal strictures placed on paupers. Now was the time, he said, to honor veterans by erecting "monuments worthy of their deeds and fame." He told the legislators he hoped the flags being returned to the state by disbanding regiments would be "conspicuously displayed in the halls of your deliberations." They should serve as a reminder of the soldiers' devotion and "our own obligation to sacredly preserve the fruits of their sacrifices." Nearly two years after the battle of Gettysburg, the bodies of only forty-nine New Hampshire soldiers killed there had been found and only twenty-seven identified. "This can be but a small part of our heroes who sleep upon that consecrated field," Smyth said. He asked legislators to consider what more could be done "to rescue from oblivion the names of those as yet unrecognized, whose memory is part of our common glory, and will be cherished as long as our race endures."

Smyth supported the Thirteenth Amendment but wanted more. "I shall feel that the great purpose of this war is not attained, the great lesson of this punishment not learned until free schools, free churches and a free ballot are established wherever the federal authority extends," he said. "Let us take courage and make the brutal assassination of our most noble President— that most wicked fruit of a barbarous system—a synonym for universal suffrage, under such safeguards as wise legislation may provide." Denying freed slaves the vote would make it easier for southern traitors to regain power, he said. He found black people inferior but able to learn. "The weakness, dependence and ignorance of the race whose broken shackles have paved our way to victory," he said, "are so many reasons why its condition should not be left uncertain or insecure." Not just slavery but the spirit of slavery must be crushed. "If we would have an enduring and prosperous peace, we shall level every obstruction, concede nothing to the prejudices of slavery, and give the freedman the right to assert that manhood peacefully at the ballot box which he has so nobly proved on the battlefield," Smyth said.

The new governor's calls for abolition and suffrage for freedmen would have been unthinkable four years earlier, when the war began. In Governor Nathaniel Berry's inaugural address before the first battle was fought, he had avoided any mention of slavery. But even a fifer like Ransom Sargent understood and accepted the change the war had wrought. The previous fall, Maria had asked which presidential candidate he favored. He had left New London thinking he was fighting to restore the Union, he answered, but now realized there would be no permanent peace "with slavery existing." He was a Lincoln man.

It is unlikely such thoughts occupied Sargent's mind as he returned to camp after the parade and speeches. His first concern on June 8, 1865, was the same as nearly every other soldier's. He just wanted to go home. Home was the farm his father Seth had bought when Ransom was two years old, a place so idyllic that a local historian would one day write that it "flows literally with milk and honey." Sargent was tired of pen-and-paper romance. He had been married for 1,031 days, but he and Maria had been apart for 1,014 of them. It was time to catch a train to New London and leave the war behind. The Eleventh was paid off two days after the big parade, and Ransom Sargent packed up his fife and did just that.

WHAT HAPPENED TO THEM

LIBERTY BILLINGS, the abolitionist officer shot in the hands on a raid in 1863, bought property in Fernandina, Florida, after the war and participated in Reconstruction politics. He was a Florida state senator from 1871 until his death of yellow fever in 1877.

M. ANNIE BUZZELL and her husband FRANK, who re-enlisted in the Fourth New Hampshire without telling her, were married for more than half a century.

WILLIAM E. CHANDLER, who helped JOSEPH A. GILMORE win the 1863 election for governor, was secretary of the navy in President Chester Arthur's Cabinet and served as a U.S. senator. He died in 1917. Chandler's brother GEORGE, who witnessed the surrender of Vicksburg, left the army after his Spottsylvania wound. He graduated from Harvard Law School in 1867 and practiced law in Baltimore. He returned to Concord in 1883 to care for his ill mother and died of a heart attack shortly after her death. He was forty-four.

CHARLES CARLETON COFFIN, the *Boston Journal* correspondent, returned to New England in 1865 and wrote several books about the war. He later broadened his literary pursuits, writing biographies and novels. He died in 1896 at the age of seventy-two.

ELBRIDGE J. COPP, the Third New Hampshire officer who witnessed the Grand Review in May of 1865, returned to Nashua and married Sarah Eliza White. They had two daughters. He ran a book business, E. J. Copp & Company, and served as colonel of a state reserve unit. He died in at seventy-nine in 1923. In 1890, Copp's older brother CHARLES, who accompanied him to the second day of the

ELBRIDGE J. COPP, CIVILIAN

Grand Review, received the Congressional Medal of Honor for bravery at Fredericksburg.

CLARK CRAGIN, the Fifth New Hampshire private who lost a testicle at Gettysburg, split time between the regiment and the hospital for several months until his enlistment was up. He married in 1875. Two years later a surgeon stated that Cragin's "sexual powers are good, as is evinced by a baby now eight months old—and, as he says, his wife is again pregnant." Clark and Martha Cragin had six children. He died in 1918.

EDWARD E. CROSS, who was killed at Gettysburg, had as many enemies as admirers. A drive to raise money for a statue of him in Concord failed, and officers he had ousted from the Fifth gloated over his death. But as he had predicted, most of his boys missed him. Cross was buried on a hill in Lancaster, and an obelisk was later erected in his memory near the site of his boyhood home. His portrait hangs in the New Hampshire State House along with the sword and silver spurs his officers presented him. The Fifth's monument at Gettysburg stands on the spot where he was fatally wounded.

JOHN A. CUMMINGS, the Sixth New Hampshire officer who lost his wife KATE in the collision of the *West Point* and the *George Peabody*, became a newspaper publisher after the war and was mayor of Somerville, Massachusetts. He died in 1887 at the age of forty-eight. The names of KATE CUMMINGS and SOPHIA SCOTT are listed with the war dead on Peterborough's Civil War monument.

DROWNED BY SINKING OF STEAMER ON POTOMAC RIVER
SOPHIA WIFE OF LT COL. CHARLES SCOTT.
KATIE WIFE OF CAPT JOHN A. CUMMINGS.

KATIE CUMMINGS AND SOPHIA SCOTT ARE REMEMBERED ON PETERBOROUGH'S CIVIL WAR MONUMENT.

FERDINAND DAVIS, who wrote a memoir of his service with the Seventh New Hampshire, returned to Lebanon after the war and married Eliza A. Thompson. He resumed work as a carpenter but soon gravitated to his real passion: architecture. He moved to California, settled in Pomona, and designed several churches, dwellings, fraternal clubs, and downtown buildings. He also grew oranges.

ORLANDO W. DIMICK, the Eleventh New Hampshire officer who escaped from a southern prison camp in 1864, taught in the South after the war. Later he became an educator in the Boston area, serving as principal of Watertown's Wells School and an officer in the Perkins Institution, a school for the blind. He died in 1917.

OBED DORT, who lost his wife JULIA in the sinking of the *West Point*, returned to Keene and worked as a druggist for many years before becoming a bank officer. In 1863 he married Sarah Jane Haile, daughter of a former governor. He lived to be eighty-eight.

SAMUEL A. DUNCAN, who commanded a black brigade and fell in love with JULIA JONES by mail, served as a U.S. Treasury agent and a patent official after the war. He married Jones in Washington, D.C., on Christmas Day of 1867, three years after their romantic wartime holiday together. They had five children. Samuel Duncan later worked in his brother's patent law office in New York City, and the Duncans lived in Englewood, New Jersey. Samuel died in 1895 at the age of fifty-nine, Julia in 1919 at seventy-seven.

RICHARD S. EWELL, the captain who commanded Fort Buchanan in Arizona and rode with EDWARD E. CROSS before the war, resigned on May 7, 1861, to join the Confederate army. He lost his right leg in August 1862 but fought on, rising to lieutenant general. He was a farmer in Tennessee after the war until his death in 1871. Ewell's lieutenant at Fort Buchanan, RICHARD S. C. LORD, fought for the Union at Gettysburg and was severely wounded two days after the battle. He died in Ohio in 1866.

ROBERT O. FARRAND, who was blinded at Olustee and survived six months at Andersonville, returned to Fisherville (later Penacook). In 1868 he married Sarah Story, the widow of Warren Story, a soldier of the Sixteenth New Hampshire who died of typhoid and malarial fever a few days after the regiment returned home to Concord. Farrand had a house built on Pleasant Street and became a bookseller. He and Sarah lived mainly on Robert's pension, which rose over the years to $100 a month. He died in 1907.

GEORGE WASHINGTON GORDON, the Second New Hampshire captain killed at Cold Harbor, was remembered at home long after the war. In Suncook, his hometown, veterans named the Grand Army of the Republic post after him. The cannons in the park at Pembroke, a neighboring town, were given in his honor.

WALTER HARRIMAN, whose candidacy as a War Democrat in 1863 helped keep a Republican in the governor's office, was captured while leading the Eleventh New Hampshire at the Wilderness on May 4, 1864. Released in an exchange for rebel officers after three months, Harriman campaigned for President Lincoln. "I do not fight for one thing in the field and vote and act for another thing at home," he said. He joined the Republican Party after the war and won two terms as governor.

DR. ESTHER HILL HAWKS, who treated wounded black soldiers in South Carolina and Florida, returned south with her husband MILTON after the war. They started the short-lived Florida Land and Lumber Company, which employed freedmen. After returning to New England alone in 1870, Esther established a successful medical practice in Lynn, Massachusetts, and supported women's suffrage and other causes. Her diaries were found in the trash in 1975, sixty-nine years after her death.

MARTIN HAYNES, the Manchester private who chronicled the Second New Hampshire's first three years in his letters to CORNELIA LANE, wrote two histories of the regiment, one in 1865, a fuller version in 1896. His letters to Lane were also published.

FRANK HERSEY and MARSHALL HURD, the two First New Hampshire privates wounded during the riot at the *Democratic Standard* in Concord in 1861, joined the Fifth New Hampshire. At Fair Oaks, Virginia, on June 1, 1862, the nineteen-year-old Hersey was killed. "The bullet entered his eye and passed through, the blood spirting in jets," wrote Private Alonzo Allen, his neighbor from Croydon. Hurd, who was twenty and lived in Lempster, was shot at Antietam three and a half months later and died the next day.

ALVAH HUNTER, who spent a year as a cabin boy on the monitor *Nahant*, served out the war in the Army Signal Corps. He later married, had four children, started a poultry farm, and edited two trade journals. He wrote accounts of his time aboard the *Nahant* and of his New Hampshire boyhood. Hunter died in 1933.

RICHARD W. MUSGROVE of the Twelfth New Hampshire founded and ran the *Bristol Enterprise* after the war. He and his wife Henrietta Gould of Newport had six children. Together they became the singing Musgrove family. Musgrove served on the committee that oversaw the creation of his regiment's monument at Gettysburg. He spoke at its dedication ceremony on September 29, 1887, saying: "These men from the old Granite State assisted those memorable days in July, 1863, in making history that will be even more enduring than this block of granite."

NAPOLEON B. PERKINS, who lost his leg at Chancellorsville, moved in with his sister, Carrie Ticknor, and her husband in January 1864. He later attended Kimball Union Academy. He married Jennie W. Shedd in 1873, bought a harness business in Groveton, and served as postmaster there during Benjamin Harrison's presidency. The Perkinses had three children. By 1902 he had fallen and injured his left leg and required an attendant. His pension, initially eight dollars a month, rose to sixty dollars. He died of stomach cancer in 1913 at the age of 69.

FRANKLIN PIERCE, the fourteenth president, lived on South Main Street in Concord when the war ended. On the rainy night that Lincoln died, a crowd visited his house and taunted him for failing to display a flag or any sign of mourning. He emerged, told the crowd he was sorry Lincoln had been killed, and defended his patriotism and loyalty to the Constitution and the Union. Pierce died four years later at the age of sixty-four.

OSCAR D. ROBINSON, the Ninth New Hampshire soldier who threw away his food but kept his pen and paper during his first battle, became principal of Albany High School in New York after the war. In the 1890s, he served on the Committee of Ten with the presidents of Harvard, Vassar, and several state universities. The committee was charged with improving and standardizing secondary school curricula nationwide to meet the needs of both college-bound and working-class students.

ELDAD RHODES, who was shot through the lung at Antietam, left the army a few weeks after returning to the battlefield with his brother FREEDOM. Back home, he married and served as town engineer in Claremont. He died in 1913 at the age of seventy-two. His daughter attributed his death to his wound half a century before. Freedom died in 1881.

JOHN L. RICE, who was left for dead at first Bull Run, later served as a captain in the ill-fated Sixteenth New Hampshire and a lieutenant colonel in the Seventy-fifth U.S. Colored Troops. In 1886 he visited the Bensons, the Manassas couple who had nursed him back to life. Learning the Sudley Church had been destroyed during the war, he raised $235 through his local newspaper to pay the final bills to replace it.

SUDLEY CHURCH, PHOTOGRAPHED BY GEORGE N. BARNARD.
JOHN RICE RAISED MONEY AFTER THE WAR TO REBUILD IT.

LUCIEN B. SMITH, the Fourth New Hampshire soldier whose opinion of former slaves changed with experience, was killed at the Battle of the Crater in Petersburg on July 30, 1864.

EDWARD E. STURTEVANT, the state's first volunteer, died at Fredericksburg. His body was stripped and buried where he fell. He is named on the family gravestone in his native Keene, and his portrait hangs in the State House. Concord's post of the Grand Army of the Republic bore his name.

HERBERT B. TITUS, who fought with the Second New Hampshire at Bull Run and the Ninth at Antietam, was promoted to brevet brigadier general in March 1865. He was in charge of ten regiments, including the New Hampshire Sixth, Ninth, and Eleventh, at Appomattox. For three years after the war he worked as a special agent recovering Confederate ships in Europe and captured and abandoned property in southern states. He later practiced law. Titus died in 1902 at the age of sixty-nine.

CHARLES WEBSTER WALKER, the Second New Hampshire lieutenant afforded a huge funeral in June 1861, lies in an unmarked grave at Concord's Old North Cemetery. Either the elements or vandals took his gravestone. The grave's location is recorded in an old handwritten ledger at the New Hampshire Historical Society.

THOMAS WIER, sentenced to hang for murdering Shaker elder Caleb Dyer in 1863, escaped the noose. After an appeal led to a second trial, he pleaded guilty to second-degree murder and was sentenced to thirty years in prison. Sympathizers petitioned for his release, and in 1880 they succeeded. Wier returned to Enfield, collected his accrued military pension of $952.57, and bought a farm on Shaker Mountain. He died in 1898.

=

The eleven Sixth New Hampshire soldiers who drowned when the *West Point* sank on August 13, 1862, were Luther Cass of Centre Harbor, Oliver J. Young of Sunapee, Henry W. Bryant of Newmarket, Stephen Brooks of Littleton, George W. Marsh of Keene, John S. Simonds of Concord, Charles E. Barker of Hancock, William Kimball of Ossipee, Philemon W. Cross of Peterborough, Samuel Plaisted of Holderness, and George W. Derby of Troy. All were privates except Sergeant Derby.

=

In 1913, fifty years after Franklin Pierce's angry antiwar speech in Concord, a Democratic governor and Legislature approved a statue of him near where he spoke that day. Many Republicans opposed the idea, and sculptor Augustus Lakeman's heroic bronze likeness was ultimately placed on a far corner of the State House yard. One Republican who did support honoring Pierce was William E. Chandler, by then a seventy-eight-year-old former U.S. senator. Speaking at the dedication on November 14, 1914, Chandler fondly recalled Pierce's visit to his Concord bedside during a boyhood illness and the fee-collecting job Pierce gave him early in his legal career. Chandler had known twelve presidents, he said, and Pierce was among the most gracious of them and "one of the gentlest and most joyous of men." Chandler said it was time to forgive and forget the southern tilt of Pierce's politics. Pierce was due credit, he said, because he truly believed the controversies caused by slavery would lead to the breakup of the Union. "As people grow old, they need not change their opinions, but they ought to moderate their animosities and recognize the good that is in all men," Chandler said.

———

Elbridge J. Copp, a veteran of the Third New Hampshire, returned to Charleston in the fall of 1905. From the walls of Fort Sumter he gazed out on the islands from which the Union army had threatened the city. Copp was chagrined to learn from his official escort, a young army lieutenant, that although the man was a Virginian, his uniform marked him as a "damn Yankee," and Charleston society snubbed him.

Copp visited the Shaw Memorial School, which northern admirers of Robert Gould Shaw, colonel of the Fifty-fourth Massachusetts Volunteers, had founded in his memory. Shaw had been killed at Fort Wagner leading his regiment. The school opened in 1865 with black pupils, white teachers from the North, and an operating budget financed by northern philanthropists. When Copp visited, the Charleston school board had long since taken it over on the condition that only black teachers work there. Copp went to a classroom where "some fifty or more niggers, as they were called," drilled in the alphabet and spelling. "A bright mulatto young lady" taught children ten to twelve years old in the next room. Assembled to sing, the student body was "of all shades of color, from the African jet black to young ladies as white and fair as any of the white race," Copp wrote. He noticed several fair ones with blond hair, but "here they were all known as niggers. . . . The taint of the African blood ostracizes all such from the society of the white race." Copp found his visit to the school "novel and most interesting."

The Shaw Memorial School lasted until 1938. The building was later demolished, and a Boys and Girls Club was built on the site.

=

A year after the war's end, a federal army detachment was sent to Olustee, Florida, to see what had become of the Union dead. Wild hogs had unearthed them, and buzzards had picked their bones clean. The federal troops found bones and skulls spread across the field and skeletal hands and feet protruding from the ground. The soldiers filled two wagons with bones and buried them nearby in a mass grave, which was fenced and marked. In time the fence and marker disappeared. Somewhere on or near the battle-field the mingled dust of black soldiers and white still lies under the earth.

ACKNOWLEDGMENTS

LIFE IS SO UNPREDICTABLE. Mark Travis and I wrote *My Brave Boys* together during the 1990s and talked for years about a second collaboration. Meanwhile, Mark wrote a fine novel (*Pliney Fiske*) and I co-wrote four books. In the spring of 2010, while driving back from a speaking engagement in Vermont, we finally hit on the idea for *Our War* as a joint project. We parted at an interstate park-and-ride, and on the way home I fell asleep and totaled my car. Miraculously, I suffered only a cut on my hand and a spooky recurring dream. A month later, Mark was diagnosed with acute lymphoblastic leukemia. As he underwent withering treatment, I moved ahead with research and writing. I visited him often and, through my surgical mask, blabbed on and on about the evolving manuscript. Mark was a captive audience—a dream come true for a storyteller. He rooted for me and guided me. When he began to gain strength, he critiqued chapter drafts one by one. Just before returning to his job as publisher of the *Valley News* in Lebanon, he wrote two chapters that he had begun researching before his illness: on the ship's boy Alvah Hunter and on the murder of the Shaker elder Caleb Dyer. Mark and I have been friends for more than thirty years. Maybe we'll even write another book together someday.

Many other people read my manuscript as it took shape. As usual, my wife Monique put up with my writer's obsession and provided a reality check. She has no tolerance for tangents, a keen eye for clarity, and a kind way of speaking her mind. My former colleague Felice Belman, editor of the *Concord Monitor*, read three versions of the manuscript for me. She and old friend Michael Birkner, a Gettysburg College historian, gave me sage advice all along the way. Another former colleague and Civil War scholar, Tony Benjamin, graciously shared his insights. Mim Anne Houk, my high school English teacher and friend of nearly half a century, tidied up my prose. My poet friend Donald Hall growled about my halting voice and tangled chronology, pushing me to revise, revise, revise. After seeing reworked chapters, he began a note to me with these words: "It's wonderful." Another poet friend, Wes McNair, an American studies professor in an earlier life, seemed to understand my every intention in writing *Our War*. Abigail (Wilson) Julien, whose late father George hired me and brought me to New Hampshire in 1978, focused her superb editorial eye on the manuscript. Her husband Aaron, president of Newspapers of New England, agreed to publish it.

The generosity of strangers inspired some of *Our War's* richest chapters. After *My Brave Boys* came out in 2001, I heard from several readers who owned letters written by ancestors who had fought in New Hampshire regiments. The first was Fred Goodwin, of Nampa, Idaho, who emailed me the letters and diary of Eldad Rhodes. Later Fred sent Rhodes's drawing of the lean-to where he recovered at Antietam and a photo of the shirt he was wearing when he was shot. Tom Jameson, a Texan with New Hampshire roots, sought me out and let me use the letters of his ancestor, Frank Butler. Butler wrote the best firsthand account I have found of Colonel Edward E. Cross's death. Tom also put me in touch with Sally Anne Schmidt, archivist of John L. Nau's collection, who sent me copies of Nau's New Hampshire soldier letters. The story of the Durgins of Fisherville came to me via the family archive of Marcy Fuller in Connecticut. Grace Forest lent me the letters of George Washington Gordon, Sue Bucknam and her family the letters of George Bucknam, Bette Paine the letters about the missing Louville Brackett, and Retta Presby Weaver the letters of the Colby family of Henniker. On a trip to Florida Monique and I had the good fortune to find Richard J. "Dicky" Ferry, a nearly lifelong student of the battle of Olustee. He was generous with his time and allowed me to use letters and photographs from his collection, including his wonderful pictures of the Farrand brothers and other members of the Seventh New Hampshire.

Thank you to three people who made special contributions to this book. Charlotte Thibault, my brilliant former colleague at the *Concord Monitor*, researched and drew the maps. David R. Sullivan of Newmarket, an excellent watercolor artist whom I met at the Civil War Institute at Gettysburg College, helped me find, assemble, and prepare the photos. And Robert Grandchamp, who came on a 2010 tour I led at Gettysburg, shared a wealth of new information about Cross. Robert is a relentless researcher whose biography of Cross is just out.

I must mention six archives I visited: the New Hampshire Historical Society, where Peter Wallner, the former library director, and his assistant Bill Copeley gave me excellent help; the Rauner Special Collections Library at Dartmouth, a state-of-the-art archive where all the librarians were courteous and efficient; the Peterborough Historical Society, whose executive director, Michelle Stahl, helped me find vital pieces of the story of the sinking of the *West Point*; the Historical Society of Cheshire County (Keene) and its executive director, Alan Rumrill; the New Hampshire State Archives, where Benoit Shoja helped me find hidden gems; and the Library of Congress, where the staff was smart and patient in leading me through the vast Civil War holdings. Thanks also to Jim Burgess and Ray Brown at Manassas National Battlefield Park, historian Bill Marvel, collector Leigh A. Webb, and Fifth New Hampshire re-enactor Dave Morin. As usual, Sid Hall showed skill, flair, and patience in preparing the book for print.

Many people helped from afar. Alec MacGillis, a former colleague at the *Monitor* and now a staff writer at the *New Republic*, dug up Ferdinand Davis's memoir and letters at the University of Michigan's Bentley Historical Library. The resourceful Amy Bertsch of Alexandria, Va., made a special trip to the National Archives to find pension records for me. Longtime friend Robin Wagner, head librarian at Gettysburg College, sent me articles and showed me the way to other material. Bob Korkuc tracked down new details about Charles Phelps, a soldier who has an important cameo role in *Our War*.

Writing a book can be a lonely journey, but these people and many others have made mine a pleasant one. Their contributions enriched the story I set out to tell. Any errors of fact or judgment in the text are mine, not theirs.

SOURCES

Footnotes and bibliography for Our War can be found at our-war.com.

PHOTOGRAPH CREDITS

Abbreviations: BF – Courtesy of Bucknam Family; DM – Courtesy of Dave Morin; DRS – David R. Sullivan photo; EJC – from Col. Elbridge J. Copp: Reminiscences of the War of the Rebellion; *FG – Courtesy of Fred Goodwin; GF – Courtesy of Grace Forest; HSCC – Historical Society of Cheshire County; LB – Courtesy of Larry Brown; LOC – Library of Congress; MF – Courtesy of Marcy Fuller; MAH – from Martin A. Haynes:* A Minor War History Compiled from a Soldier Boy's Letters to "The Girl I left Behind Me," *1861-1864; MP – Mike Pride collection; NC – Courtesy of Nancy Colburn; NHHS – New Hampshire Historical Society; PHS – Peterborough Historical Society; RJF – Courtesy of Richard J. Ferry; RRL – Courtesy of Richard R. Long; TJ – Courtesy of Tom Jameson; USAMHI – U.S. Army Military History Institute (Carlisle Barracks, Pa.).*

x – HSCC	94 – USAMHI	217 – NHHS
xi – MP	96 – USAMHI	218 – LOC
2 – NHHS	100 – NHHS	220 – MP
5 – MP	111 – DM	223 – GF
10 – LB	112–13 – FG	227 – USAMHI
11 – NHHS	117 – FG	229–30 – USAMHI
14 – USAMHI	119 – LOC	231 – NHHS
20 – USAMHI	123 – USAMHI	232 – TJ
21 – NHHS	124 – LOC	236 – NHHS
22 – HSCC	126 – USAMHI	238–39 – MF
24 – HSCC	130 – NHHS	241–42 – MF
25 – HSCC, USAMHI	137 – DM	245 – RJF
28 – MP	140 – MAH	246 – USAMHI
29 – LOC	142 – NHHS	248 – RJF
30 – HSCC	143–44 – MP	254 – NHHS
36 – NHHS	145 – HSCC	259 – USAMHI
47 – MP	150 – NC	263 – LOC
51 – MP	154 – LOC	266 – MP
52–53 – NHHS	166 – NHHS	269 – LOC
56–57 – NHHS	168 – NHHS	272 – LOC
59–60 – NHHS	173 – MP	274 – EJC
64 – HSCC	175 – LOC	275 – LOC
68 – BF	187 – NHHS	281 – USAMHI
69 – HSCC	191 – EJC	284 – USAMHI
71 – PHS	192 – USAMHI	285 – DRS
72 – PHS, USAMHI	198 – RJF	288 – NHHS
82 – MP	208 – MP	289 – LOC
88 – RRL	211 – NHHS	
91–92 – USAMHI	212 – USAMHI	

INDEX

Fry, James B., 39
Fryeburg, Maine, 16
Fuller, Henry W., 179
Garland, Samuel, 114
Geary, John W., 234
General Lyons, 229
General Meigs, 130
George, George Washington, 116
George, John H., 109, 118, 120, 124–25
George Peabody, 73, 285
Georgia troops: 5th Infantry, 117; 8th Infantry (Rome Light Guards), 64
Gettysburg, 140, 158, 162, 164, 184, 190, 223–24, 233, 276, 282, 285–86, 288; New Hampshire infantry regiments at, 139–54
Gillmore, Quincy A., 168–70
Gilmore, Joseph A., 119–24, 126–27, *126*, 177–79, 184, 212, 279–80, 284
Gilmore, Joseph H., 177–78, 201
Godfrey, John S., *21*, 21, 22, 22, 32–33, 35
Goings, Charles, 106
Goings, Claude, 106
Goings, Mary, 106
Goldsborough, N.C., 262
Goodwin, Ichabod, 9
Goodwin Rifles, 16, 17, 21, 146
Gordon, Angeline, 223–26
Gordon, Etta, 223, 226
Gordon, George Washington, 223–26, *223*, 227, 231
Gordon, George Jr., 223, 226
Gove, George S., 96–98, *96*, 150–51, 153, 235
Gove, Nathan M., *53*, 57
Governor's Horse Guard, 11–12, 17, 280
Graham, Charles K., 145–46, 148
Grand Army of the Republic, 286, 290
Granite Guards, 8
Grant, Fred, 276
Grant, Henry B., 258
Grant, Ulysses S., 158, 159, 162, 164, 183, 207, 211–13, 272, 275–78
Greensboro, N.C., 255

Greyhound, 260
Griffin, Simon G., 17, 28–29, 35, 212, *212*
Grosvenor, Harold Chapman, 51
Grover, Frank, 133–34
Grow, Galusha, 62
Gurley, Phineas, 270
Hadley, Amos, 8, 9, 46, 177
Haile, Sarah Jane, 286
Hale, Charles, 143–45, *144*, 149–50, 153
Hale, Edwin B., 237
Hale, John P., 249
Haley, Thomas, *198*
Hall, Alonzo P., *208*
Hall, Eddy, 104
Hall, Edward F., 58, 60, 104
Hall, Maria M. C., 216
Hall, Susan, 58, 104
Halleck, Henry, 269
Ham, John F, *208*
Hamilton, Andrew Jackson, 121
Hanby, John, 216
Hancock, Winfield Scott, 143–45, *145*, 276
Hanson, Howard M., *217*
Hapgood, Charles, 150–51
Harper's Weekly, 190
Harriman, Walter, 123, *123*, 126, 279–80, 287
Harrington, George, 271
Harris, Hubbard, 205
Harris, Joseph K., 195–96
Harrison, Benjamin, 288
Harrison, William Henry, 163, 271
Hart, Charles, *208*
Hart, Charlie, 271
Harvard College, 289
Harvard Law School, 284
Hawks, Esther Hill, 101, 107–08, 132, 174–6, *175*, 197–99, 287
Hawks, Milton, 107, 174, 199, 287
Hawley, Hattie, 195
Hawley, Joseph, 195, 274
Hawthorne, Nathaniel, 156, 158, 218–22, *218*
Hawthorne, Sophia (Peabody), 219–22
Hawthorne, Una, 221
Hay, John, 193

Haynes, Cornelia (Lane), 35, 140–41, *140*, 146, 148, 152, 225–26, 287
Haynes, Martin A., 21, 26, 28–29, 31–33, 35, *140*, 224–26, 287; Gettysburg campaign, 139–42, 145–148, 152
Hayward, Allen, 231, *231*
Head, John M., 103
Hell Gate (New York City), 187
Henry Hill (Bull Run), 29–30, 64–66
Herald of Freedom (Concord), 122, 163
Hersey, Frank, 45, 287
Higginson, Thomas, W., 108, 128–29, 132, 174, 197
Hill, D.H., 165
Hill, John M., 45
Hill, Sylvester J., *217*
Hilliard, Henry S., 61–63
Hilton Head, S.C., 54, 55 (map), 58, 104, 108, 128; slaves at, *100*; wharf at, *59*
Holmes, Charles, 32
Holmes, Oliver Wendell, 220–21, *220*, 222
Holt, Henry (original member of 2nd New Hampshire), 26
Holt, Henry (later member of 2nd New Hampshire), 226
Hooker, Joseph, 116, 121, 134
Hopkins, Stephen, 113
Holden, Wyman, 148
Holman, William C., 256
House, Jerome B., 166–67, 170, 173–74
Houston, Sam, 6
Howard, Daniel E., 179, 181, 183
Howard, Oliver O., 104, 165
Howard, William A., 124–25
Howe, William, 148
Hoyt, Christopher, 105
Hubbard, George, 17, 32, 34–35
Hudson River Railroad Company, 68
Humphrey, Mason W., 233
Humphrey, Moses, 17
Hunter, Alvah, 185–191, 287
Hurd, Charles E., 104–05
Hurd, Marshall, 45, 287
Huse, James, 204
Huse, Webster, 254–55

Story, Sarah, 286
Story, Warren, 286
Stovall, George T., 64–65
Straw, Ezekiel A., 279–80
Stubbs, R.F., 231
Sturtevant, Edward E., 5, 44, 66–67, 79, 94, 290; background of, 5–10; death of, 96, 98
Sudley Church (Manassas, Va.), 32, 37, 289, *289*
Sumner, Charles, 46, 249
Swain, Charley, 31, 37
Swain, Josiah S., 31, 33, 37
Swift, Frank, 97
Sylvester, George, 151
Sylvester, Silas G., 151–52
Syracuse, N.Y., 175
Tallahassee, Fla., 195, 244–45
Taneytown, Md., 140–42
Tappan, Mason, 13–14, *14*, 16
Texas, xi, xiv
Thackeray, William Makepeace, 221
The Scarlet Letter, 218
Thirteenth Amendment, 279, 282
Thompson, Ai B., 9, 22, 24, *25*, 25–26, 29–35
Thompson, C. B., 9
Thompson, Charles, 178
Thompson J. H., 9
Ticknor, Carrie, 288
Ticknor, William Davis, 220
Tilton Academy (New Hampshire), 142
Tissot, Peter, 38–41
Titus, Elliott, 51
Titus, Herbert B., x, 26, 36, 63–66, *64*, 83, 85, 290
Titus, Herbert T., 49
Towle, George H., xi, xiv, 106–07, 128
Townsend, Luther, 181–82
Tracy, George, 213, 215
Treadwell, Thomas P., 9
Trostle, Abraham, 164
Turner, Thompson M., 48–51

Tyler, John, 205–06
Union Army corps: *2nd*, 143, 153, 213, 255, 276; *3rd*, 139, 144, 146, 148–49, 153, 276; *6th*, 149, 152; *9th*, 82, 87, 254, 276; *12th*, 142, 234; *18th*, 232–33, 235
Union Hospital (Georgetown), 90–91, 111
U.S. Capitol, 20, 78, 268–72
U.S. Constitution, 18, 43, 62, 105, 110, 120, 155, 157, 218, 288
U.S. Christian Commission, 231
U.S. Sanitary Commission, 175
U.S. Treasury Department, 271, 286
Vallandigham, Clement, 155, 157
Valley Cemetery (Manchester), 229
Vasser College, 289
Vera Cruz, Mexico, 52
Vermont troops: 2nd Infantry, 41; 9th Infantry, 256
Veterans Reserve Corps, 271
Vicksburg, Miss., 158, 159–60, 162, 177, 183, 212, 254, 266, 284
Walker, Abiel, 16
Walker, Charles W. xii, 15–18, 32
Walker, Galen, 16
Walker, Lyman, 16, 17
Walker, Timothy, 18
Walker, William, 49
Walker, William H., 37
Ward & Humphrey (hardware store, Concord), 238
Warren, Dixie, 133–35
Washington, D.C., 7, 16, 29, 32, 34–36, 38, 62, 65, 76, 78–80, 90, 113, 141, 164, 189, 211, 213, 238, 268, 274, 286.
Washington, George, 155
Washington House (Fisherville, N.H.), 238
Watertown, Mass., 286
Webster, Daniel, 129, 155
Webster, Sidney, 155–56

Weehawken, 189–91, *191*
Weekly Arizonian (Tubac, Ariz.), 48
Weitzel, Godfrey, 265
Weld, Theodore Dwight, 121
Welles, Gideon, 270
Wells School (Watertown, Mass.), 286
Westfall, John William, 270
Weston, Ephraim, 28, 31–32.
West Point (steamer), 73, 75–76, 285–86, 290
Wheatfield (Gettysburg), 145, 147 (map), 149–50, 164
Wheelock, Edwin M., 110
Whipple, Thomas, 52
Whitcowmb, Marcien, 184
White, Armenia, 119
White, Nathaniel, 119
White House, 76, 78, 155, 218, 268, 270–72, 273, 276
White Mountains, 144, 221
Wier, Ellen, 202–04
Wier, Mahala, 202–03
Wier, Sarah, 202–04
Wier, Thomas, 202–07, 290
Wilderness, 266, 278, 287
Willard's Hotel (Washington), 211–12
Williamsburg, Va., 223
Wilmington, N.C., 261
Wilmington River, Ga., 189
Wilson, Henry, 164
Winser, Henry J., 261
Wirz, Henry, 246
Wood, Julia, 78
Wood, Marshall P., 78–80
Woodward, E.W., 239
Worcester, Mass., 177–78
Worthen, George E., 149
Wrightson, William, 51
Wyatt, John G
Yates, William, 116
York River, Va., 226, 229
Young, Hiram A., 67.
Young, Oliver J., 290

About the Author

MIKE PRIDE is a historian and journalist. He is editor emeritus of the *Concord Monitor*, where he ran the newsroom for thirty years. For nine of those years, Pride served on the Pulitzer Prize board. He has co-authored several books, including *My Brave Boys*, a history of Colonel Edward E. Cross and the Fifth New Hampshire Volunteers. Pride graduated from the University of South Florida and was a Nieman Fellow at Harvard University and a Hoover media fellow at Stanford University. He has been a presenter and tour guide at the Civil War Institute at Gettysburg College, where he also co-taught a seminar in presidential politics. He lives in Concord with his wife Monique.